ON DECEMBER 8, FOUR DAYS AFTER THE DIS-
APPEARANCE OF REAL ESTATE AGENT JULIUS
DESS, Corpus Christi resident Michael Chaney
caught sight of a group of coyotes while beachcombing with his neighbor near the dunes just south of the
barricade at Padre Island. Chaney wandered up toward them. Suddenly, he stopped.

"Joe!" he yelled. "Come look at this!"

Joe Walker ran to where his friend stood gazing
down at a decomposing body. It was a grisly sight.
The coyotes had eaten away the toes of one foot and
the flesh of the genitalia, the thighs, and all but the
upper arms and legs. Pieces of intestine lay scattered
about, and blood had stained the sand a pinkish hue.

The surrounding area was covered with animal
tracks and a curious assortment of personal items,
including a partially burned business card with the
name—"Dess, J. A."

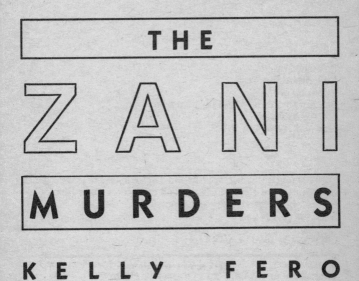

THE ZANI MURDERS

KELLY FERO

A DELL BOOK

Published by
Dell Publishing
a division of
Bantam Doubleday Dell Publishing Group, Inc.
666 Fifth Avenue
New York, New York 10103

Zani photograph which appeared in *The Daily Texan* is reproduced here courtesy of *The Daily Texan* and the Barker Texas History Center, the University of Texas at Austin.

ISBN: 0-440-20898-X

Reprinted by arrangement with Texas Monthly Press, Austin, Texas

Printed in the United States of America

Published simultaneously in Canada

June 1991

10 9 8 7 6 5 4 3 2 1

Vuela para ti, Maria,
por tanto haber aguantado, aguantado

ACKNOWLEDGMENTS

To those who endured hundreds of hours of interviews, follow-up questions, visits, phone calls, snatches of conversation in bars, and the nuisance of recalling moments they would rather have left alone, I am grateful.

To Robert Martinez, who told me the story during a night on patrol and suggested that "it'd make a good book," I hope it has. To Paul Ruiz, who worked closely with me over a three-year period to push for fairness and accuracy, and to Joe Turner, who helped decipher the legalese with an eye toward the literary, a special thanks. None of them asked me to shade the truth or spin a scene, but each may properly take credit as a coauthor.

To those who advised and consented—Craig Hattersley, Rosemary Sheffield, Scott Lubeck, Cathy Casey Hale, David Lindsey, Bill Shearer, Bob Rosenbaum, Ken Case, John Taliaferro, and Betsy Williams, editor extraordinaire—I'm indebted.

To my Maria, Mary Elizabeth, whose insights I hope are evident in these pages, and to my daughters, Kate Smith and Caitlin Newlands, whose contributions too often took the form of sacrifice, thank you.

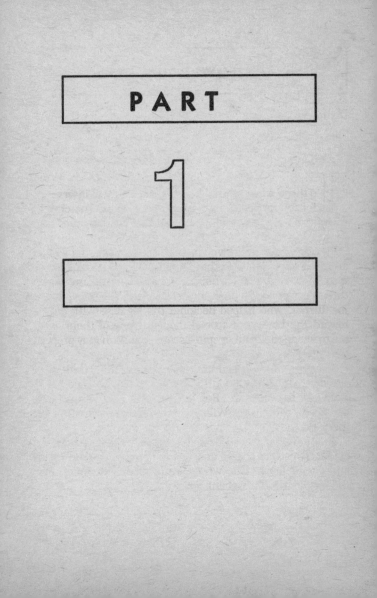

PART

1

ONE

Nuevo Laredo in the mid-sixties drew young gringos in for the kill. A lazy inertia of sin, the hum and buzz on the streets, that vague threat of violence behind every doorway. It was a sacked and plundered backdrop for dark people in dark bars brewing dark deals, a used-up border city existing for no other reason than itself.

The promise of pleasure brought college students from around Texas to its back alleys and *bodegas*, its brothels and billiard halls. A generation of Texans looked to a collective rite of passage down I-35 to the border and, then, to that red-light district of Nuevo Laredo known as Boys Town—the wildest bit of Mexico this side of Juárez, it was said.

Covering several square blocks west of the main plaza, Boys Town was a sanctuary where any young man with a few bucks in his pockets was encouraged to drop them on the local economy. The stench of illicit danger mingled with the sticky persistence of flies. It insinuated itself into the lardish nourishment fried up by peasant women on the street corners, flavored the more temporal sustenances offered by other ladies, and lent the air a disagreeable hint of contamination.

Though little of its dim appeal remains today, Boys Town achieved legendary status in its heyday. It's stock-in-trade was prostitution, outlawed in all but two Mexican states but tolerated as both a tourist attraction and an important source of revenue for local officials, who provided Boys Town with political protection in return for a piece of the action—financial or otherwise. Word was that ex-governors and former mayors automatically inherited stock upon leaving office. As a result, Boys Town impresarios could count on little interference in their business affairs and minimal enforcement of health regulations or other laws.

Street after street in Boys Town sported garish entrances and narrow doorways competing for the party crowd. Behind each lay a different delight. One well-known block alone boasted half a dozen dance halls. An eight-piece mariachi group played standards as the musicians' sisters hustled the *turistas* for overpriced drinks. A swing band pounded out Glenn Miller classics while teenage girls leaned into their dance partners, a peso per tune. In a small cantina across the street, American veterans spent their disability checks on tequila and bad brandy, climbing down from the bar now and then to feed the jukebox or urinate into the cement trough in a corner of the room.

Next door, fraternity brothers from Houston and Dallas applauded a rock band's latest psychedelic set, their arms draped over one another's shoulders. And at the corner, just past the marimba bar and *restaurante tropical*, a company of comics, dancing girls, and leering emcees worked to revive the days of vaudeville with a full revue of live entertainment.

Some sex clubs featured middle-aged women well practiced in the art of sucking coins, cigarette lighters, and other small objects from the stage with parts of their anatomies. After the rise of Tijuana's famous Donkey Lady in the late fifties, more than one establishment rushed to hire its own local version of the woman and her animal act. Other clubs presented the usual array of bored dancers whose splits and gyrations seemed little more than bad gymnastics, or cabaret singers shaking fat asses on tabletops to the tune of tired accordions.

In short, Boys Town's entertainment was to eroticism what

mud wrestling would later be to the performing arts. It took a whole lot of booze to get worked up about it—which was precisely the point, as far as the club owners were concerned. Though some young men drank too much, yelled obscenities at the stage, and wound up on the sidewalk with their heads bleeding, the audiences were generally quite tame.

Regular visitors, however, knew that the real action was out on the streets, amidst the nightly free-form choreography of people moving from one place to the next, drinks in hand and false bravado turned up loud. Hookers patrolled their strolls on the lookout for johns, most of whom whistled back while safely sticking to the curbs in groups of three or more. In the whorearchy of Boys Town, the best women broke luck in the early evening, swindling a bit from some young man's dreams, while the rest resigned themselves to watching the sun come up in some hot-sheet hotel, flatbacking their nightmares away.

But what really set Boys Town apart from other erogenous zones along the border was the hole-in-the-wall. This infamous attraction was nothing more than an open doorway hollowed back from the sidewalk, just far enough to accommodate a single mattress or cot. Passersby were treated every few feet to glimpses of languid young girls, their legs splayed toward the street. For a handful of change, a young man could step inside and spend his cheap, quick love in full view of the street.

Hole-in-the-wall whores were usually recent arrivals from some village in Mexico's interior—just this side of puberty and not yet well enough connected to find work inside the clubs or brothels. For many, life in Boys Town was a leap up the social ladder from their even more squalid beginnings.

One such young freelancer was Irma Serrano Reyes. Born on March 9, 1943, Irma had grown up in the grinding poverty of a misnamed collection of squatters' shacks known as a *colonia hogar moderno,* or "colony of modern homes," ringing the hills that overlooked Acapulco, where thousands of families strained at the seams of their cardboard and adobe huts.

Her father had been a subsistence farmer in the nearby mountains of Guerrero, Mexico's poorest state, where he cleared the terrain with a self-possessed fatalism that both ruined his own dreams and fueled those of his children. In the early forties, he moved his family to the coast upon hearing of the government's plan to turn the sleepy fishing village of Acapulco into a lush resort for the international jet set. But like hundreds of other campesinos, he found only occasional work as an unskilled laborer on the construction sites of the sudden playground springing up on the shores of the Pacific.

Irma's mother struggled to put food on the table for her children—Irma, another daughter, and three sons—through a variety of odd jobs, the most frequent of which was apparently as a *bruja,* or witch. She offered herbal remedies, predictions of the future, and other services traditional to the practice of *brujería* among Mexico's peasant class, many of whom believe strongly in the power of magic spells, amulets, and other dimensions of witchcraft. Her customers were drawn mainly from the area's sizable black population, descended from two boatloads of African slaves who escaped and settled in the region a century and a half earlier, and from the predominantly Indian residents of the surrounding neighborhoods.

But her customers all had one thing in common: Their families were as impoverished as Irma's own, so payment for the wisdom her mother dispensed was often slow in coming.

Ironically, Irma reached her teenage years about the time that another young Irma Serrano was beginning a career that would soon turn her into one of the most popular entertainers of the era among Mexico's peasantry. Known as La Tigresa, Serrano the singer had become the courtesan of Fernando Casas Alemán, cousin and business partner of ex-president Miguel Alemán. A former governor and senator of Veracruz, ambassador to Greece and Italy, mayor of Mexico City, and Alemán's personal choice to succeed him as president, Casas Alemán was engaged in countless tourism ventures in Acapulco. He introduced La Tigresa to powerful people in the entertainment industry who granted her auditions as a favor to her lover, though most agreed that the plump, somewhat slutty woman with the wildcat mascara had no discernible talent as a singer.

By the late fifties and early sixties, La Tigresa's private life was every bit as public as the short, tight country-girl outfits she wore onstage. It was an open secret, for example, that her lovers included everyone from the muralist Diego Rivera to Gustavo Díaz Ordaz, who was sworn in as Mexico's chief of state in 1964. Devotees of the national gossip columns delighted in each new report of her exploits, particularly an incident at a birthday party for Mrs. Díaz Ordaz during which La Tigresa punched out the president.

Patterning herself on her famous namesake, young Irma Serrano Reyes set about the business of improving her own social standing. She left school after the sixth grade, and by age seventeen she had added two illegitimate children to the household, the products of casual liaisons not uncommon among her social class. Already, sheer endurance had begun to carve its traces into her face. She came to realize that the options were limited for a poor teenager from the shabby port, its once-shimmering waters long since gone to gray, like suntan oil on turbid tourist skin.

One day a friend of the family drove up the rutted road in front of 12 Río Bravo and announced that he knew of a place where Irma could earn more money than she had ever dreamed. He put her on a bus bound for Boys Town, Nuevo Laredo.

At four feet ten inches, with her black hair trimmed in a modified page-boy framing her high cheekbones, flared nostrils, and wide brown eyes, Irma managed to appear both innocent and hard, both childlike and mannish. It was easy to imagine her as the exotic foil for many an adolescent's ambiguous sexuality. She had learned to undulate slowly, not so much thrusting her hips to and fro in the standard bump-and-grind as letting the movement shiver through her. When she narrowed her eyes, they looked inward with a fierce, almost angry expression made all the more striking by the felinelike mascara that stained her cheekbones in the muggy border heat. Soon, Irma was earning enough to send money orders home regularly, and they quickly became essential to the family income.

Almost from the beginning, though, she had discovered in herself a rootless quality that allowed her to pick up and go at a moment's notice, a kind of steadfast detachment that enhanced the improvisational nature of her life. When the internecine battles of Boys Town flared, when traffic was slack, business slow, and competition tough, she would wander along the border region, settling for a week or two in a different spot.

Ciudad Acuña, a couple of hundred miles upriver, became a favorite refuge. It was really no more than a dusty cluster of buildings across the border from the Texas city of Del Rio—not at all like the tropical abundance that had stopped just short of her family's home on the outskirts of Acapulco—but it retained something of the slow pace of her childhood. Crickets echoed in the night air and fireflies illuminated the web of shin-high scrub grass surrounding the town, so steeped in humility and patience. In Acuña she could drift in the lull and let the undemanding days wash over her.

During the spring of 1967, Irma spent more and more of her time shuttling between the two border towns. She made herself increasingly unavailable to the subterranean world of tricks and turnouts, working just enough to wire money home before disappearing again. A photograph from that time reveals a weary, freeze-frame look rippling across her face. She seemed battleworn and randomly scarred beyond her years.

So it startled her when a twenty-three-year-old part-time translator at the University of Texas in Austin tracked her down in Acuña to propose marriage. Robert Joseph Zani had visited her in Boys Town in recent weeks, whenever he scraped together the gas money for the trip in his sky-blue 1963 VW Bug. She had enjoyed the attention he paid her, enjoyed how his legs thrashed about on the bed, making the mattress squeak like the soles of his tennis shoes. She had enjoyed half-listening when he wooed her in passable Spanish with stories of the adventures they would have someday. She had enjoyed it all, but she hadn't taken it seriously.

Still, as they traveled to Mexico City to marry on June 28, 1967, Irma Serrano Reyes entertained the cautious thought that the union might endure. And as they spoke their vows before a civil judge, she wondered if the young man at her side regarded her as anything more than a dirt-poor Mexican whore. That night she sat on the far side of her honeymoon bed in a cheap hotel and peeled her stockings off as if she were skinning herself, stockings darned so often they were no more than a series of runs sewn together. She looked at him over her shoulder and allowed herself to imagine that she might wrest a little legitimacy from the world after all.

What Irma never imagined was that Robert Zani had found in her the first of his twisted fantasies made flesh. By pledging to honor and obey, she had handed him the key to other, far grislier fantasies. She didn't know it, but she was just what he had been looking for to get back at the world— a world to which she hoped to belong but from which he wanted to flee. He could see his mother's face even now, contorted in anger when he brought his new bride home. The image gave him a great deal of satisfaction.

In the end, it may have been Irma who unwittingly nudged Robert toward murder. Not just a little killing now and then, but out-and-out, bone-chillingly murderous murder. Strolling into a room at random, putting a gun to some stranger's head, and pulling the trigger, then strolling back out before the brain matter hit the floor. Over and done with in less time than it took him to drag one of his Raleighs down to the butt.

Years later, a lieutenant with the Austin Police Department would say: "Zani was a nobody. A guy like him, he could have gotten a job as a bookkeeper or whatever, gone back and forth to work for thirty years, drawn a pension, and died. Without that little old gal he had, he never would have amounted to anything."

TWO

I t was just three weeks later, shortly before 6:30 on the morning of Sunday, July 23, 1967, when Tom Mantle's wife shook him awake. Low clouds had moved into Austin overnight, trapping the muggy air close to the ground, and the temperature had already hit the 77-degree mark. Mary Mantle, unable to sleep in the stillness, finally stopped trying, climbed out of bed, brewed some coffee, and dressed for her job at Seton Hospital. Now it was time to wake her husband.

Tom Mantle liked to sleep late on Sundays. Since June 6, he had managed store number 121 of the locally owned Town and Country convenience store chain, opening the doors just after dawn seven days a week. But everyone deserved a morning off now and then, so Mantle had asked George Vizard, his old friend and co-worker who normally worked the afternoon and evening shifts, to begin opening the store on Sundays. This morning was to be their first run at the new arrangement.

Because store policy allowed only the manager and his supervisor to carry keys, Mantle had hung his set on a nail near his front door before going to bed the night before. Vizard could stop by for them on his way to open the store—without disturbing Mantle. Not that it mattered now. Mantle had forgotten that his wife's schedule called for her to be at work by 7:00 a.m. all week. He would have to get up early anyway and drive her to the hospital.

Mantle cracked the front door and noted that the keys were gone. He told Mary that they should swing by the store at 3310 Northland on the way to the hospital just to make sure that Vizard had everything under control. As they pulled into the parking lot about 6:40, the store was still dark. Puzzled, Mantle turned the car around and headed back toward the house, wondering if he should phone Vizard or open the store himself.

At the corner of Koenig Lane and Burnet Road, a major intersection about one mile east of the store, the Mantles spied Vizard on the opposite side of the street, pedaling his bicycle in the direction of the Town and Country. Mantle slowed to a crawl and leaned out the window.

"Did you get the keys, George?" he hollered.

Vizard looked up and smiled when he saw his boss across the street. Pulling to the curb, he propped himself on one leg, fished first into the pocket of his white short-sleeved shirt, then into the pocket of his dark dress slacks, and, holding the key ring in the air, jangled it.

Mantle smiled back, relieved. "Everything all right then?"

Vizard nodded and pushed off from the curb, while Mantle steered the car south toward Seton through the sparse Sunday-morning traffic, a little embarrassed at having doubted his friend's ability to open the store alone.

Tom Mantle and George Vizard had known each other for years. They had met on campus while attending the University of Texas, each more interested in the student activism of the day than in studying for some stultifying career. They became close friends, though Mantle had to admit that it was sometimes difficult to keep up with the pudgy Vizard. In an era when radical beliefs were as common as blue jeans, George's politics were tailored to the extreme, and Mantle knew that his friend enjoyed another circle of asso-

ciates far wider and more radical than Mantle's own. He
admired George's fire and commitment, but they also made
him just a bit uneasy.

George John Vizard IV was born in McAllen, Texas, on
November 24, 1943, and was raised in San Antonio. He once
entertained thoughts of becoming a priest, but after moving
to Austin in mid-1963 to attend UT, he fell in with the small
group of earnest young activists that formed the local chapter of the Students for a Democratic Society, or SDS. He
joined the Communist party, using his membership to duck
the draft, and then devoted himself more or less tirelessly to
the agenda of the left, imagining himself to be one of
Austin's most important student leaders.

Vizard and his cronies didn't fully realize it, but the
chaotic social movements of their time marked a break with
history. They were the children of the most prosperous and
culturally tolerant segments of society, and now they were
staging a moral revolt that did not, on the whole, extend to
working men and women. They were students, after all;
they felt alienated, not exploited. They represented neither
blue-collar folks nor minorities, but they were all too eager
to act on their behalf.

In fact, SDSers and other student activist were the true
minority. That spring a Gallup poll found that 49 percent of
U.S. students identified themselves as hawks, and only 35
percent called themselves doves. The dramatic swing of
opinion that would see those figures flip-flop was still two
years away.

In other cities, Vizard complained to friends, an occasional ghetto burned and thousands turned out to protest
the escalation of war in Southeast Asia. But in Austin, no
matter how many lost their lives, there were still hordes of
young men left to ship off to Vietnam, even after all the
deferments were granted to the sons and lovers of important
people. The most prominent local display of dissatisfaction
had come eleven months earlier, Vizard often said, when a
young gun enthusiast and Marine Corps hopeful named

Charles Whitman climbed to the top of the UT Tower and gunned down fourteen random victims in broad daylight.

In his black horn-rimmed glasses, rumpled clothes, and on-again, off-again shaggy mustache, Vizard became a fixture at meetings and demonstrations, trying to shake loose the indifference he saw around him. He dropped in and out of school, explaining to his parents that he just couldn't seem to find the time—though he was always among the first to volunteer to help organize a rally or leaflet a crowd. "Your first responsibility is to your own head," he told his listeners.

On December 18, 1965, Vizard married a sleepy-eyed fellow student named Mariann Exia Garner. They had met in late May of that year when George, accompanied by a black woman, strolled into a campus hangout known as the Chuck Wagon and spied Mariann seated at a nearby table with a black fellow student named Ronnie Bookman. The two couples converged on Roy's Lounge, a segregated bar across the street, and, as expected, were refused service. Vizard was arrested, charged with simple assault, and released after posting a $20 bond. The action helped spawn a month-long series of protests by the SDS, culminating in a confrontation with rock-throwing members of the anti-integrationist Young Americans for Freedom, or YAF, of which Robert Zani was a member.

It was a heady beginning to George and Mariann's relationship. But the rent came due the first of each month, even for those who called themselves revolutionaries. Vizard worked a variety of minimum-wage jobs to finance the young couple's political activism—and, less frequently, his own college education. He supervised mentally disturbed clients at the Austin State Hospital for a time and made local deliveries in a Yellow Freight Line trucking company van. He clerked in the downtown substation of Homestead Laundry and Cleaners, leaving after a dispute over a missing $600. Most recently, he had quit his bartending job at the New Orleans Club, a bluesy music venue where musicians and employees were paid primarily in tips, if they were paid at all. So when his friend and fellow SDS member Tom Mantle called to offer him the three-to-eleven shift at the Town and Country, Vizard hastened to accept.

Now, about three blocks from the hospital, Mantle felt the steering wheel lurch to the side—the right front tire had gone flat. Because Mary was already a few minutes late for her shift, he drove the rest of the way to Seton on the flapping rubber, depositing his wife by the emergency-room door so that she could sign in. He then eased the car ahead, searching for a level spot in the parking lot to change the tire, and had just taken the spare from the trunk when Mary reemerged.

"George is on the phone," she said. "He's inside the store, but he's forgotten the combination to the safe."

Mantle recited the series of numbers and turns to her, and Mary walked back inside to relay the message to Vizard. *George may open the store a few minutes late today*, Mantle thought, *but what's the harm? A couple of lost coffee-and-doughnut sales to Northwest Austin churchgoers and little else.*

Mantle glanced at his watch. It was 7:10. After wrestling the spare tire into place, he drove home, climbed back into his pajamas, and promptly fell asleep.

The call came in to Austin police headquarters at 8:17 a.m. Fifty-three-year-old Richard Furlong, a professor in the civil engineer department at UT, was on the line. He lived at 2304 Northland, a few blocks from the Town and Country, he explained, and had gone into the store to buy a pack of cigarettes. He stood at the counter for several moments, but no attendant came. As he waited, four men who had come in before him put their items on the narrow counter, pushing aside a pile of merchandise that had already been placed there. Having gotten off to a late start for their fishing trip that morning, they stood behind Furlong, shifting their weight impatiently.

Though he was in no particular hurry, Furlong too had finally grown impatient. "Hey, anybody home?" he called out. He walked to the back of the store and peeked into the large walk-in cooler, looking for the clerk. *He must be out of earshot*, Furlong thought. He was.

George Vizard was lying facedown on the floor of the cold-storage unit, his arms folded under his chest and his horn-rims jarred loose from behind one ear. A pair of slip-on shades lay shattered beneath his knees, along with a dark blue ballpoint pen featuring the Morton's advertising slogan. There was a trail of blood leading down an improvised aisle formed by boxes of canned drinks and foodstuffs stacked opposite the spot where Vizard had collapsed. It stretched to within approximately four feet of the end of the cooler and returned up the other side of the aisle to the body.

Vizard had evidently been shot as he bolted toward the padlocked back door. At twenty-three, he had become one of the first in a nationwide rash of clerks killed in the walk-in coolers of the convenience stores they manned for a minimum wage of $2.65 an hour. One bullet had entered the left bicep, breaking the bone and exiting along the underside of the left upper back. Another bullet, apparently fired astray while Vizard scrambled for cover, had struck a carton of Coke, piercing one can and lodging inside a second. The sticky brown liquid was still oozing down the side of the cardboard box when the first investigators arrived on the scene.

In what appeared to be an execution-style shot delivered as the killer loomed over him, a third bullet had been fired into the back right shoulder blade, penetrating the heart, the left lobe of the liver, and the sixth rib, then exploding out through the top of a pack of cigarettes in the left front pocket of Vizard's shirt. A lead fragment was found on the floor beneath the body; later, when Vizard was undressed at the funeral home, the rest of the bullet fell from his blood-stained shirt.

It was unclear whether the shots had come from a .38 special or a .357 magnum. But there was little doubt that one shot, probably the third, had killed him.

Patrol officer Willie Pribble pulled into the Town and Country parking lot at 8:20 a.m., three minutes after the report was phoned in. Furlong and the four men who had been in the store before him were waiting on the walk outside. Moments later, another officer arrived, and while Pribble entered the store, the second cop pressed Furlong and the others into service, securing the area against the curiosity hounds who were even now beginning to gather.

Pribble walked directly to the cooler and checked the body for signs of life. There were none. Radioing the police dispatcher, he requested that the justice of the peace Bob Kuhn be summoned to conduct an inquest. He began cataloging the evidence in the rest of the store.

The cash register drawer was open. It contained seven $1 bills and assorted change, plus two $20 bills hidden under the tray—a total of just under $60. Several items were sitting on the counter, including a 10-cent package of Baker Boy fudge brownies; a one-pound loaf of Mrs. Baird's bread; a six-pack containing one bottle each of Coke, 7-Up, Mountain Dew, Pepsi, Grapette, and Dr Pepper; four August issues of *Playboy* magazine; and a roll of butter-rum Life Savers.

APD's fingerprint expert, John Williamson, was called to dust the scene. Williamson worked in his usual, quietly thorough way. With the indifferent gestures of a man dining alone in a restaurant, he covered the cold-storage unit, the merchandise shelves, and the entire register area with powdery gray chemicals. Then he gathered up the items on the counter, put them in a paper sack, and drove back to headquarters to dust for further prints.

By now, cops had begun arriving from all sectors of the

city, drawn by the sudden activity on a sultry Sunday morning. Gene Freudenberg, a portly young sergeant (now retired) who would later head up APD's vice squad, questioned the employees of two nearby gas stations. One of the men offered little help; by the time he opened for business, he said, the police were already poring over the murder scene next door. The other man recalled that a white Ford Econoline had driven through his driveway and parked in front of the Town and Country at about 6:55, but he could provide no further details.

Another officer checked the open fields of scraggly bushes that grew yellow and gnarled in the sandy soil at the east and north sides of the store, with negative results. His partner interviewed a delivery boy for the *San Antonio Express,* who stated that he seldom entered the store when he dropped off his newspapers in the coin-operated machine outside. The route manager for the *Austin American* remembered using the pay phone on the west end of the building sometime between 6:30 and 7:00. But he hadn't noticed anything unusual, he said, or even if the store was open.

Shortly, police sergeants Robert Kelton and Bill Landis arrived. They had been assigned to the case by Captain Harvey Gann, a lumbering, aggressive cop for whom the cliché "ice water in his veins" seemed to have been invented. Though he would later become Austin's most notorious narc, Gann's experience with murder cases was limited; he was merely covering for Lieutenant Merle Wells, the grizzled chief of APD's homicide detail who had recently suffered a heart attack and was not yet fully recovered.

Gann strode into the store, which was now filled with officers picking over the shelves and tilting their heads from one side to the other like museumgoers. Taking charge of the investigation, Gann contacted the news media, asking them to broadcast information about the murder, with instructions that anyone who had made a purchase at the store between 7:00 and 8:15 that morning get in touch with the police.

Next, Gann sent Kelton to recheck the outside of the building. Kelton found three pennies lying on the ground and promptly announced that they had probably been dropped by the assailant as he fled. As for Landis, Gann told him to call Chuck Dinges, a Town and Country district manager and Mantle's immediate boss, and tell him to come to the store.

When Dinges arrived, he said he had been promoted two months earlier to supervise ten of the nineteen Town and Country stores in Austin. He had hired Mantle at that time and trained him to take over the Northland location. As Landis scratched down notes, Dinges counted the cash in the register and reported that no money had been stolen. They never opened with more than $60 anyway, he explained.

Dinges neglected to mention the floor vault, which was encased in a concrete block beneath the counter and covered by a rubber mat. The receipts from Friday night and all day Saturday—probably some $1,500 to $2,000—had been left inside, and store policy prohibited him from publicly divulging the amount.

Justice of the peace Kuhn rushed to the scene, apologizing for the delay. Kuhn, who would lose a 1970 bid to become county judge by fourteen votes before starting a successful private practice, quickly pronounced Vizard legally dead and released the body to an ambulance driver and his assistant, who had been waiting in the parking lot since first hearing the report of the murder on their police monitor. They loaded the body into their vehicle and sped off toward the Weed-Corley Funeral Home on Lamar Boulevard. Kelton and Landis followed. It was 10:00 a.m.

At Weed-Corley they were joined again by Gann, who brought with him a disheveled Tom Mantle. The store manager was led to a back room, where Vizard's bloody corpse lay covered by a sheet. Still dressed in his pajama tops and obviously shaken, Mantle choked out a positive ID of his friend. Gann returned to the station.

Dr. Coleman DeChenar, a private physician who performed most of the autopsies for local law enforcement agencies, prepared the corpse while Kelton and Landis took a statement from Mantle in a nearby room. By the time they walked him to his car, the store manager had recovered sufficiently to assure the officers that he would phone Mariann Vizard. Three hours after the crime was first reported, someone had finally thought to notify the victim's wife.

Back at the Town and Country, Kelton and Landis sent several officers out to comb the area, telling them to question and then requestion every potential witness they could find. The cops fanned out in a widening circle around the store, but the leads they gathered were unusually poor—and dutifully recorded.

According to the offense report, for example, a man who had been watering his lawn about 7:00 that morning recalled seeing a tan Chevelle Super Sport with a black racing stripe come from the direction of the Town and Country "at a very high speed." It was driven by a white male, 20 to 35 years of age, wearing a dark jacket and a light shirt without a tie. You could tell the driver wasn't dressed for church, he noted.

A caretaker for the Highland Park Baptist Church stated that he had been passing by at about 7:30 when he noticed a white car hauling a boat and trailer pull up to the store. A man dressed in shorts had gotten out and gone inside, he said, while a woman waited in the car.

Someone else claimed to have seen two black males race through the area in a late-model Buick. Maybe they were the murderers, he suggested.

A woman who lived down the street reported that she had come out of her house when she heard the sirens. She saw a white man, six feet tall and slender, with a half-moon scar on his right cheek, standing on the corner directly across from the store. A friend of his had just died, he had told her, and now he was waiting for his minister to pick him up so that the two could break the news to his friend's wife.

In a case file that would soon run to two hundred pages, entry after entry began: "This officer, called to assist in the investigation, interviewed . . ." Reading them, one began to understand the reason behind the old adage that half the trick to being a successful cop is learning how to write a report even a superior officer will read.

It was standard police procedure to cast as wide a net as possible in the wake of a homicide, but the catch so far seemed distressingly small.

The truth was, APD had once boasted one of the best murder-clearance rates of any city in the United States. In recent years, however, the department had developed a reputation as a hub of illegal activity. Certain officers were known to jack up innocent citizens, usually on the city's poorer east side, and it was not uncommon to cover for a fellow cop's minor infraction by fudging reports. Austin cops had been brought up on a series of charges ranging from excessive force to padding expense accounts and shaking down illegal aliens. During a drug run to Latin America, one member of the force had even been nabbed by *federales*, who politely mailed his badge back to the department.

Old-timers particularly liked to tell the one about the traffic cop who would curb motorists and, if hassled, eat their driver's license, informing them, between chews, that he was now also going to have to write them a ticket for driving without a license. Lamination, went the punchline, finally cured him of the habit.

So although random brutality and corruption were not generally considered part of the local law enforcement repertoire, everyone knew that the cops might still gorilla you a bit on a bad day. This taint of impurity had permeated the community, leading to less cooperation from residents—and fewer crimes solved.

Still, two reports that seemed rather substantial did come in later that day. About 3:00 in the afternoon, a man phoned the station and told the officer on the desk that around 8:00 that morning he had seen a white late-model pickup parked at a 7-Eleven store two blocks from the scene of the murder. There were two white females and three white males inside, he said, one of whom sported a beard. Several cases of orange juice were resting in the bed of the truck, along with sacks filled with other grocery items. The caller, who had overheard the store attendant mention that he had just sold the bearded man two hundred pounds of ice, thought it strange to purchase such a large quantity of orange juice at one location and then buy the ice somewhere else, "close to the scene of the murder at 3310 Northland."

Three hours later, Sergeant Landis received a call from the Reverend Ray C. Burchett. Burchett explained that he had been ill for some time, and his doctor had advised him against holding services at his church that morning. About 7:35 he went to get a *Dallas Morning News* from the rack outside the Town and Country. A light-colored pickup was backed in on the east side of the store, with two young women seated in the bed of the truck and a gray-haired woman "who looked Latin American" inside the cab. When he entered the store to break a $1 bill, Burchett continued, he overheard a bearded man asking the clerk where to buy two hundred pounds of ice. The clerk, whom Burchett recognized as a regular employee of the store, had directed the man to the 7-Eleven down the road. Oh, and by the way, Burchett added, there had also been a second customer present, a young man with dark hair and no beard and dressed in a maroon shirt and khaki trousers.

Landis made a note of the call, circling Burchett's description of the second customer and drawing a line to the margin of the report, where he jotted down the word "suspect."

The most intriguing lead of the long day was given to

Kelton just after 10:00 that night. An informant known by both Kelton and Lieutenant Wells stated that he had been in the Town and Country at approximately 7:45 that morning. He had observed a slender white male with dark hair and dark trousers, about thirty years old, spreading out a city map on a rack of magazines and showing an unidentified man how to get to the Lockhart Highway, southeast of Austin. Operating the cash register was a stocky man about twenty-seven to thirty years of age, wearing a solid light-colored shirt and white jeans. The informant had noticed the white jeans because he had never seen a Town and Country clerk wear anything but the required dark dress trousers. It wasn't much, he concluded, apologizing for the sketchiness of his information, but maybe it would help.

Late that Sunday night, low clouds rolled in and an unseasonal rain threatened, followed by a brisk wind that swooped down from the sky and shooed the clouds away, somersaulting scraps of paper, leaves, and other debris across the empty streets of downtown Austin.

By the time they left the station well after midnight, it was becoming abundantly clear to Kelton, Landis, and the other investigators in homicide that they were going to need all the help they could get on this one.

THREE

On the night of August 1, a self-described intellectual and campus regular named Paul Pipkin made a discreet call to Austin police headquarters. Lieutenant Burt Gerding, night commander of APD's criminal investigation division and a man regarded as the premier police authority on local radical groups, answered the phone. For some time, a number of students had helped finance their university education by providing Gerding with information on UT's activists and their plans, earning as much as $500 per month from a secret FBI account. Pipkin had offered his services, but Gerding had declined, considering him too untrustworthy to become a paid informant.

"Yeah, Paul," Gerding whispered into the receiver. He had been in touch with Pipkin on several occasions since the events at the Town and Country nine days earlier. Pipkin claimed to have intimate knowledge about where Mariann Vizard had been at the time of her husband's murder, and for once Gerding believed him. Another source had already told the lieutenant that he himself was with Mariann, and Gerding had used the confidential information to steer the investigation away from his fellow homicide officers' routine suspicions of the victim's wife.

Pipkin was a real prize. With his pipe and black overcoat, he hovered at the fringe of student demonstrations, pretending to be part of the action while simultaneously lording his pretensions over the movement's more earnest members. He was romantic and pompous, acquaintances said, and probably the last person in town to be trusted.

Mariann was a willowy, self-serious blonde, the oldest of five children born to a Fort Worth potato-chip manufacturer and his wife. Through the years, she had attempted to discard her middle-class upbringing by adopting a cynical avidity that didn't quite fit her. Friends said she embraced the movement's emphasis on free love, though just how committed she was to the deeper revolutionary ideals professed by her husband and his cohorts remained open to question. If George was energized by a vision of social transformation, they said, Mariann seemed more resigned to a brotherhood of another sort, without illusions.

Gerding knew more about these dynamics of student politics than many of the students themselves. He had joined the force in 1950 as one of nine cadets, the largest graduating class in the department's history at the time, proudly taking badge 163 from longtime police chief Boss Thorpe during a brief ceremony on the steps of the Municipal Building. "Boys," Thorpe had warned the recruits, "this badge will get you more pussy than anything in town. And pussy'll get this badge quicker than anything else."

Known at first as a greasehead, a derogatory term used to describe cops who sported the then-unusual credentials of a college degree, Gerding had gone on to distinguish himself during eight years on the forgery detail, learning the intricacies of banking fraud and white-collar crime. He made invaluable contacts within the ranks of the Secret Service, the FBI, and other federal law enforcement agencies. And as the civil rights movement gained local momentum in the early sixties, he found himself with a new assignment. His only charge: "Keep the lid on it."

Gerding accepted the task with relish. Chief R. A. Miles, having succeeded Thorpe, detested the Bull Connor image of Southern cops, an image that found approval among a great many of his veterans who liked to take rookies aside and advise them that there was a "whole lot of justice at the fat end of a club." Miles discouraged the use of excessive force and snarling police dogs, and he argued against taking sides in the social conflicts then beginning to fray the fabric of the nation. For his part, Gerding was aware that some of those conflicts not only threatened Austin, but also originated there, and he resorted to more creative methods of damage control.

Gerding's exploits were legendary. He subscribed to a dozen underground journals, kept detailed lists of names, and compiled a surprisingly incisive history of some of the most memorable local protest groups. He once sneaked into the basement of an SDS member's house and dismantled just enough of the group's printing press (stolen a year before from atheist Madalyn Murray O'Hair) to render it inoperable. Another time, he outfitted a dead cockroach with a tiny antenna from an old transistor radio and had it placed beneath a chair in the front row during an SDS gathering in the YMCA meeting room across the street from campus. The meeting broke up when the students, already convinced that they were under constant surveillance, discovered the "bug."

"It was a healthy rivalry in those days," Gerding later recalled. "Like a chess game, we moved our players around the board and played cat and mouse. But whenever I saw an opportunity for checkmate, I took it. Much of my time was spent keeping their kings in check."

In the process, Gerding, the Vizards, and Pipkin had frequently crossed paths. Indeed, the lieutenant had been the arresting officer in Vizard's simple-assault charge at the off-campus restaurant in May 1965, and he had been present when the pudgy SDS member was booked into the Travis County jail for "causing a disturbance" and "arguing and cursing at a security guard" during a protest march on the grounds of the state capitol in January 1967. Pipkin, too, had been there on those and other occasions, loitering as always at the edges of the student movement.

Now Pipkin was on the phone, telling Gerding about a recent demonstration in Houston during which the Committee to End the War in Vietnam had been assaulted by a group of Marine reservists. Among the counterpickets had been a man closely fitting the description given in local news reports of the unidentified person behind the counter at the Town and Country on July 23. Pipkin urged Gerding to obtain the man's name and photograph from the *Houston Chronicle*, which had covered the demonstration. Gerding never did.

On August 5, Walter Haase, an employee of the Retail Credit Company, contacted the Austin police to say that he had been called to investigate George Vizard's $7,000 life insurance policy. Originally purchased in 1962 by George's parents, the policy had recently been changed so that Mariann, not George's brother Ed, became the beneficiary after the young couple assumed the premium payments.

The police suddenly had a possible motive to go along with the person who was shaping up, despite Gerding's best efforts, as their principal suspect: the victim's wife, Mariann, was asked to submit to a polygraph test and readily agreed. An appointment was set for August 10.

Mariann Vizard had spent the days since the murder hiding out from news reporters at the Austin home of Woody Ashwood, an old friend who had been released some months earlier from Leavenworth, where he was serving time for military desertion. The press had seized on Vizard's killing as a symbol of the confrontation and violence that characterized the times. Daily headlines in the *Austin American,* as well as stories in the *New York Times* and other national publications, fueled talk that the SDS leader's killing was more than just a spur-of-the-moment murder committed during some attempted robbery at a convenience store; this was political assassination. Letters and telegrams poured in from around the country, expressing sympathy for Mariann and pledging solidarity in the wake of another fallen brother.

After the murder, the Austin Area Dubois Club, a small leftist movement known for its uncompromisingly socialist views, printed and distributed a rather sententious four-page flyer entitled "Who Killed George Vizard?" in which members second-guessed APD's investigation and, after digressing into a general indictment of modern-day America, concluded with the notation "This leaflet has been approved of by Marianne [sic] Vizard" prominently displayed across the bottom. The flyer read:

George Vizard, a leader of Austin's equal rights, free speech and peace campaigns was shot to death on the morning of Sunday, July 23, in the cold storage room of the drive-in grocery where he worked. To this day nobody knows who was responsible for the murder. Opinion here is parted between two camps, one holding that his murder was politically inspired, the other contending that it was purely the result of an armed robbery.

Because George was a well-known leftist, because in the past his life had been threatened, because early morning and Sunday holdups both defy the patterns of armed robberies; for at least these reasons there are those who style George's murder a political assassination. It is also no secret that paramilitary groups of the ultra-right train in guerilla warfare on weekends in the countryside near where George worked. Added to this is the possibility that his murder was carried out with a .357 magnum pistol, whose destructive capability rules out its use by any but the most informed and desperate. Those who see political motives behind the murder do not find it incredible that an assassin might also steal. . . . Those who rule out political motives in the killing often do so by saying that an inexperienced bandit might have fired and fled, panicked by factors known only to him.

The two cases are summarized in a single statement: that the man or men who murdered George Vizard were either well prepared reactionary fanatics, or unsure and incompetent bandits. In the absence of more certain details, we feel that neither case is worthy of support to the exclusion of the other. . . .

As a man, George Vizard was a gentle and perceptive person, and was therefore devoted to the cause of peace and socialism. He had come to realize that under an economic order where one's foremost duty in life is to compete for the "privilege" of consumption, men are *needlessly* pitted against one another, and come to see themselves, not as partners in a cooperative endeavor, but as beings engaged in ceaseless hostility. . . .

George Vizard was not satisfied with the lessons that capitalism teaches, not content with a heritage of exploitation and bloodshed advanced under the cover of "freedom" and "patriotism." And he was vocal in voicing his discontent. If his voice was silenced for political reasons, the implications are clear. . . .

No matter which motive we examine, one point is clear: that in either cases [*sic*], the teachings of capitalism informed and inspired the act which led to George Vizard's murder. Therefore, the question we should pose is not "Who killed George Vizard?" but "What brought about his death?" For in either case, the man who murdered George Vizard was merely an unconscious instrument of an economic system which oppressed him just as much as it did his victim—just as much as it does us all. There cannot be a world free of poverty, war and crime until man is freed of capitalism. This is the lesson that George Vizard taught in life, and this, above all, is the social meaning of his death.

By the time she arrived at police headquarters to take her polygraph test, Mariann had become a lightning rod for those and others of the movement's many conspiracy theorists who used her husband's murder as a means to publicize the larger evils of America. Accompanied by Paul Pipkin and her attorney, Mariann told investigators that Allen Hamilton, the chief of the University of Texas police, may have had something to do with George's death, according to word on the street. Hamilton had threatened her husband's life, she said, when he and a state trooper arrested the activist during a speech by Secretary of State Dean Rusk on the grounds of the state capitol earlier in the year. At the booking desk of the county jail, an angry Vizard had supposedly turned to Hamilton and hissed, "I'm going to get me a heater and burn the next sonuvabitch who puts his hands on me."

APD officers, who generally squandered little love and even less respect on the campus police, quickly hauled Hamilton in for questioning. He told them he had spent the night of July 22 and the day of July 23 with friends and family at his cabin on Lake Travis. What was more, he said, two business associates from town had come out early that Sunday morning to help him round up several head of cattle from an adjoining property so that they could be sold at auction later in the day. Hamilton had first learned of the events at the Town and Country that night, when he turned on the ten o'clock news. No fewer than eleven relatives, friends, and neighbors would vouch for him, he said.

Meanwhile, Kelton and Landis tried to patch together a pattern from the disparate leads gathered on the day of the murder. With Merle Wells still ailing and Harvey Gann only nominally in charge, the two veteran police sergeants knew that the success or failure of the investigation lay largely in their hands.

Early on the Monday following the murder, Kelton sat down to draw a general diagram of the Town and Country and its cold-storage unit, showing where the body had been found. He read through the report, trying to make some sense of it. Landis sent routine Teletype messages to police departments around the state, asking for information on a number of perennial suspects he had culled from APD files. But both men knew they were grasping at straws, biding their time until a break in case A69421 presented itself.

Even the name of Richard Furlong, the UT professor who first called in the murder, turned out to have been misrecorded. Page 1 of the offense report read: "This writer received a phone call from Carl Burnette stated [sic] he had found a man shot in the cooler of the Town & Country Store at 3310 Northland Drive."

The entry had been made by Landis himself, who discovered the error only after he finally got around to answering several phone messages left by the real Carl Burnette. At 8:50 on the morning of the murder, Burnette told Landis, he had seen a man walking briskly in the 4200 block of Venado Drive, about a mile northwest of the Town and Country. He was wearing a light-colored shirt and khaki trousers, and he carried a paper bag tucked under his arm. He seemed suspicious, said Burnette, who immediately returned to the area after hearing news of the murder. By then the man was gone.

Kelton then spoke to Mary Stallings, who said that she and her roommate had left their home at approximately 7:55 that Sunday morning en route to Lake Travis. She was sure of the time, she explained, because when she had called her friends at the lake to tell them she and her roommate were on their way, she asked the time. She stopped at the Town and Country for ice and a bottle of Sea and Ski suntan lotion sometime just before 8:00. While her roommate put the ice in the trunk of her 1964 Buick Riviera, Stallings went inside for the Sea and Ski and to pay for the ice, hoping to have enough change left over for a newspaper. Unable to raise the attendant, however, she returned the suntan lotion to the shelf and went back outside to the car. She sounded the horn several times before giving up and driving off in anger.

Stallings was sorry, she added, but it had just occurred to her that she had never paid for the ice. Kelton smiled and promised not to tell.

Other investigators in the small homicide unit were also being drawn into the case. Sergeant Donald Kidd received a call from a Department of Public Safety officer. A fifteen-year-old named Tom Foster had just enrolled in a DPS driver's education class, the DPS officer explained, and had approached him to confide that he might know something about the Vizard case. According to the boy, he and two buddies, Mike Joyce and Dana Martin, had attended a Boy Scout camp meeting on the night after the murder. They had been discussing their friend Russell DeCamp, who had committed suicide earlier that day, when Joyce mentioned that DeCamp had recently complained of being ejected from the Town and Country by Vizard.

On Tuesday, Kidd drove to the camp to interview Joyce and Martin, who were working there as counselors for the summer. The teenagers were frightened. Casting a nervous glance toward Joyce, Martin stammered that he really hadn't known DeCamp all that well. Joyce admitted that he and DeCamp had been friends, but the last time he had seen the troubled teenager was two weeks ago. They had spent the day together, going into the Town and Country sometime during the late afternoon.

Hesitantly, Joyce recalled how DeCamp had taunted Vizard, holding a Coke bottle out in front of him and asking the clerk what would happen if the bottle "accidentally" dropped and shattered on the floor. Vizard had tried to ignore him. But when DeCamp began walking around the store, picking up items and repeatedly asking their prices, Vizard lost his temper and told the boys to get out. "We're leaving now," DeCamp supposedly sneered back over his shoulder at Vizard, "but I'll come back and visit you again."

Compulsively now, the nervous boy began to ramble,

describing other incidents involving DeCamp, as Kidd scratched down notes. Once, Joyce said, they had been playing with DeCamp's .22 in his friend's backyard when a Piper Club flew overhead. "Two bits says I can hit it," DeCamp had bragged, and Joyce remembered the ping of the bullet richocheting off the underside of the plane. Another time, DeCamp had put the loaded rifle to Joyce's head and hissed, "I'll blow your head off if you move." He was always doing something like that, Joyce said; that's why Joyce had quit running around with him.

After the interview, Kidd drove back to headquarters, convinced that he had found Vizard's murderer, motive and all. He pointed out to anyone who would listen how ironic it was that the killer's body should be lying on a cold slab at Weed-Corley all the while, probably right next to Vizard's.

Finally, on Wednesday, July 26, George Phifer, then captain of the criminal investigation division (now assistant chief of police), interrogated Jerry DeCamp, the dead boy's father. Kidd was also present. Yes, the bereaved DeCamp admitted, Russell had access to a .32 revolver and two .22 rifles, one of which he had used to kill himself. On the morning of the murder, however, DeCamp had awakened his son at 7:00 so that the family could attend services at St. Matthew's Episcopal Church. They had remained at the church until 8:30. The assistant pastor, who had filled in for the vacationing reverend that day, would be more than happy to verify it.

Despite what seemed to be a solid alibi—to say nothing of the fact that police already believed Vizard had been slain with a .357 or a .38, not a .32 or a .22 rifle—Kidd remained skeptical. He continued to pursue the DeCamp angle until someone, probably Phifer, quietly cleared the teenager as a suspect in the official file. In time, Kidd lost interest in the case altogether.

* * *

Years later, a retired APD lieutenant who had worked closely with Kelton, Landis, and Kidd commented on his former colleagues.

"Remember, these were all friends of mine," he cautioned, gazing across his living room to a fireplace on the opposite wall. "But you could take all three of their heads, and I'll guarantee you, their skulls combined would be thicker than them bricks over there. Kelton was good, but unimaginative. Landis? When he decided that someone did something, he never changed his mind. And Kidd was worse than that; he was thick-headed and racist. I mean, he didn't even like the Germans or Irish. Whatever any of the three of them could find out on the telephone was enough. They didn't leave the office much, except for lunch."

Landis especially was regarded as having a flair for the mediocre. Another retired officer who was part of the six-man homicide squad in those days remembered working a robbery investigation with Landis just before the Vizard murder: "It looked like it matched a whole string of cases he'd had. I talked to him about it. He said, 'Nope. Not my boys. Some guys from Fort Hood [a military base in Killeen, north of Austin] did mine.' Well, they pulled another robbery, and through an informant, I got them caught. They sat down and gave me a full confession, in detail, including some of Landis's cases. I went into his office to give him a copy—you know, to help him clear his cases—and he wouldn't even look at it. 'I don't want to read their lies,' he said. 'Couple of soldiers from Fort Hood pulled *my* robberies.' He never did clear his cases."

Nevertheless, in a town where murder was still front-page news, Landis and Kelton were left alone to work the Vizard case full-time, and the leads they followed grew more bizarre as the days dragged by. On Wednesday night a woman called to report that she had been visiting her son near the Town and Country on the morning of the murder. She and some friends were driving by the store at about 10:55 on their way to a fishing trip on the coast when she saw a "beatnik character" standing across the street. Her description of the man was indicative of both the times in Austin and what even the best officers were up against as they tried to sort fact from fancy: "One white male, age 25 to 30, five feet ten inches, medium build, auburn or chestnut hair worn foolishly long. Subject had a mustache and bushy, kinky hair about two inches long. The beard did not quite touch the mustache. Subject wore an olive khaki shirt with the tail out and dark-color trousers. His hair was long, similar to the 'California' type, but not quite as long, not down to his shoulders."

The woman assured the sergeant who took the call that not only was this their man, but she also planned to be in town until Friday morning and would be happy to come down and identify him after the police picked him up.

On Thursday morning Tom Mantle was brought to the station and fingerprinted in an effort to eliminate his prints from those found at the scene. Two days later, he was given a polygraph test. By then the store manager had begun to hedge his story, insisting that the investigators make note that Vizard had often opened the store alone on Sundays. In fact, he said, George's daily schedule had shifted between mornings and afternoons. It wasn't as if he had left an inexperienced clerk in charge that Sunday.

Nevertheless, Mantle passed the polygraph test and was released. On his way out, he met Mariann Vizard, who had come to pick up the contents of her husband's billfold—two $1 bills, 60 cents in change, a driver's license, assorted receipts, and telephone numbers scrawled on scraps of paper and matchbook covers—and the two went off to discuss the whirlwind of events since Vizard's graveside services four days earlier at the Mission Burial Park in San Antonio.

* * *

At 8:00 on Sunday morning, July 30, nine men assembled in the lineup room at police headquarters. Landis and Kidd asked them one by one to record what they had observed at the Town and Country exactly one week earlier.

Richard Furlong was first. He repeated his shock at discovering the body in the cold-storage unit. Then, the four men who had entered the store before Furlong to pick up supplies for a fishing trip—Clifford Wolff, Alex Connley, Sam Smith, and Walter Carrington (one of Austin's principal land developers)—remembered the confusion at the scene after the first officers arrived.

Norman Higgins was next. Speaking into the recorder with slow, deliberate precision, he recalled how he had stopped in front of the Town and Country to buy a block of ice about 7:30 on the morning of the murder. Finding the blocks melted together, he went inside to ask for help. The clerk, a slender white male about nineteen years of age with dark hair and glasses, reached under the counter and handed him an ice pick. Higgins had just emerged from the store when two men, who appeared to be father and son, drove up. While the younger man waited in the car, the older man offered to help Higgins. After several moments, they freed a block, and Higgins went back inside to ask the clerk for tongs to lift the ice into the trunk of his car. The clerk disappeared into the cold-storage unit to look for a pair. "He was a long time in bringing the tongs," Higgins recalled, "but he eventually brought them." Higgins paid for the ice and left.

Finally, Jerry Mogoyne, Sr.; his son, Jerry Junior; and their friend Dewey Dungan recorded their recollections. According to the elder Mogoyne, the three had stopped at the Town and Country for ice and snacks on their way to install an air-conditioning unit in the Lake Travis home of Louis Shanks, the owner of a well-known local furniture store. The stop had become routine for them because of the volume of electrical work required in the residential developments springing up west of town that summer.

Mogoyne continued his story, nodding toward Higgins. As Mogoyne had driven into the parking lot that morning, a man was struggling with blocks of ice in the outside cooler. Mogoyne helped him break them apart and then joined his son and Dungan inside the store.

Dungan agreed with Mogoyne's account, adding that he had selected a sandwich, a bag of chips, and a soda water and placed them on the counter. He noticed that the cash-register drawer was open and began looking around for the clerk, who finally came out of the walk-in cooler. Dungan could provide little more than a vague description of the young man who gave him change, but he did recall a sense that the man never rang up the purchase.

The younger Mogoyne volunteered that a second man, approximately twenty years of age, five feet six inches to five feet eight inches tall, 130 to 140 pounds, and wearing black pants, had also been in the store. He seemed to be assisting the clerk, Mogoyne said, having unfolded a city map to help a customer find his way to some location.

With the exception of the Reverend Ray Burchett, who was still ill, everyone known to have been present in the store around the time of the murder had now corroborated their original statements to the police. (A week later, Burchett was feeling healthy enough to come down to the station and repeat his version of events, as well.) Based on their recollections and those of Mary Stallings, Landis and Kidd established the time of death at somewhere between 7:50 and 8:05 in the morning.

As they were winding up the interview session, Kelton rushed into the room and suggested that they try to come up with a composite sketch of the clerk who had waited on Higgins, Dungan, and the Mogoynes. Though he had no drawing experience, Kelton sat down with a sketch pad and began asking questions. Higgins was little help. Dungan and the Mogoynes, however, each described a young man of medium build, wearing a solid light-colored shirt and white jeans or khakis. He was not the regular morning or afternoon attendant they were used to seeing, they agreed, though he did seem to know his way around a cash register.

Kelton finished his sketch and proudly showed it to them. Hard to say, they hesitated, not wanting to offend the investigator's artistic sensibilities. Perhaps if they could see an actual photograph of the deceased? Kelton reluctantly fished a photo of Vizard from his briefcase and tossed it on the table. Immediately, Dungan and the Mogoynes came alive. Yes, they exclaimed simultaneously, that was one of the clerks they knew from their regular stops at the Town and Country—but it was not the one who had been behind the register on July 23.

That afternoon, Kelton dropped his composite sketch off at the offices of the *Austin American,* urging that it be published to assist the police in their investigation. When the drawing appeared on the front page two days later, some thought the sergeant had signed his name across the bottom with a bit too much flourish.

On August 2, Fred Rymer, the chief of the firearms section at DPS, submitted the results of his ballistics tests on the bullet fragments found at the Vizard murder scene. During a career that already spanned some thirty years, Rymer had earned a reputation as one of the top weapons experts in the country; he was rarely, if ever, wrong.

Rymer's report was succinct. "Bullet is either a .38-caliber or possibly a .357-caliber . . . eight lands . . . right," he concluded, adding that it had been fired from one of two weapons—a .38 special or a .357 magnum.

By mid-August, the investigation was veering toward the absurd. On the morning of August 14, an APD officer contacted the chief of police in San Marcos, a quiet college town 24 miles south of Austin that was best known as the home of Southwest Texas State University, President Lyndon

Johnson's alma mater. Two youths, seventeen and fifteen years of age, had been arrested in connection with an armed robbery there three days earlier. One was nabbed in Galveston, the other after a shootout with the police on a lonely highway near the city of Del Rio, across the border from Ciudad Acuña. They had given written statements and been released, even though the seventeen-year-old had been found with a virtual arsenal in his possession—including two M1 carbines, a couple of sawed-off shotguns, a .357, and half a dozen other pistols—and had confessed to a Wisconsin liquor-store holdup in which the attendant was shot point-blank in the face.

For several days, Kelton and Landis single-mindedly sought information on the two teenagers. After a sergeant in the Del Rio Police Department sent word that the older boy had been out of the state on the day of the Vizard murder, they turned their attention to the fifteen-year-old and traveled to San Marcos to interview him when he unexpectedly showed up there, accompanied by his mother, who had come from Willow Springs, Illinois, to retrieve her son. She confirmed that both boys had been at her Illinois home on July 23.

More time was wasted on a background check of Richard Leslie Cooper, a twenty-seven-year-old New York native who also used the name "Richard C. Armenti." Cooper boasted a lengthy police record, having been arrested in various parts of the country, including Houston, where he was charged with assault with a deadly weapon in 1960. On March 12, 1967, while serving time for murder, he had escaped from the California state penitentiary at Chino. Witnesses had fingered him as the suspect in an April 11 homicide downstate in Santa Maria, California, where the gun used was a .357 Ruger magnum with .38-special ammunition. He had last been seen in El Paso some days later.

This time, at least, Kelton and Landis believed they had a possible ballistics match. But they quickly lost interest in the lead, complaining that the California authorities were reluctant to provide more information. The background check on Cooper, like others before and after it, soon dried up.

Now and then, as the new year came and went, a tip materialized, reviving hope for a final resolution. The officers pursued each tip for a time, then tucked it away with the rest of the unanswered questions that were yellowing in the George Vizard file—by now the oldest unsolved murder case in Austin and Travis County.

On the first anniversary of the murder, the *Austin American* published a lengthy review of the case in which Tom Barry, a staff reporter who would one day be promoted to editorial page editor for the newspaper, asked, "Murder or Assassination?" After strongly hinting that Vizard's murder might fall into the latter category, Barry concluded: "Whatever it was, the police are no closer now to solving the death—they call it 'murder'—than they were on that Sunday morning when a customer found Vizard's body."

In the late summer of 1969, there was a flurry of activity surrounding a man named John McCaleb, who had been wounded during an armed-robbery attempt in Houston. McCaleb told Merle Wells and Donald Kidd that he had left his native Oklahoma with his wife and children sometime in mid-1967, committing a series of robberies along the way to finance the trip. He wanted to cooperate, he assured the officers, but his memory wasn't what it once had been, because of his recent injuries. Maybe he had come through Austin, but he couldn't be sure.

Within a few days, it was discovered that the hapless McCaleb had not left Oklahoma until Thanksgiving, four months after the events at 3310 Northland Drive.

*   *   *

Over the next few years, the principals in the investigation went about their lives. Austin was changing, transforming itself into what a Dallas newspaper proclaimed "a bustling, go-ahead metropolis," replete with high prices, heavy traffic, and increasing crime rates. During the late sixties and early seventies, the number of University of Texas students doubled, while strikes and demonstrations on behalf of civil rights and against the Vietnam War became commonplace.

Austin police officers gradually found themselves patrolling a major city with major problems. Their duties became broader and more contradictory and slowly began to encompass more than just a concern with criminal behavior. The unsolved murder of a student activist and convenience-store clerk was pushed even farther toward the back of the files.

Bill Landis was transferred from unit to unit, winding up his career as an investigator in the theft detail. One night he suffered a heart attack in his sleep. When word filtered back to the department that Landis was dead, one of his former colleagues looked up from a stack of paperwork and deadpanned, "How can they tell?"

His partner, Robert Kelton, went back to his desk in homicide, where he continued to maintain a low profile and a small workload. In time, he transferred to the general assignments detail, then to theft. Well into middle age, he became a father and determined to hang on to his job as long as possible. He was eventually put in charge of the department's property room.

Donald Kidd also resumed his unspectacular career. Several years later, he was transferred to the forgery unit, from which he retired and sat back to collect his pension. Few on the force missed him.

Mariann Vizard used a portion of the $7,000 settlement from her husband's life insurance policy to travel to the Soviet Union, then returned to help a friend finance *The Angry Jigsaw: A Novel of the New Left,* which was published by a vanity house in New York. One morning Burt Gerding opened his front door and discovered a copy of it on his porch. The inscription read: "To Burt Gerding, who keeps the lid on it. Paul Pipkin."

On January 13, 1972, the $57.04 taken as evidence by the police from the Town and Country register nearly five and a half years earlier was released to the City of Austin General Fund.

Later that year, Lieutenant Merle Wells, who had never fully recovered from his heart troubles and had recently retired, attended the funeral of another former officer. "We're dropping like flies," he whispered to a friend at the gravesite. The following morning, Wells received his first retirement check in the mail, and the day after that, he too passed away.

FOUR

On March 28, 1980, APD officer Paul Ruiz fired up a Carlton and let its blue serenity burn in a tin ashtray. His partner, Robert Martinez, lit a Marlboro, and their tiny, windowless office filled with smoke. It was just before three o'clock on a Friday afternoon, and the two veteran cops were beginning to wind down a week of loose ends, busywork, and quiet boredom. Martinez was on the phone with an informant, and Ruiz, his feet propped on the room's single desk, grinned each time his partner rolled his eyes toward the ceiling at the worthless information the snitch on the other end of the line was trying to peddle in return for some pocket change to make it through the weekend.

Suddenly, Lieutenant Bobby Simpson, the head of the department's organized crime unit, or OCU, appeared in the doorway, clutching a sheaf of papers. "I know it's late on a Friday afternoon," he said, "but we need a couple of warm bodies for a little stakeout."

Ruiz and Martinez looked at each other. They had been friends longer than either could remember, growing up in the barrio of East Austin and, after losing touch for a number of years, winding up together again on the fifth floor of the Twin Towers East, one of a pair of office buildings in northeast Austin. Under the direction of new police chief Frank Dyson, the city had recently built a tall, modern centerpiece downtown and moved the police department there from its cramped quarters in the old Municipal Building. But they had already outgrown the new facility and been forced to rent additional space in several of the new buildings springing up on the skyline of what was then one of America's fastest-growing cities. The Twin Towers became home to the department's narcotics, organized crime, and special crimes units, where Ruiz and Martinez reported to work each morning.

As the first Hispanics and the first officers below the rank of sergeant ever selected to serve in OCU, Ruiz and Martinez had earned the respect of all but the most bigoted cops on the Anglo-dominated police force. Their uncanny knack for solving crimes long after other units had given up was described by some as magic, though a few dismissed their talents as simple luck, griping that they concentrated far too heavily on "misdemeanor murders," as homicides involving Mexicans were derisively known. Simpson, however, knew that the two officers depended on a simple concept for their clearance rates: hard work. They seemed personally offended by certain crimes, finding them difficult to forget at the end of the working day.

"They were an extraordinary pair," Simpson later recalled. "Paul seemed like the leader because Robert was so quiet. But, really, both of them were just bulldogs. Once they got hold of something, it didn't make any difference how many hours of work they could see ahead. They took it. The main thing I had to do with them was try to slow them down."

Sitting on the back porch of his retirement home on Lake Travis, where his days were now spent with hook and line, following the flight of fish and feeling the fine rush of air off the lake in the early mornings, Simpson lost himself in a reverie of his long career patrolling the streets of Austin till a quarter past who-gives-a-damn.

"I got into police work in 1949," he continued, " and I got sick and tired of reporting to my supervisors only to hear them say, 'Well, that's not the way we do things.' I told myself that if I ever got into a supervisory position, I wouldn't work the cases. Instead, I'd spend my time providing my men with the resources they needed to do the job. And I'll tell you, if I was chief of police somewhere today and had the authority to start a homicide unit, Paul Ruiz and Robert Martinez would be the first two men I'd recruit. That's how much I think of them and their abilities. They were the best—never afraid to try something new."

Ruiz and Martinez were sometimes viewed as a single entity by their fellow officers, but the success of their partnership was marked as much by the differences between them as it was by their common background.

Ruiz had been born thirty-six years earlier in the Santa Rita projects on Austin's east side, where, thanks to the efforts of a young U.S. congressman named Lyndon Johnson, families with average incomes of about $600 had been moved into the first three federally funded low-rent housing projects in the nation: Chalmers Courts for whites, Rosewood for blacks, and Santa Rita for Mexican Americans. The third of four children, Ruiz often accompanied his mother, Trine, to the homes of wealthier West Austinites, where she worked as a domestic. At night he sometimes ate with the rest of his family in the kitchens of the Mexican-food restaurants where his father, Sam, a former amateur boxer, waited tables.

It was a bare-bones, segregated existence, but young Paul, cushioned by the comfort of a household as loving as it was poor, didn't seem to mind. "Don't be a Mexican all your life," his father would preach, urging his son to speak English as well as Spanish and to work hard at deflecting the Anglo image of Hispanics as lazy or slow.

At school Paul served as a lieutenant on the safety patrol, wearing the red-and-silver badge of his rank with boyish pride. Weekends, he played second base for a Little League team or gathered with other kids his age for a pickup game of football on the wide grassy medians of East Avenue, now I-35, which then, as today, divided the city along both racial and economic lines. He once sat entranced by Gene Autry and his horse, Champ, who had come to perform at a festival on the shores of Town Lake. And sometimes, late at night when he was supposed to be in bed, he would steal to the stoop and wait for his father to arrive home from work in one of the "two-nickel" cabs that operated independently of the city's taxi companies.

There were occasional moments of drama to punctuate their lives. One night the family heard a banging at the front door, and through the glass they saw the silhouette of a man who seemed to be trying to break in. Paul crouched behind a chair and watched as his father grabbed a small-caliber pistol. Just when the intruder seemed about to break the door down, Paul's father pulled the trigger. There was a leaden click as the firing pin hit the bullet, and then silence. The gun had jammed.

"It's your father!" the man shouted, and when they opened the door, there stood Paul's grandfather, uncharacteristically drunk. Early the next morning, Paul's father took the family into the backyard and aimed the gun at the ground. This time, the bullet fired perfectly, burying itself in the dirt.

Through the years, however, the Ruiz family settled into a quiet and modest middle-class routine. Sam grew into one of the finest maître d's in town and came to know personally many of the well-heeled businessmen and local officials he served. Trine secured a license from the state to operate a small day-care center. They moved out of Santa Rita, by now a dismal slum that poverty had integrated in a way no federal legislation could achieve, and some years later rented themselves a tiny A-frame on a shaded street in South Austin.

By the time Paul reached high school, his interests had widened considerably. Curious and outgoing, he was a popular student, lettering three straight years in baseball and his senior year in football, when he was also captain of both varsity teams and set a short-lived city record for field goals. He was known for constantly arguing politics with his father, a devout Democrat who couldn't understand his son's more independent philosophy. The rest of the family would know that the discussion had gotten out of hand when both men moved to the kitchen and the elder Ruiz began to cook, a practice his son continues today.

Paul's interests had also widened to include the opposite sex. But his popularity with girls—especially with the Anglos he often dated—didn't always extend to their parents. The subtle forms of discrimination that had somehow escaped his attention until now were finally brought home to him when he began dating the daughter of a city council member who seemed to Paul as interested in keeping the young Hispanic away from his house as he did in conducting municipal affairs. The couple was forced to sneak around to avoid detection and made to feel cheap and dishonest, all because of Paul's ethnic background.

After his high school graduation, impatient and anxious to prove himself, Ruiz decided to escape town by joining the Army Reserve. Two days later, he was on his way to Little Korea, a basic-training camp in Missouri. Although it hardly qualified him as a world traveler, the six months Ruiz spent in the camp helped to broaden his perspective. He was away from home for the first time in his life, meeting other young men from around the country and hearing about their lives in places as far-flung as the Pacific Northwest and New York City.

When he returned to Austin, Ruiz found a job as a business manager for a local interior design firm. With his father's help, he placed a down payment on a small house in South Austin and had soon saved enough to buy a new Ford Mustang. One day in 1964 he aimed it toward California with his girlfriend at his side—she was another Anglo whose parents disapproved of her choice in men. Somewhere along the way, they stopped at a pay phone, and she called her parents collect to tell them they had eloped. Her parents were not pleased.

Ruiz found a job as a bank teller in Los Angeles and later moved on to computer work in the financial institution's data processing department. A son was born, then a daughter. But the Ruiz family quickly grew tired of the earthquakes, the smog, and the riots in Watts, so Paul and his wife began scouting for jobs back in Texas. When Lockheed offered him a position at the Manned Space Center in Houston, the couple leapt at the chance. Four years in California had been quite enough.

After the moon-landing projects of the late sixties wound down, life in and around the NASA complex lost much of its appeal. Not coincidentally, so did the Ruiz's marriage. Paul found himself thinking back more and more to his grade-school ambitions of becoming a cop. He wrote to the City of Austin for information on the police department and was invited to take the civil service exam, which he promptly failed. With his characteristic refusal to accept defeat, he pulled some strings and was allowed to retake the test. This time he passed, and in November 1972 he moved his family back to Austin. Four months later, Paul Ruiz was handed his commission, badge 179, and the keys to a blue-and-white, pausing just long enough to officially bring his marriage to an end.

Robert Martinez was also born on Austin's east side, the sixth of thirteen children raised by Tomás and Clotilde Martinez, on December 27 one year earlier than Ruiz. Tomás, whom everyone called Tom, was a self-educated farmer who had lost his land during the Depression and moved to town to wash dishes at the venerable Driskill Hotel, where Clotilde worked as a maid. Despite such inauspicious beginnings, the hardworking couple managed to buy a house in the 2000 block of East Seventh Street and build a stable life for their family.

Though each of his parents and his older brothers and sisters spoke adequate English, young Robert wasn't really pressed to learn the language until he entered the first grade. His boyhood activities tended to revolve around church rather than school. Every Sunday, at the insistence of his father, he trudged off to the first Mexican-American Baptist church in East Austin. Often he emerged from the service to find Paul Ruiz, a member of the same church, waiting for him on the sidewalk. Sometimes the two boys played hooky from Sunday school, spending the few coins their parents had intended for the collection plates on ice cream down at the corner drugstore. And when Robert's church-sponsored ball team got together for games on Saturday afternoons, Ruiz was frequently the star second baseman.

As a teenager, Robert felt like the black sheep of the family, a tough, streetwise kid who was known as a gang leader in the days when such a reputation implied more of a simple territorial imperative than the involvement in hard drugs and criminal violence associated with gangs today. Still, his family was concerned about him; increasingly, it seemed, the other teenage boys from the neighborhood were falling into trouble with the law.

One night, while attending a Fats Domino dance at the City Coliseum with his high school sweetheart, Mary Ann, and another couple, the fifteen-year-old Robert pulled a pint of Seven and Seven bourbon from his coat. He had just started to doctor his friends' cokes when a police officer tapped him on the shoulder. "You're under arrest for possession of an alcoholic beverage," the cop told him.

Unable to convince the officer that he was a minor, Robert was taken to city jail and booked. Three days later, he was released to the custody of his worried family, whom the police had refused to notify until their slow-motion check of the youth's background revealed that he had been truthful about his age all along. Though his brothers and sisters delighted in taunting him about the incident, calling him jailbird and con, the incident proved to be a turning point in Robert's life.

"One of these days," Martinez resolved, "I'm going to show them I'm the best at something. I'll let them read about me in the newspaper."

To help him on his way, Robert's sister found work for him, sacking groceries in a local grocery store. With a job after school and on weekends, the teenage gang member had little time to hang out on the corners of East Austin with his friends. Unfortunately, he also had little time to study. But with Mary Ann's assistance, Robert managed to graduate from high school in June 1961, and the next month the two longtime sweethearts married. Ten months later, their first child, Robby, was born, and then a daughter, Roxanne. (Robby, like his father, would distinguish himself as an Austin police officer. In the early hours of February 25, 1989, while en route to a disturbance call in East Austin, he was killed when his patrol unit struck a tree as he swerved to avoid a pickup that had run a red light. He was twenty-six.)

Meanwhile, Martinez had been promoted to assistant manager of the grocery store, in charge of buying and personnel. One day in 1966 he hired an Austin policeman to work security at the store a couple of days a week during his off-duty hours. He was fascinated by the cop's commanding presence, the crispness of his uniform, and the stories he would tell about ankling down alleyways after crooks. Martinez began to wonder about joining the force. Though he was earning $725 per month at a time when Austin patrol officers were paid only $350, he knew that he stood a better chance of showing his family what he had made of himself as a member of the police force than he did working the rest of his days in some grocery store.

With Mary Ann's blessing, Martinez took the civil service exam. Like Ruiz, he failed the first time and had to wait to take the test again. But in December 1967, six months after George Vizard was slain, Robert Martinez, only the third

Hispanic officer in the history of the force, donned badge 373 and hit the streets.

In the wake of the Watergate break-in, which had been discovered by a plainclothes officer in a federal law enforcement program that made it possible for local police departments to send officers in unmarked cars into high-crime areas, APD initiated the first of its permanent undercover units not solely dedicated to the fight against narcotics. Martinez was selected to be among the first dozen officers to man the new TAC squad operation.

Not long afterward, Martinez and his partner, Frank Castillo (now with the Texas attorney general's office), backed up a burglary call in north-central Austin, Martinez knew the uniformed officer. Frank Maxwell, who had arrived first on the scene, and he thought he recognized Maxwell's partner as well.

"Aren't you Paul Ruiz?" he asked, remembering the boyhood pal with whom he had played ball and skipped Sunday school.

The two renewed their friendship, and Martinez learned that during his few years on the force, Ruiz had achieved one of the highest arrest rates by a uniformed officer of people connected with major crimes. When a position opened up on the TAC squad in 1978, by now renamed special crimes, Martinez urged Ruiz to put in for the job, then lobbied for a spot on the review board slated to approve the applicants. To the astonishment of no one, Ruiz was tapped, and he and Martinez formed a working partnership that required no little accommodation from both. One was brash and headstrong, the other quiet and methodical. But the remarkable results they achieved in the cases made the effort to put up with each other very much worthwhile.

Now Bobby Simpson needed their help. In his office across the hall, the lieutenant and three of his men—Sergeant Jimmy Brown and patrol officers J. W. Thompson and Robert

Chapman—were playing host to an agent for the local office of the Century 21 real estate firm. Larry Flood had spent twenty-two years in the military, surviving combat duty in two foreign wars before retiring to Austin to try his luck in what was rumored to be the nation's best real estate market. Yet it was difficult not to notice that the soft-spoken, dignified man in his mid-fifties was scared to death as he related his story to the officers.

The previous fall, Flood explained, agents in Austin's real estate community had expressed concern about a couple—a white male and a Hispanic female—who had asked to see several expensive, owner-occupied homes listed in the newspaper. With their unkempt hair and shabby clothes, the couple seemed unlikely prospects to purchase property in the price ranges they insisted on viewing. But what had really made the agents nervous was the man's practice of isolating them in one part of the house while his wife wandered into the other rooms alone. Virginia Dinan, president of the Austin Board of Realtors, had gone so far as to mimeograph a bulletin and distribute copies to all area real estate offices, warning the agents to be careful. But after a few days, when the couple stopped calling for appointments, the matter had been forgotten.

According to Flood, however, there again seemed to be a similar scam afoot. Aware that the local market had hit a temporary dry spell and that agents, chasing after commissions, might tend to be less cautious than usual, Dinan had sent around another flyer describing an unshaven man in dirty clothing who seemed to have no visible means of support. Then, on the previous Sunday, March 23, one of Flood's colleagues had asked him to pick up a potential client at the Ramada Inn North and take him to see some exclusive properties out on Lake Travis. Having nothing on his schedule, Flood had agreed.

"I called to confirm that a Richard K. Womack was registered there," Flood recalled, "and I arrived at the hotel promptly at ten o'clock. When I drove up, I looked to the second floor because I knew his room number—219. A man came out of the room and wagged his finger at me. 'I'll be down in a minute,' he shouted. I could tell that he was somewhat irritated."

This Womack fellow had been quite specific about what he wanted: a three bedroom, three-and-a-half bath, one-story, 2,300-square-foot family-type home on a half acre of land in the Lakeway area, all for $130,000. During the drive, Flood learned that the client had already placed a contract on a house of this type.

"I asked him why he hadn't followed through on the contract," Flood recalled, "and he told me that he'd had a disagreement with the agent. That made me feel rather concerned. "If you want to go see this same house,' I told him, 'you'll have to understand that the ethics of the profession require that the original agent has a right to the commission.' He said he wanted to look at it anyway. 'I'm not going to have anything to do with that other agent,' he said. He was very adamant about this."

Flood tried to find out more about Womack as they wound their way through the Hill Country west of Austin. What was his financial situation? What requirements did he have for his family, schools, church, work? Womack volunteered that he had been in Austin about a week, having accepted an offer to join his father's business as a wholesale distributor of mobile homes. He had recently separated from his wife and planned to live here with their two children, whom he would enroll in a Catholic school. Flood was not to concern himself with these matters because they were of no consequence.

After five hours of driving around the area, with Womack trying unsuccessfully to find the home he had in mind and Flood repeatedly suggesting that they stop to eat, the two returned to Flood's office, where Womack launched into a discussion of Texas history. Finally, the hungry and tired realtor succeeded in setting up a tentative appointment with

Womack for Friday, March 28, and then dropped him back at the Ramada Inn.

"He may have been a bit odd, but I never connected him with the recent flyer from Virginia Dinan," Flood told the officers. "He was very quiet, intelligent, and dressed in a new shirt, new tie, and new trousers. In fact, when he was sitting in my office, he crossed his legs, and I noticed that the soles of his shoes were scratched only to the extent that he had gotten in and out of my car."

It was Dinan who finally insisted that Flood get in touch with the authorities. On Friday, March 21, two days before Flood's first appointment with Womack, one of Dinan's agents had shown several homes to a man named Bob Hays. He had asked the agent, Louis Parkington, to pick him up at the University of Texas library, where he claimed to be doing some research. When Parkington walked into his house after a fruitless day of driving Hays around Lake Travis, the phone was ringing off the wall. It was Dinan. Parkington told her that Hays was "different," but he intended to take him out again the next morning.

This time Hays asked to be picked up outside the Stephen F. Austin Hotel, at the corner of Seventh Street and Congress Avenue, in the heart of downtown Austin. When Parkington arrived. Hays jumped into the car and demanded to go directly to the offices of Amelia Bullock, an established local realtor whose reputation was said to stem at least in part from her having been married—not once but twice—to Bob Bullock, the powerful Texas comptroller. Inexperienced and slow to disappoint a potential customer, Parkington agreed. But when he got back to his own office and reported to Dinan, she was furious. She called Jean Shearer, an agent who worked for Bullock, and asked if she had shown a home to Bob Hays from Houston.

"No," Shearer replied, "but I did have some weirdo in here

by the name of Ray Richeda. His body odor was atrocious, and his clothes were filthy."

Sensing trouble, Dinan asked Shearer to let her know if she heard from the man again.

Later that night, Dinan was catching up on some paperwork in her office when the phone rang. Without any opening comment, the voice on the line said, "My client has been robbed!" It was Jean Shearer. She had taken Richeda to view a home in Oak Hill, in the southwest part of the county. Now the owner was complaining that some jewelry and a wallet containing three credit cards were missing.

Dinan asked Shearer if she had left Richeda alone at any time while they were in the house. "I was with him every moment," Shearer replied, "except for when he went into the bedroom. He just went in there by himself and then came right back out."

After comparing notes, the two women realized that Womack, Hays, and Richeda were one and the same man. Dinan advised Shearer to report the theft immediately to the Travis County sheriff's department. She then phoned APD, where she was put in touch with none other than Harvey Gann, the captain who had been in nominal charge of the original Vizard investigation.

"That's hearsay," the aging captain said, after listening to Dinan's story. "We can't do a thing."

Gann was nearing the end of a long career that had turned controversial several years earlier, when the department refused to foot the bill for his defense after he was sued for illegally wiretapping a suspected drug dealer (he was eventually exonerated). Now Gann seemed to be coasting, putting in his time until retirement. Dinan called back a number of times, speaking to at least three other officers. But each referred her to the captain, patiently explaining that he was the senior watch commander that night and would have to sign off on any investigation.

Dinan spent a sleepless Saturday night. Someone was out there, someone who had access to almost every expensive home on the Austin market through an endless stream of hungry real estate agents. By early Sunday morning, she was alarmed enough to call Travis County district attorney Ronnie Earle, who happened to be a tenant in one of her duplexes. Earle tried to reassure her.

"Don't worry about it, Ms. Dinan," he said, his tone more than a little patronizing. "Everything'll work out all right."

Dinan hung up. But the more she thought about it, the more dissatisfied she was with Earle's response. She called back a few moments later, only to be politely put off again. The DA didn't want his Sunday morning disturbed, she decided.

A former state representative and Austin municipal judge who had been elected district attorney on a reform slate of liberal Democrats, Earle had disappointed some voters with what they perceived to be a reluctance to act. The joke around the courthouse was that Earle, who bore a slight resemblance to Al Pacino, had something else in common with the actor—neither had ever tried a case in district court. Earle countered such charges by pointing to the county commissioners' well-known refusal to provide his office with an adequate budget. Still, when Dinan phoned back a third time, the DA took note of the disturbing edge of frustration in her voice. He agreed to check into the matter.

During the next two days, as she waited for word from Earle's office, Dinan spoke to dozens of real estate agents. She learned that a surprising number of them had dealt with a client fitting Womack's general description in the past two weeks. One knew him as Bob Palasoto, another as Buck Womack, still others as Don Rossini from Jennings, Louisiana, or Don Cecerilli from a small town near Baton Rouge. To one agent, the client confided that he needed rest because he had lost fifty pounds in the past five weeks. He told another that his wife and mother-in-law had recently tried to poison him. Someone else learned that he would be in Laredo on business for a few days but would be back "to close the deal."

"It's not unusual to find out more about your client than a psychiatrist would," Dinan later explained. "They reveal a lot. But with the kinds of things he was disclosing, I really began to wonder if he might be a mental case."

By late Monday, Dinan had grown so impatient that she told her assistant to distribute another flyer, which only brought in more reports from still more agents. Sifting through their comments, she was puzzled that Womack was described as unclean and belligerent by some, and well-read and immaculately clean by others.

Then, on Tuesday, after he had received the latest Board of Realtors flyer, Larry Flood phoned Dinan with a theory. If Jean Shearer's client had lifted some credit cards on Saturday, March 22, from her client's home in Oak Hill, wouldn't it have been possible for him to run up charges at a clothing store and register at the Ramada Inn in time for Flood's appointment with him Sunday? That would explain the unscuffed shoes Flood had noticed, as well as the very different descriptions of Womack given by agents who had been with him before and after Sunday. Dinan agreed, asking Flood to try his hand at finding a sympathetic ear at APD.

The ear belonged to Lieutenant Simpson, chief of the organized crime unit, an umbrella unit set up four years earlier through federal, state, and local grants to encourage cooperation on major criminal investigations among the seventeen member law enforcement agencies in its eleven-county jurisdiction. Simpson asked Flood to come by the Twin Towers right away.

During that first meeting, Flood intended to tell Simpson of his suspicions and add that he had made a tentative appointment to meet Womack again at three o'clock the next Friday. "I thought I was just going by to discuss the situation as I knew it then with Lieutenant Simpson," Flood later recalled, "but I walked into this roomful of plainclothes detectives, and it shook me up a little. In a matter of minutes, they had narrowed down the information I gave them and hatched a plan to capture this guy."

The plan called for Flood to keep his Friday appointment with Womack. Flood was to pick up his client at the Ramada around three o'clock and take him to view a home on Kemp Drive in Cedar Park, a bedroom community on the northwest outskirts of Austin. Special-crimes officer Robert Chapman would be watching television in the living room when they arrived, dressed in jeans and an old sweatshirt and playing the role of the owners' teenage son. Sergeant Jimmy Brown would be hidden in the closet of the master bedroom, the door cracked just enough to afford him a view of the dresser, where several hundred dollars in twenties and fifties were to be strewn. Officer J. W. Thompson, carrying a walkie-talkie, would be stationed in a clump of trees outside the home to alert Brown and Chapman as Flood and his client drove up. Given half a chance, they reasoned, Womack would take the bait and pocket the bills on the dresser; when he did, the officers would pounce.

Flood called Womack from the OCU office to confirm the Friday appointment. "I don't have any appointment with you," Womack insisted.

Knowing that the setup depended on his ability to get Womack to accompany him to Cedar Park, Flood pressed on, reminding his client that they had agreed to look at more houses. "I don't have the time," Womack snapped, his temper flaring.

Simpson told Flood to go home and keep trying. Finally, after a number of calls on Thursday in which nothing was resolved, the nervous realtor suggested to Womack that perhaps Flood could come by the hotel the next afternoon, and if Womack was a little late, Flood would simply wait for him in the lobby. It was the best he could do.

* * *

It was now a few minutes before three o'clock on Friday, March 28—time to set the plan in motion. Ruiz and Martinez ambled across the hall to Simpson's office, where they were briefed on the situation and introduced to Flood. Simpson asked them to follow the realtor to the Ramada, where he would pick up Womack; then the officers were to tail them to Cedar Park.

The two officers shrugged. This little plan would take an hour at most, they assured each other as they headed down to the parking lot and climbed into their unmarked white-over-green Plymouth Duster. Having conducted their share of sophisticated surveillance operations—some involving airplanes, night scopes, and intricately coordinated timing—the current plan seemed hardly worth a second thought. They knew they would be off duty soon, probably by five o'clock, and they were ready to enjoy their first free weekend in some time.

An hour and a half later, Ruiz and Martinez were still sitting on the curb of the freeway access road in front of the hotel, drawing vague patterns with a stick on the white walls of the tires they had recently mounted on the Duster to make it look less like an undercover cop car. In the absence of any breeze, the late afternoon sun bore down with unseasonable intensity, and they wiped the perspiration away as the Friday rush-hour traffic rumbled by. They could see Flood's automobile parked near the lobby, where the realtor was waiting for Womack to show. Now and then, the walkie-talkie they had placed between them on the curb crackled with the impatient voice of Jimmy Brown from the home in Cedar Park.

At about a quarter to five, Flood emerged from the hotel and approached the officers as nonchalantly as he could. "I don't think he's going to keep the appointment," he told them, a mustache of concern moistening his upper lip. "Should we wait?"

Ruiz and Martinez radioed Brown, who advised them to let Flood go about his business. Flood thanked the officers, apologized for wasting their time, and, with a look of clear relief, headed toward his car.

As they watched Flood drive away, Ruiz and Martinez discussed the failure of the setup in a case about which they knew only the sketchiest details.

"We could've gone home and the whole thing would have been over," Ruiz later recalled. "I mean, what the hell did we have? We just had time. But, you know, sometimes you get a rush, a kind of hot flash. You think, *Something's wrong here.*"

Martinez agreed. "Me and Paul were already there, so we decided to stick it out," he explained. "We wanted to know who this bastard was."

The partners walked into the lobby of the Ramada and asked the woman behind the desk to call the manager. As it turned out, James Gooch was something of a police groupie, only too happy to provide the officers with whatever information they needed. Sure, he told them, there was a Richard K. Womack registered in this hotel. He had checked in last Saturday night, a real weirdo who left his room early every morning and didn't return till late. So far, Gooch said, he had racked up a bill of $217.

Martinez looked at the registry. Noticing that Womack had supplied a Visa number as payment, he asked if the credit card had been cleared.

"Why, no," the startled young manager answered. "Do you think it might be stolen?"

A quick telephone check from Gooch's office revealed not only that the Visa and two other credit cards had been lifted six days earlier from a home in Oak Hill belonging to one Richard K. Womack but also that the theft had been reported to the sheriff's department that same night, Saturday, March 22.

"After the hit on the credit cards, the little bit of extra time and effort we'd spent seemed worthwhile," Ruiz later remembered. "It'd been a bullshit case till then. Now we had something to go on. Not much, I admit, but at least we knew we could salvage something."

While Martinez verified the stolen credit-card report, Ruiz phoned Bobby Simpson to let him know what they had: three probable counts of credit card theft and one count of credit card abuse.

"Where's Brown?" the lieutenant wanted to know, wondering why the two officers had been left at the scene without a supervisor.

Ruiz told him that Brown, who had driven to the Ramada after the setup in Cedar Park failed to come off, had gone home. Angry that Brown had abandoned the officers, Simpson assured them he would call the sergeant and order him back to the hotel. Meanwhile, Ruiz and Martinez were to stake out room 219 until Womack—or whatever his name was—returned.

Hotel manager Gooch lived in an apartment that opened onto the east wing of the second-floor balcony. They were welcome to wait there, he told the officers, where they would have a clear view of room 219 down the way. Ruiz and Martinez sat near the double sliding glass doors of Gooch's apartment, sipping soft drinks and coffee supplied by the manager from the restaurant downstairs. They were soon joined by a disgruntled Jimmy Brown.

Just after five-thirty, while regaling the eager Gooch with cop stories, they heard the scrape of shoes on the outside stairwell to the second-floor balcony.

"That's him!" the manager shouted. "That's Womack!"

He was about five feet eight inches tall, a slight mid-thirtyish man wearing black horn-rimmed glasses and carrying a tan imitation-leather briefcase. Though they looked new, his clothes fit him poorly, as if he had lost considerable weight during the past few weeks. He seemed jittery as he climbed the steps, his eyes darting back and forth and over his shoulder, like a rabbit just before it's seized by the scruff of the neck.

Ruiz, Martinez, and Brown jumped to their feet, arriving at the sliding glass doors just as the suspect walked by on his way to 219. He was startled by the movement inside the manager's apartment and bolted down the hallway. Ruiz tried to pull the door open, but it wouldn't budge. As the suspect ran toward his room, Martinez and Brown pitched in to help Ruiz with the door.

"It must be locked," Gooch suggested, wide-eyed at this turn of events that had suddenly placed him in the center of a real live police chase.

"Then unlock the sonuvabitch!" Ruiz yelled.

Snapping to, the young manager found the lock and yanked the glass aside just as the suspect reached the door of his room. Martinez was the first one into the hallway.

"Hey! Police officers!" he shouted. "Hold on a minute!"

By now the suspect was fumbling with his keys. Glancing back at Ruiz, Martinez, and Brown as they sprinted toward him, he unlocked the door, stepped inside, and slammed it behind him. For what seemed like several minutes, the officers stood outside and pounded on the door. At last the suspect opened it a crack and demanded to know who the three men dressed in sweatshirts and jeans were.

"We're police officers," said Ruiz. "What's your name?"

"Womack. Why?"

That was all they needed to hear. The stolen-credit-card report and a positive ID by the hotel manager had given them probable cause to take the man into custody right then and there. They kicked the door open, slammed his hands against the wall, and patted him down. His thin cotton shirt was half untucked, and his lightweight khakis, hanging from his hipless frame, seemed about to crumple around his ankles at any moment.

Inside the right front pocket of the soiled suede jacket he was wearing, the officers discovered a U.S. passport issued to a man named Robert Joseph Zani, whose photograph matched the man in the Ramada. They found another passport, issued to his wife, Irma; a receipt from Snooper's

Pawn Shop near the university, where the subject had recently purchased a .25 Sterling Arms automatic; and three live rounds of .25 ammunition.

"Is this your real name, Mr. Zany?" Martinez demanded, the first in a long line of cops, prosecutors, and news reporters involved in the case who would assign the buffoonish mispronunciation to the suspect's surname. By now, however, Zani was rigid and uncooperative. He refused to respond.

While Ruiz cuffed and mirandized Zani and informed him that he was under arrest for suspected credit card theft and credit card abuse, Brown and Martinez surveyed the hotel room from the doorway. It seemed curiously unlived-in, as if he had managed to stay there for the past six days without leaving more than the most superficial mark on his surroundings. A lime-green necktie lay on the floor, a bottle of Listerine mouthwash and a can of Right Guard aerosol deodorant rested on the nightstand, and the briefcase they had seen him carrying earlier sat open on the bed. From the doorway, they could see that it contained assorted papers, legal documents, and pages torn from the Yellow Pages of a phone book, many of which, they would later see, were filled with a cramped scrawl and elaborate doodles in the margins.

Knowing they needed a search warrant before touching a thing, Brown summoned Gooch and told him to padlock the room with a special safety lock used by hotels when they've evicted a guest. Gooch headed down the hallway, and the three officers led Zani to the parking lot. As they secured him in the back seat of the Duster, Ruiz turned and looked up at the hotel manager, who was still standing on the second-floor balcony.

"We're taking this guy down," Ruiz called to him, "but we'll be back with a search warrant."

Then, as the Duster lurched into gear, Ruiz leaned out the window and turned his best smile on the bewildered Gooch.

"Don't go away, sir," he added. "This could turn into a very long night."

FIVE

"**A**guantando," Robert Zani snarled. "*Estoy aguantando.*"

He had refused to say a word during the six-minute drive from the Ramada to police headquarters. As Jimmy Brown followed in his own car, Ruiz needled the Duster through traffic, the suspect strapped into the front passenger seat beside him and Martinez keeping a watchful eye from the back. With the windows rolled up, Zani's body odor was inescapable. Martinez thought he smelled like a goat and, noticing a small bloodstain on his shirt collar, wondered why Zani would have taken the time that morning to shave but not shower. They walked their small-time credit card crook from the parking lot in silence. There didn't seem to be much to say.

Once inside the station, Brown disappeared into his office to begin drawing up a list of the probable cause necessary to persuade a municipal judge to interrupt his Friday evening and come down to the station to sign a search warrant. The handful of officers present on the second floor of APD headquarters lifted their eyes with practiced indifference as Ruiz and Martinez led Zani to an interrogation room at the end of a quiet hallway in the back corner of the homicide unit.

At first Zani was the very picture of detachment, his handcuffed wrists resting casually behind his head as he tipped his chair against the south wall of the narrow room. He viewed Ruiz and Martinez with the cold expression of a man whose duty it had become to make it known he intended to oppose them every step of the way. Their preliminary questions were greeted with obvious disdain. He considered them to be part of the usual clumsy approach of the law enforcement "profession"—he fairly sneered the word. Cops, he believed, had a distasteful habit of forcing all but the lowest common denominator into oblivion.

After about an hour, Martinez was fed up. "What's the big deal, man?" he asked. "How come you're not cooperating? I mean, all we've got you on is a bullshit credit-card-theft charge."

Zani shifted in his chair, as if expecting a fire alarm. With wry little jerks and smirks, tics and twitches, he glanced to his side and paused to gaze out an imaginary window in the windowless room. Suddenly, his temper flared. Slamming his cuffs on the table in front of him, he grunted in the language of a man accustomed to talking to himself a good deal more than he did to anyone else.

"*Aguantando,*" he repeated. "*Estoy aguantando.*" His eyes ran back and forth between the cops. Then, with clear contempt, he focused in on Ruiz. "Do you know what that means?" he taunted.

The two Spanish-speaking officers exchanged puzzled looks. They knew the literal translation of *aguantando*— "withstanding"—though they had no way of knowing what Zani intended by his use of the word now. Perhaps he meant that he could endure their interrogation—and anything else they hurled his way.

Soon Zani was rocking back and forth in his chair, his eyes loosely locked in a trancelike flutter. He began to babble about the hatred he felt for his mother-in-law. "She's a witch," he whispered, his face contorted in low-keyed fury. "*Bruja! Bruja!*"

He was alternating between attitudes that Martinez later described as "friendly" and "fuck you." In a thin, rushed voice, he complained that his wife was putting too much pressure on him, that he was consumed with fear for his children's welfare, that none of it mattered in the end because he was suffering from cancer and had only a short time left.

Martinez sat up straight and tried to sound sympathetic. "Man, I feel sorry about that," he said. "Have you seen a doctor? We can take you to one right now if you like."

"No!" Zani snapped, his eyes fluttering like moth wings as he leaned back in his chair. *"Estoy aguantando."*

Ruiz realized that Zani had taken an instant dislike to him, though he seemed to have found some common ground with Martinez. He excused himself, explaining that he wanted to check on Brown's progress with the search warrant.

"Zani was playing us against each other," Ruiz later explained. "I knew that if Robert could get close to him, we might find something out. But I didn't want any part of it."

Alone with Zani now, Martinez leaned forward and glared into his eyes with a frightening look that the veteran interrogator reserved for only the toughest of cases.

"What's your problem, man?" he asked in a quiet, firm tone that was somehow more menacing than if he had screamed, the overfriendly sort of voice a man uses to call a dog he fully intends to kick in the ribs. "We're just carrying on a friendly conversation here, just trying to pass the time while they draw up the damn search warrant. We're talking about everyday events, man. Why are you being such an asshole?"

Zani turned cold again and stared away. Then, with an almost audible grinding of mental gears, he looked at Martinez. "You know what?" he asked casually. "Your partner may be a smartass, but you remind me of Dizzy Dean."

"You mean the baseball announcer?" Martinez asked, thrown off balance by the continuing ups and downs of their conversation.

"Yeah, the guy from Arkansas," Zani nodded. "Dizzy Dean

tried to sound dumb, but he was really very smart. And now you're trying to come off like a dummy, too. But you're smart. You're very smart." Stiffening, he seemed to sense that he had gone too far. "You may be a nice guy," he added, his upper lip curled arrogantly, "but you're still trying to take me for a chump."

Martinez couldn't help thinking that some ninety minutes had gone by in which he and his partner had failed to extract the slightest bit of useful information from this man. True, it was a minor case thus far, hardly requiring the bringing to bear of his or Ruiz's renowned skills for getting confessions. But as much as he tried to shrug this and other comments off, his curiosity had been piqued by their apparent inability to draw Zani out. As he waited for Ruiz to return, Martinez asked a number of pointed questions, each of which Zani either answered with a question of his own— "It doesn't really matter, does it?"—or brushed off with a repeated challenge: "You can find that out. You can find that out."

Meanwhile, Ruiz was rechecking with Visa's regional office in Houston to verify that credit card number 4666 023 175 502, issued to Richard K. Womack and good through the last day of June 1981, had indeed been reported stolen. He called the Travis County sheriff's department and learned that two other credit cards belonging to Womack—Master Charge number 510 51011 332 880 and American Express number 3734 700188 91006—had also been flagged. He passed this information to Brown, who added it to his growing probable-cause list and waved Ruiz away.

While running down the credit card information on the phone, Ruiz glanced through the passport confiscated from Zani in the hotel room. Several curious notations were written on its wrinkled pages. Signed "R. J. Zani," the passport had been issued by the U.S. embassy in Mexico City on March 28, 1979—exactly one year before to the day—and indicated that the bearer, born in Tulsa, Oklahoma, on February 26, 1944, had no spouse and no minors.

According to the document, Zani had traveled to a surprising number of locales for a drifter with no regular paycheck. During a five-month period in 1979, for example, he had entered and exited Mexico on various occasions and at different cities. On April 5 he crossed from Mexico into Belize, clearing customs at Corozal in a 1973 Ford pickup; five days later, he re-entered Mexico at Chetumal. On May 8 he landed in Tripoli, Libya. Though the tight Arabic scrawl in the passport was difficult to decipher, it seemed to indicate that he had departed one month later, on June 9. There was an immigration stamp dated June 10 showing that Zani had arrived at Heathrow in London and another dated the following day to show that he had departed from Gatwick, that city's second airport. The latest entry had him arriving in Mexico on September 22, 1979—at Nuevo Laredo.

By the time he stepped back into the interrogation room, Ruiz had lost all semblance of civility with the suspect. He grabbed a chair, straddling it backwards. "Tell me about Mexico," he demanded. "Have you ever been to Mexico?"

"Have you?" Zani asked.

"What were you doing there?" Ruiz insisted.

"What does anyone do in Mexico?" Zani shot back.

Ruiz pressed on with a series of questions, each angrier than the last. He felt close to that spark of truth he had felt in other interrogations, the one that fires the pulse and sends occasional charges through the nervous system.

But Zani continued to fix him with that maddening half smile. "You can find that out," he said. "You can find that out."

The air-conditioned interrogation room was crisp, but the officers could see sweat starting to bead on Zani's forehead, erupting like fever blisters as it caught the light from the overhead bulb. He was working hard to find out how much the officers knew before divulging anything himself. More than three hours had now gone by since they brought him in, and slowly the suspect was turning the interview session around.

Finally, Ruiz stood up and put his hands together in the universal sports gesture for time-out. He called Martinez out of the room.

"Robert," he asked, "do you get the feeling that *we're* the ones being interrogated?"

Martinez agreed. "Man, we're fixing to confess to *him*. We need to back off this motherfucker because he ain't telling us shit."

In hushed tones, the partners conferred in the hallway, stifling their nervous laughter at the absurdity of it all.

"While you were out of the room," Martinez said, "he talked about his 'world travels' to Belize and Libya and God-knows-where-else. Said he was detained in some communist country. They released him after a high-level U.S. diplomat intervened on his behalf."

Ruiz nodded, recalling the entries in the passport. "I'll tell you what," he whispered. "This guy has had some CIA training or something. He keeps looking at us as if to say, 'You're nobodies, and I'm going to out-smart your ass.'"

They were stumped. Suppose Zani really was a CIA agent. Suppose they had stumbled into the middle of some intelligence operation. This could be a test of their police professionalism. *We need to go by the book on this one*, they warned each other. *We need to do this right, brother—hang this interrogation up and see what he's got back at the hotel*.

Locking Zani in the room, they headed down the hall to the coffee machine. Even another cup of APD mud held more attraction than the prospect of listening to Zani's snide remarks. They stood in the hall, sipping from the Styrofoam.

It was almost midnight by the time municipal judge David Phillips arrived to sign off on the search warrant Jimmy Brown had prepared. A simple case of credit card theft had become something more—though just *what* was still far from clear.

Years later, neither Ruiz nor Martinez would be able to pinpoint the precise moment when they stopped treating the case in an offhand way. Each, though, had felt the tug of adrenaline rise gradually in his gut and slowly felt the instinct of their training supplant mild curiosity. What Martinez described as "that little grip of fear" had kicked in.

"Zani was such an asshole," he recalled. "I couldn't understand why he wanted to make it so tough on himself. I told Paul, 'Listen, partner, we need to find out more about this guy.'"

Ruiz needed no encouragement. Never one to pack it in before all alternatives to going home had been explored, he knew already that he was in for the long haul on this case. Zani had responded to their questions once too often with a challenge to "find that out." Now Ruiz resolved to do just that.

At 12:15 in the morning, they headed back to the Ramada Inn to search Zani's room. Brown drove them in his gray, four-door Ford sedan, the handcuffed Zani riding shotgun and Martinez and Ruiz in the back seat. As they pulled into the parking lot of the hotel, the headlights played along the balcony like searchlights. Ruiz, who had spent the short drive staring at the back of Zani's head and trying to control his seething anger, leaned forward and tapped the suspect on the shoulder.

"Let me tell you something, asshole," he said, waving the search warrant over Zani's shoulder. "I don't care who you think you are or what the fuck you're *aguantando*. Before this thing is over, we're going to find out everything there is to know about you."

Zani fidgeted in his seat as Ruiz took a long drag on his Carlton and let it out in a quick burst. "We're going to find out things even you don't remember."

Hotel manager Gooch unlocked the door to 219 and let the officers in. Then, excusing himself, he disappeared into his apartment, the desire for sleep having long since overcome his initial excitement at being involved in a true-to-life police drama.

With Gooch out of the way, the officers pushed Zani down into a small armchair and told him to stay put. He sat facing the bed, where his battered briefcase still lay open, and a fleeting look of alarm passed over his features. Truth, he had read somewhere, devours her lovers if they dare look her in the eye. Now, with Brown rummaging through the jumble of papers inside the briefcase while keeping a watchful eye on him, Zani seemed to turn dim and molelike, as if the truths he knew they were about to discover were just a prelude to some larger disaster.

The contents of the briefcase formed an odd collection. There were three pages torn from the Yellow Pages of the Austin phone book, two of which featured ads for local Mexican-food restaurants and pizza parlors, the other a list of area coin dealers. Jagged clips from the real estate section of the *Austin American-Statesman* advertised rural properties and homes, their margins filled with cramped doodles. Several realtors' business cards lay scattered on the bottom of the briefcase, including one from Louis Parkington at Dinan and Company on which Zani had scrawled the name "Bob Hays," apparently to remind himself which pseudonym he had used with the agent. Brown took note of a recent Ann Landers clipping in which the Chicago-based columnist advised a young couple who had been cheated in a family real estate transaction to "forgive and forget." There was more, but the sergeant knew it would have to wait until they were back at the station.

Martinez, meanwhile, had walked directly to the bathroom. After years of working organized crime and narcotics investigations, he considered it second nature to check the toilet tank; almost without fail, he had learned, addicts and dealers ditched their works there as soon as the authorities came knocking on the door. He lifted the ceramic top and placed it gently on the floor. Floating on the surface were the three plastic credit cards—Visa, Master Charge, and American Express—all issued to Richard K. Womack. A sixty-day temporary driver's permit, filled out by a DPS officer fourteen days earlier, lay waterlogged on the bottom of the tank. It listed Zani's address as Route 1, Box 101, in the South Texas city of La Feria, just outside Harlingen.

Martinez chuckled to himself. Tearing a length of toilet paper from the roll, he wrapped the items in it and walked back into the room.

"Lookee here, Paul," he said. "I believe we done got ourselves some credit cards." He shot a sardonic smile Zani's way and slipped the bundle of evidence into his shirt pocket.

Ruiz had thrown open the doors to the closet, startled at first by the sound of empty wooden hangers clacking against each other in the disturbed air. Something caught his eye. Two pillows lay next to a small pile of linen on the top shelf. One of the extra pillowcases was folded neatly, but the other appeared to have been tossed onto the shelf in haste. Ruiz reached for it and immediately realized that it was heavier than it should be. He hauled it down and peered inside. It contained the .25 Sterling Arms automatic and thirty-five shiny shells noted on the pawnshop slip they had found in Zani's coat pocket earlier.

It was time to head back. Ruiz and Martinez gathered the remaining contents of the room and placed them in a plastic Ramada Inn laundry bag. They didn't know it, but the brief inventory of items was the dreary sum of Zani's possessions: the mouthwash, deodorant, and necktie they had seen earlier; a single carpenter's glove, a toothbrush, a comb, a leather belt, a disposable razor, a needle and thread, and a bottle of Family Formula Multi-Vitamins. On the nightstand were a sterling silver money clip, two pennies, a handful of Mexican coins, and a spent match. All was scooped into the bag as possible evidence.

As they left, Brown paused on the balcony, closed the door behind them, and inhaled deeply, relieved to be back in fresh air. "What did you do in this room?" he asked, frowning at the nauseating smell.

They knew what was coming before Zani opened his mouth. "You can find that out," he replied.

The booking desk was busy with the usual assortment of drunks and barroom brawlers from a late Friday night, early Saturday morning in Austin. Two surly men in lumberjack shirts, arrested during a disturbance in an East Austin bar, sat on the narrow bench, staring at a man wearing bright orange pants and an earring who had been brought in moments earlier from one of the gay bars a block east of the police station. The sergeant in charge roamed the corridor, checking to see which drunks had sobered up enough to be released so that others could take their places in the cells.

Hoping to dump Zani as quickly as possible, Ruiz and Martinez muscled him up to the front of the line.

"Name?" asked the clerk, without looking up.

Zani ignored him.

"Name!" the clerk demanded, fixing Zani with a withering look. He was unaccustomed to taking guff from prisoners.

Martinez stepped forward to supply the information while Ruiz quickly fingerprinted the scowling suspect and turned his pockets inside out to make sure they hadn't missed anything. Placing the items in a wire basket, the clerk cataloged them, arching his eyebrows at the odd collection: 80 cents in change, a wadded clump of Kleenex containing a single black pubic hair, and, in the cuff of his soiled khakis, a small Mexican coin mounted in gold-leaf clusters. He handed Zani a paper receipt and moved down the counter to attend to the next officer with a Friday-night collar.

After declining the standard offer of a phone call, Zani was led by a jailer through the large metal doors toward a crowded cell, shoved inside, and told to await the arrival of his court-appointed attorney. Zani slumped on the edge of a cot and stared blankly at his cellmates, who bent their heads and read the floor closely, their faces full of an accumulated, hard-won privacy. From the din of the cell across the corridor, someone shouted a sarcastic greeting to the new arrival. But Zani's eyes had already narrowed and gone dead, like two fist holes in the dirt.

Back in Brown's office, the sergeant prepared a notice to be sent to police departments around Texas and the Southwest first thing Monday morning. He wanted to get word of the arrest out as quickly as possible, before Zani made bail.

Across the room, Ruiz and Martinez spread on a desk the evidence they had brought from the hotel. A sheaf of papers immediately caught Martinez's eye. On a scrap of yellow legal paper, a number—5-53-33-33—was scribbled. *Looks like a Mexican phone number,* Martinez thought.

Next, he found two typewritten pages below the heading "List of Attorneys within the Mexico City Embassy's Consular District." Five names were circled in blue ink, their addresses given as "Acapulco, Guerrero." A wrinkled piece of paper was filled with more names and numbers, all of which seemed to be Mexican, as well as a notation for a Ron Urbanek, followed by the words "American Consul."

Martinez picked up a cheap six-by-eight-inch notebook, instantly recognizing it as the type supplied to prisoners in Mexico. The first page was scrawled in Spanish with an address: "Municipal Jail #1, Cell #4, Acapulco." While Ruiz looked over his shoulder, Martinez flipped through the notebook with growing fascination. The pages were filled with quotations from Unamuno and Karl Menninger, bad poetry, and long passages from a language he judged to be Latin.

Suddenly Ruiz stopped his partner. "Go back a couple of pages," he said. "I think you just passed something interesting."

Indeed. In the same erratic scratch as the other pages, a

message had been written. This one, however, was in English and carried an urgency the other lacked: "My wife is Irma Serrano Reyes de Zani. She lives at Colonia Alianza Popular, Esq. de Calle 6 & 1, Lote 13, Manzana 5, Acapulco, Gro. She lives there with my 4 children that she *stole* away from me, *refused* to let me see, and stole all my worldly possessions. She did all this at the insistance [*sic*] of my mother-in-law, a real bitch. My wife is a killer and has confessed."

Martinez closed the notebook. "According to this," he told his partner, "Zani was arrested for something in Acapulco, Mexico. Let's call the embassy and see what it's all about."

Then, glancing at his watch, he saw that it was already past four o'clock in the morning. "On Monday," he added.

It was just before dawn when Martinez walked in the front door of the small, white frame house on a quiet South Austin street where he lived with his family. Mary Ann, a grade-school teacher, was taking advantage of the Saturday morning to sleep in. She had long since resigned herself to the fact that her husband held a job different from most; when he left for work, she often told friends, she never knew if he would come home alive. Robert had long ago quit calling to tell her he would be late, because the jangle of the phone in the middle of the night frightened her more than when she reached over to his side of the bed and discovered he was still gone.

Martinez made himself a cup of instant coffee, undressed in the living room, and padded toward the bedroom, his clothes in one hand and the cup in the other. When he awoke later that afternoon, the coffee was still resting on the nightstand, untouched.

Ruiz went home to the tiny community of Manchaca, seven miles south of town, pulling into the driveway just as the sun began to peak through the early-morning haze. His wife, Crispin, stirred when he crawled into bed. They had met during the years when she covered the police beat as a reporter for the *American-Statesman*. Now, she was director of communications with the Austin chamber of commerce, but she had never forgotten that her husband's work frequently involved unpredictable hours. Their relationship had survived the trials of her writing exclusive stories about the police department that everyone suspected were leaked by her husband, though people who knew them well were aware that Paul never gave her any tips that could be traced back and used against him in the xenophobic atmosphere of APD.

"What's going on?" Crispin asked.

Ruiz knew better than to answer. His wife, still a reporter at heart, never stopped at one question. Besides, how could he explain the increasingly bizarre circumstances that now surrounded what was supposed to have been a simple case of credit card theft?

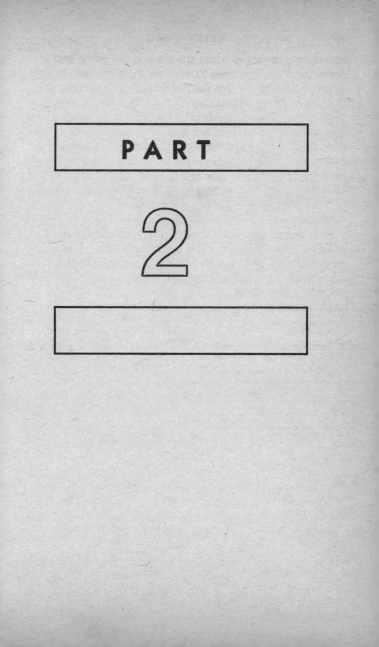

PART

2

SIX

When Bexer County OCU investigator John Bustos strolled into his San Antonio office on Monday, March 31, after several days and a weekend off, he took one look at the pile of paperwork that had accumulated during his absence and went for coffee. Clearing a space in the center of his desk, he emptied a packet of Sweet 'n Low into his cup and sat down to read the newspaper.

Among the handful of cases Bustos' metro squad was working, one in particular had him stumped: the four-month-old abduction and murder of a local real estate agent in which all leads had evaporated faster than a light rain in the searing Alamo City heat. Now Bustos' eyes strayed from the sports section to a single sheet on the top of the stack of work that awaited him. It was Jimmy Brown's message, which had arrived only minutes earlier. The words "real estate agents" caught Bustos' eye, and he began to read.

The Austin police were holding a prisoner on charges of credit card abuse, the message read, though they suspected him of other minor crimes as well. Bustos couldn't help but notice that the MO of the suspect described in the Teletype closely resembled the MO in a case of his own—a drifter who had displayed an inordinate talent for talking local realtors into previewing expensive homes he had no hope of affording.

Two important details in the Teletype varied from what

Bustos had discovered in his investigation, however. No mention was made of the Mexican female whom Bustos suspected had accompanied his perpetrator, and APD clearly had nothing as serious as murder in mind when it arrested its man. Still, enough of the brief Teletype matched Bustos' murder case that he picked up the phone and called Jimmy Brown.

In Austin, Ruiz and Martinez had arrived in their office early, each deciding independently to begin checking into Zani's background as soon as possible. Brown, too, had just walked in when the phone rang. The APD sergeant took the call and, after listening for a few moments, waved at Ruiz and Martinez across the room. Getting their attention, he scratched "Zani" on a notepad and held it up for them to see. The two partners came over and hovered at Brown's shoulder, trying to listen in as the San Antonio investigator laid out a sketch of his case.

Late last year, Bustos explained, authorities had begun to receive complaints from several members of the local real estate community about a couple who, in the words of one agent, "gave us the creeps." They were dirty, abusive, and apparently quite indigent. Furthermore, the man liked to isolate realtors in one wing of the house while his wife wandered through the other rooms unattended. Half a dozen homeowners had reported personal items missing from their jewelry boxes and bedroom drawers after the couple had been shown around their homes. The details sounded all too familiar to the Austin cops.

Then, Bustos continued, on December 4, 1979, the complaints stopped coming in. It was on that day that a San Antonio real estate agent had turned up missing.

Shortly after 7:00 that Tuesday morning, according to Bustos' reconstruction, seventy-three-year-old Julius Alfred Dess, known to his family and friends as J.A., climbed into his car and angled through the residential neighborhoods and small-business areas of San Antonio, quiet at that early winter hour. When he got to the I-35 access road, he entered the freeway and headed south toward La Quinta Motor Inn on the edge of town, boosting the defroster another notch against the chill that condensed his breath on the windshield.

An experienced realtor, Dess was on his way to pick up a man named Ray Thomas, who had phoned Dess's married daughter, Betty Jo Mason, two days earlier to discuss a rural property near Poteet, some thirty miles south of San Antonio. They had made an appointment for later in the day, but at the last minute Thomas had called to cancel. His wife was at the flea market and refused to leave to keep the appointment, he said, insisting without apology that they reschedule. Anxious to unload a property that had been listed in the Dess Realty Company catalog for months, Betty Jo had willingly complied. After all, the land belonged to her father's brother-in-law, Ralph Horwedel; it deserved a little extra effort.

Twenty minutes after Dess left for the appointment, however, Thomas was on the line again to ask what was keeping the realtor. This time, Dess's wife, L.J., answered the phone in the spare bedroom that she and her husband had converted into a study for those times when they were away from their official real estate office in a downtown business park. She was proud of their home in Castle Hills, an incorporated area on San Antonio's northwest side where solidly upper-middle class families lived in quiet comfort, and she didn't mind an occasional intrusion of business if it meant the bills would be paid. As politely as she could, L.J. told Thomas "not to fret," that he husband was on his way.

Ten minutes later, Thomas called back. He was standing at a pay phone in the motel parking lot, he complained, growing colder and more impatient by the minute. "Where is he?" he demanded to know. "It's freezing out here."

Mrs. Dess advised him to sit tight because her husband would be pulling in at any moment. Just look for a stone-blue 1974 Ford Thunderbird, she suggested. The line went dead, and in the split second before she hung up the receiver, Mrs. Dess later told Bustos, a chilling thought crossed her mind. That afternoon, it occurred again. She shook her head as if to dislodge the unpleasant thoughts and returned to her paperwork, telling herself that she must be imagining things. She was wrong.

When her husband had not returned by midnight, L. J. Dess began phoning area hospitals and emergency centers, none of which had admitted anyone matching Dess's description. By five-thirty in the morning, she was beside herself. She called Horwedel, a twenty-year veteran of the San Antonio Police Department who had recently retired to prepare for what would be a successful campaign for precinct 6 constable in Atascosa County. Horwedel immediately got in touch with Steve Becker, his daughter's fiancé, and the two began a search of the rural property near Poteet. Finding nothing, they drove to Stinson Field, a private airport in San Antonio, and rented a plane to conduct an aerial search of southern Bexar County. Again, nothing.

Horwedel and his future son-in-law then went to the Dess home in Castle Hills, where Betty Jo and her husband, Jack, were waiting to discuss the family's next move. Horwedel explained that he and Becker had already made a land search of the property and an aerial search of the general vicinity. His years with the police department had taught him that the next place to look for the car would be the parking lots of the various shopping centers in town and, after that, the San Antonio International Airport.

About nine o'clock that night, December 5, Horwedel discovered J.A.'s Thunderbird sandwiched between two large vans in the airport's long-term parking lot. He sent Becker to notify the police and then peered into the car by the light of his flashlight. He could see that the seat belts had been cut and the glove compartment forced open. The CB radio was propped on the console between the two front seats, and the floorboards were covered with sand. On the backseat, several strands of matted gray hair were caked to the upholstery in dried and jagged pools of what appeared to be human blood that had been smeared, as if to wipe the seats clean.

On December 8, four days after the disappearance of Dess, Corpus Christi resident Michael Chaney caught sight of a group of coyotes while beachcombing near the dunes just south of the barricade at Padre Island National Seashore's North Beach. He watched with mounting fascination as they trotted on a straight line headed north—the loneliest direction, he liked to say—their noses thrust in the air and their thin, howling shapes barely visible through the vaporous spray near the waterline. They they broke into a gallop and disappeared. Though the noisy arrival of the early tide made it difficult to hear, the coyotes seemed to be just beyond the dunes, whimpering and growling at some urgent scent.

Chaney and his neighbor Joe Walker had driven out to the beach that morning to take advantage of the quiet and, they hoped, to catch a little sun in the relative lull of the off-season. Now, with Walker sticking close to the water's edge, Chaney wandered up toward the dunes, attracted by the sound of the coyotes and what looked to him like a pile of debris left over from some campsite. Suddenly he stopped.

"Joe!" he yelled. "Come look at this!"

Walker ran to where his friend stood gazing down at a decomposing body curled into a fetal position. It was a grisly sight. The coyotes had partially exhumed it from its shallow grave, eating away the toes of one foot and the flesh of the genitalia, the thighs, and all but the upper arms and legs. Pieces of intestine lay scattered about, and blood had stained the sand a pinkish hue. Though the skeletal structure seemed intact, not much else remained—other than a gold and brown necktie and the shreds of a white Van Heusen shirt cuff buttoned around the right wrist.

The surrounding area was covered with animal tracks and

a curious assortment of personal items, including a burned left boot, a CB antenna, seven pairs of panty hose, and a small shovel with an address inscribed on the handle: "Gunter Bldg. 517, San Antonio." A partially burned business card, melted in from the corners like celluloid, listed the same address, a telephone number, and a name—"Dess, J. A."

On April 1, 1980, Ruiz, Martinez, and Brown drove to San Antonio to meet with Bustos, who had promised to contact local real estate agents and have them in his office to discuss the case with the Austin investigators. For nearly two hours that afternoon, they interviewed a stream of nervous realtors, taking statements from each in a tiny room where a lineup of five photographs lay spread out on the table. Without fail, the agents picked photo number 3—Robert Zani.

After the interviews, Bustos sat the Austin cops down to discuss the status of the case. There was a problem, he said. Investigators now believed that Dess had been killed either outside the town of Poteet, in Atascosa County, or next door in Wilson County—both poor, rural areas with few local resources and even less law enforcement expertise. As a result, the Texas Rangers had been asked to step in, and Bustos could no longer assure the Austin officers of much cooperation. He wanted to help, he said, but he could see that his metro squad was increasingly being squeezed to the sidelines in the case, its only involvement stemming from the fact that Dess had been a San Antonio resident and his car had been discovered at the airport, inside city limits.

Nevertheless, Ruiz, Martinez, and Brown decided to drive immediately to Corpus Christi to see what they could learn from the authorities who had handled the discovery of Dess's body, certain now that they were all on the trail of the same man—Robert Zani, who sat in a city jail cell back in Austin, wordlessly challenging them to make a case against him. Braving San Antonio's afternoon rush-hour traffic, they headed southeast, stopping midway through the 150-mile trip to buy toothpaste, toothbrushes, deodorant, and underwear at a K mart along the highway.

"We just took off," Ruiz later recalled. "I mean, even to this point, we didn't have much. A murder in San Antonio and a body buried near Corpus. It wasn't even our case. But we did have a two-bit credit card thief jailed back in Austin. So we just took off—and then we kept going."

The next morning, April 2, they burst into the Nueces County sheriff's department in Corpus Christi and announced that they were investigating a murder, drawing blank stares from those on duty. But the officers had remembered to phone Lieutenant Simpson back in Austin the night before to fill him in on their plans, and Simpson had called Nueces County sheriff Solomon Ortiz to let him know that three of his investigators would be dropping by the next day.

Simpson had once helped Ortiz and his chief deputy, Florencio Rendon, set up an organized crime unit, and they had remained friends. Brown, too, had worked a case with Rendon—known to many in the area by his affectionate nickname, "Lencho." Rendon's burly build and scowling looks belied a reputation as a thorough professional. Now Rendon was summoned, emerging from his office to greet the officers warmly. Yes, his department had conducted the original investigation, he told them. But because Dess's body had been found on a national reserve, the FBI had taken charge of the case.

Ruiz and Martinez winced. The Texas Rangers and the FBI were now the principal agencies involved. The two men had limited dealings with Washington, but they were well aware of the FBI's reputation for arrogance toward local police departments, especially the street cops who peopled their ranks. As for the Rangers, the officers had firsthand experience with the sometimes brutal frontier tactics of Texas' pioneer law enforcement agency.

Still, four months had now passed since the killing of

Julius Dess, and as Martinez noted, if it was going to take a couple of "Mexican shoeshine boys from APD" to shake something loose, then so be it.

Rendon quickly agreed to run interference with John Newton, the FBI case agent stationed in Corpus, and later that morning, Ruiz, Martinez, and Brown were ushered into Newton's downtown office. No sooner had they seated themselves, however, than Ruiz and Martinez began to suspect that Newton was recording their conversation. They could see a red light flash from time to time on the face of a portable recorder behind a picture frame. The meeting had gotten off to an icy start from which it would never recover, and after a half hour of vague conversation during which each side circled the facts it had gathered in the case without divulging any to the other, Ruiz, Martinez, and Brown left in barely disguised anger. They drove back to San Antonio that afternoon.

There Bustos put them in touch with Dess's daughter and her husband. A quiet, thoughtful couple in their mid-thirties, Jack and Betty Jo Mason had grown bitter and frustrated at the lack of progress in the investigation. As far as they could see, nothing had been done. On the day of her father's funeral, Betty Jo recalled, the local FBI agent originally in charge of the case, Pedro "Bruce" Yarborough, sent "an entire SWAT team" to the graveside, explaining that he thought the old man's murder might be part of a broader conspiracy. Matters had gone downhill from there, she complained. The backseat of the Thunderbird, which had been removed so that it could be sent to the FBI lab in Washington for further analysis, was still sitting in a San Antonio warehouse, and what Betty Jo thought were Yarborough's repeated attempts to get her into the sack pretty much summed up the extent of his agency's interest in the case, as far as she was concerned. The one bright spot, she concluded, was that he had recently been reassigned.

"What she told us rang true," Martinez said later. "We knew Yarborough because he used to be stationed in Austin.

He was a real bastard, a hateful sonuvabitch. Typical FBI. We figured his replacement couldn't be any worse, so we decided to look him up right then and there."

Norman Stutte turned out to be the one FBI agent who seemed willing, almost eager, to accept their help with the investigation. Among other things, Stutte told the officers that he had interviewed a man named Donald Wilkey, who lived across the road from the Horwedel property near Poteet, where Dess had driven his clients on December 4, 1979.

According to the statement Stutte had taken from him, Wilkey was headed into town that morning when he saw the realtor, whom he had met a number of times, opening the gate to the property. He had stopped to exchange brief pleasantries with Dess and his clients—an Anglo man and his Mexican wife—and then driven off. Minutes later, Wilkey's wife, Barbara Ann, had also driven by and reported seeing Dess in the company of a man and a woman. The two men were sitting in the front of the car with the doors open, and the woman was behind them in the backseat. When she returned a couple of hours later, she said, they were still there.

Finally, the Wilkey's teenage son, Danny, had roared past in his pickup. He admitted that he had been paying more attention at the time to the Thunderbird, parked by then a hundred yards or so inside the gate. But the boy did remember noticing three people standing near the car: "An old guy in a suit," a younger man, and a woman with a green scarf tied over her head. The older man had smiled and waved at him, the boy recalled.

The outgoing Julius Dess had left quite a trail, Stutte had to admit. After learning that Ruiz and Martinez were holding a possible suspect in custody back in Austin, the FBI agent agreed to get in touch with Wilkey to see if he would accompany him to the capital city to view a lineup. Scratching his chin, Stutte studied his calendar like a handicapper poring over a racing form. Perhaps one morning toward the beginning of next week would be an appropriate time, he suggested.

"Next week, hell!" Ruiz shouted, coming out of his chair. "Let's do it tonight!"

Ruiz knew that a hold had been placed on Zani, a legal maneuver that allowed the Austin police to detain him for up to three days while the Travis County sheriff's department investigated the credit-card-theft charges. But Zani's bail had been set at a low, though routine, $2,000. For 10 percent of that amount—a mere $200—he could spring himself as soon as the hold lapsed. Clearly, there was little time to waste, especially now that Zani was shaping up as a suspect in a murder case.

Ruiz and Martinez insisted that Stutte dial Wilkey's number immediately and ask him to be in Austin that night. They listened just long enough to hear the FBI agent explain the situation over the phone, just long enough to see him nod his head at them, indicating that Wilkey had agreed to be there. Then they stood up and raced out the door. By the time the FBI agent replaced the receiver, Ruiz and Martinez were headed back to Austin to supervise the arrangements for the lineup.

At 6:55 that evening, a jailer led Zani from his cell to municipal judge Harriet Murphy's courtroom, where he was given the magistrate's warning and asked to sign a waiver of attorney. He refused. Murphy then appointed local defense lawyer Alberto Garcia, a former municipal judge, to represent Zani for the purposes of the lineup and whatever else might arise.

While Garcia consulted with his new client, Ruiz and Martinez drove the fifteen blocks to the Travis County jail and selected four inmates who more or less matched Zani's appearance. When Garcia previewed the lineup, however, he protested that at least two of the inmates were unsatisfactory. Homicide chief Lieutenant Roger Napier, a friend of Ruiz and Martinez's who was familiar with Garcia's methods and had made a point to be present, sent for two of his officers who resembled Zani. They were substituted for the two inmates.

Garcia then requested that the defendant be allowed to shave and shower. He was trying to alter Zani's appearance as much as possible prior to the lineup, but the officers went along out of fear that their failure to cooperate now might be found to have been prejudicial later at trial. At last, having exhausted his delaying tactics, Garcia reluctantly allowed the proceedings to continue, and just after 9:30 on the night of April 2, Zani, dressed like the other participants in white overalls borrowed from the sheriff's department, shuffled into the lineup room.

Wilkey was still breathing heavily after having sped the 120 or so miles from his home south of San Antonio to reach Austin in time. He stared through the glass, squinting to take in every detail, as the five men found their places against the wall. For several seconds, the sound of Wilkey's breathing hung in the air as if amplified by the tension in his chest. Then he stiffened. jamming his index finger into the glass, he pointed out the man standing in the third position.

"That's the guy," he whispered excitedly. "That's the guy." It was Robert Joseph Zani.

Early the next morning, April 3, Martinez phoned the Mexican consulate in Austin to make an appointment with Victor Romero Lopetegui, Mexico's emissary to the Texas capital. At sixty, Romero Lopetegui was nearing the end of a diplomatic career that had begun in his native Acapulco—where his father once served as a general in the revolutionary army of Emiliano Zapata—and had continued through tours of duty in Oklahoma City, Colorado, California, Europe, and a number of towns along the Texas border. Martinez, still intrigued by the prison notebook he and Ruiz had discovered in Zani's possession on the night of his arrest, knew that if anyone could help sort out the confusing entries it contained, Romero Lopetegui was the man.

At ten o'clock that morning, Martinez and Ruiz joined the Mexican consul and his first assistant, José Ramos, in their downtown Austin office. After looking through the notebook and other assorted papers from Zani's briefcase, the Mexicans advised them that their suspect had apparently been arrested in Acapulco on March 3, 1980, and charged with aggravated robbery and assault. This being Easter week, however, most government offices in Mexico were closed. Romero Lopetegui suggested that the officers might have better luck if they phoned the U.S. embassy in Mexico City and asked to speak to a Mr. Kuhesk. Displaying no little diplomacy of their own, Ruiz and Martinez thanked them and left, chuckling to each other only after they had reached the sidewalk that securing records from the authorities in Mexico would be something resembling a miracle itself, Easter week or not.

Still, Romero Lopetegui and Ramos had at least given them a name, so Martinez and Ruiz returned to their special-crimes office and tried to put through a call to Mexico City. After several attempts, they succeeded. Kuhesk was unfamiliar with the case, he said, but he gave them the office and home phone numbers of the American consul in Acapulco. He might be able to help, Kuhesk said.

Martinez remembered the consul's name from Zani's notebook—Ron Urbanek—and he immediately tried to get a line through to Acapulco. Two hours later, he finally reached the consulate switchboard, only to be told that Urbanek had just gone home for the day. Martinez waited a few minutes, then placed a call to Urbanek's home phone number. On the fifth try, Urbanek himself answered. No, the puzzled consul said, he had no recollection of anyone named Robert Zani. Could he call the officers back about eight o'clock the next morning, after he had a chance to get into the office and review the case?

Martinez cradled the receiver and looked at Ruiz. "That's the last we'll ever hear from *him*," he predicted.

When the phone jangled them out of their concentration at precisely eight o'clock the next morning, the two partners were taken aback. Ruiz reached across the desk and heard a faint, high-pitched voice crackle on the other end of the line.

"Officer Martinez?" the voice asked, before dissolving into a series of beeps and whirs, clarifying for a brief moment— ". . . file . . . arrest . . . charges . . ."—and then fading again into a distant, mechanical hum over which only the strongest words seemed able to make themselves heard.

"I think it's your guy in Acapulco," Ruiz said, handing the phone to his partner.

Martinez listened as the computerized vagaries of the international linkup struggled to sort themselves out. At last, Urbanek's voice came through loud and clear, as if he were sitting in an office down the hall. Yes, he told Martinez, he had checked his files. It seemed an American citizen by the name of Robert Zani had been arrested at the Acapulco home of his mother-in-law, Raquel Reyes Ventura, on March 3, 1980, after she called the local police and charged him with *asalto*—robbery and assault. Two days later, she had dropped the charges on the condition that her son-in-law be forced to leave the country. Zani had phoned the American consulate for help. That's when Urbanek had come into the case.

In a small patio outside Zani's cell, Urbanek recalled, he had listened to the prisoner's story while several state judicial police with M1's slung over their shoulders watched from a discreet distance. He and his wife, Irma Serrano Reyes de Zani, had come to Acapulco some weeks earlier to visit her mother, Zani told the consul. All had been fine until Raquel sold his truck one day behind his back, after which she kicked him out of her house. When he tried to return for Irma and the four children, an argument ensued, and his mother-in-law had called the cops and bribed them to throw him in jail.

His mother-in-law was a witch, Zani continued, and she had corrupted his wife. He leaned forward and confided what he knew Urbanek, as a representative of the conservative Reagan administration that had just taken office back in Washington, would have to regard as the ultimate proof: Both Raquel and Irma, he whispered, were members of the Mexican Communist party and the Socialist Workers Party. They had sold his belongings out from under him, he said, including several pieces of expensive jewelry, probably to finance the overthrow of the Mexican government. As for himself, Zani concluded, he had nothing now, no one to turn to and nowhere to go.

Urbanek said that Zani impressed him as a "very intelligent individual" who seemed to have a grasp of "the right buttons to push" to elicit the reactions he wanted in others. However, there was a limit to what the consul could do for him.

"I told Mr. Zani that I would secure his release on the assault charges if he agreed to immediately leave the country," Urbanek recalled. "Beyond that, I said, he was on his own."

"So what happened next?" Martinez wanted to know.

"Mr. Zani was quiet for several minutes," Urbanek continued. "Then he looked at me and asked, 'You mean they don't have any firearms charges filed against me?' I said, 'No. Did you have some firearms when you were arrested?' He said that the police had taken three guns from him—a .357, a .38, and a .25.

"He refused to answer any more questions after that," Urbanek concluded. "But I got him out of jail, gave him three hundred dollars, and put him on a bus for the border. He was an American citizen, after all."

Martinez thanked Urbanek for his cooperation and hung up the phone. *This case is getting stranger all the time*, he thought. *Guns? On a gringo in Mexico? And then, just like that, he's headed back to the States after spending only a couple days in jail?* Martinez was familiar enough with Mexican police tactics to know that it took more power and money than Zani seemed to possess for an American to get around a weapons rap south of the border.

"Correct me if I'm wrong," Martinez turned to his partner, "but don't you think there's something hinky about all of this?"

As a matter of fact, that was precisely what Ruiz thought. Hauling out their notes, the two pondered the state of their investigation. They were holding a suspect in Austin on a minor charge. They had a possible link between him and a murder south of San Antonio. They knew that his estranged wife was in Acapulco, where he had been arrested one month ago with weapons in his possession. Other than that, they agreed, very little was known about Robert Zani.

The time had now come to find out more, to gather every scrap of information they could and then close in. Knowing that Zani was born and raised in Tulsa, Oklahoma, Ruiz suggested that they get in touch with his mother. Who better to help them start piecing together the bizarre trail that had led her son to a jail cell in Austin, Texas? But Martinez and Brown warned him off.

"If we contact his mother," they said, "she may come up with the two hundred bucks to spring him. And if Zani walks, we lose him forever."

Even as dogged and single-minded a cop as Ruiz had to see the logic behind their argument. Now, as he drove home just after midnight, something stuck in his mind that Jack and Betty Jo Mason had mentioned earlier in a hectic day that had taken Ruiz, Martinez, and Brown from Austin to San Antonio to Corpus Christi to San Antonio and then back to Austin.

"No one has done a thing to solve this case," the couple

had said, the growing desperation evident on their faces. "If you will pursue it, we're willing put up twenty-five hundred dollars of our own money to pay for plane tickets or bribes or whatever you need. No questions asked. Please, just help us, won't you?"

Ruiz drove south toward Manchaca on the quiet, darkened freeway. Behind him lay Tulsa; down the way was San Antonio and, beyond that, Nuevo Laredo. He could aim the car and keep on going past Boys Town, he thought, and be in Mexico City in less than ten hours, where, he had been told, the United States maintained its largest CIA contingent. He could then turn southwest and hit Acapulco another eight hours after that. In some strange way, this road was shaping up as a thread leading through the entire investigation. Ruiz had once read that it was the longest highway in the world, stretching from Chicago to Panama and then onward to Santiago, Chile, and beyond. As a cop, he knew it had become an almost endless dominion of anonymous drifters along whose aimless white line someone could escape for years. Perhaps even Robert Zani.

As he drove, Ruiz mulled over the conversation with the Masons again and again in his head. There could be only one thing they had in mind by "plane tickets" and "bribes," he reasoned, only one direction they thought Ruiz and his partner should be looking for the next logical step in the investigation. Out of the grief over their loss and their frustration with the FBI, the Masons might just have voiced what would later turn out to be the key to the case.

Pulling into the driveway, Ruiz killed the headlights and quietly closed the Duster's door. Letting himself into the house through the kitchen, he padded across the floor like a burglar, chuckling under his breath as he reached for the phone on the wall.

"Pack your bags, partner," Ruiz whispered when he heard Martinez pick up the receiver at the other end. "I don't know just how yet, but we're going to take ourselves a little trip to Mexico."

SEVEN

"**A**capulco?" Lieutenant Gilbert Miller looked up from the paperwork strewn across his desk and tried without success to conceal his astonishment. Reaching for a fresh cigarette, he lit it from the butt still smoldering in his ashtray and let out a deep sigh. The smoke whooshed across the room toward Ruiz and Martinez, who stood with their eyes downcast and their shoulders set at an aw-shucks angle, like school kids in the principal's office.

Miller was a classic case of the street-cop-made-good, a veteran officer who had worked his way in from the beat and run the ranks to the fifth floor of police headquarters (where he is a deputy chief today). He thought he had heard just about every scam a cop could pull, but he had to hand it to these guys. In a department that balked at sending investigators even as far away as Dallas or Houston, Ruiz and Martinez were now proposing to jet off to some famous Pacific playground to follow up on a flimsy case that didn't even belong to them.

"Sure. Why not?" Miller said at last, the sarcasm almost dripping from his lips. "Maybe we should send your wives along, too. That way you can all take a week or so off. Just charge it to the department."

He waved them away with a flick of his ashes, which landed just short of the ashtray at the corner of his desk.

"Hey," he called after them as they turned to leave, "why don't you let me baby-sit your kids while you're gone, too?"

The message was clear: Miller had no intention of facilitating a trip to the tropics for a pair of patrolmen who imagined they were on to something big. There had never been a great deal of camaraderie among them anyway. Ruiz and Martinez barely disguised their lack of interest in the work Miller wanted them to do—"working whores," they called it, the type of petty street vice the city council expected its police department to concentrate on.

Settling back in their tiny office, the partners traded complaints. Whatever happened to hunches? they wondered. Whatever happened to a couple of shoeshine boys on the street who stumbled upon a lead and were then given the latitude to follow it to its logical conclusion—even to Acapulco?

The truth was, APD was in the throes of one of its periodic crises of morale. Members of the force had begun complaining anonymously to the press, and the word making the rounds was that the department was just a five-story building held together with plumbing—bad plumbing, at that. Because he was married to a reporter, Ruiz was suspected of being one of the principal leaks. And Martinez, who had made relatively few enemies over the years, found that his partnership with Ruiz was now causing some of his colleagues to have second thoughts about him.

Nevertheless, when Miller ran into Frank Dyson a couple of days later, he brought the matter up. Dyson asked the lieutenant into his office. Only the third police chief in Austin since 1929, Dyson had been hired away from Dallas six years earlier. He was a lanky, slow-moving man given to wearing cardigan sweaters frayed at the elbows. Once, he had grown a mustache and discarded his glasses in a feeble attempt at style, but he was ultimately unable to update a face that resembled nothing so much as a comfortable old blanket with twin cigarette burns for eyes. His image in the community was that of a grandfatherly boss, an image that held true for the most part among his troops as well. He ran the department in a paternalistic way, always reluctant to overtax his patrolmen or ask a great deal of his commanders. From time to time, his name was even whispered as a possible mayoral candidate.

Dyson listened to Miller's halfhearted request on behalf of Ruiz and Martinez and, as expected, nearly laughed the lieutenant out of his office.

"Acapulco?" Dyson asked. Then, as if to make sure that he hadn't misheard, he asked again, "Acapulco?" Miller sheepishly excused himself.

The lieutenant was therefore understandably reluctant to go back to the chief when Ruiz and Martinez came to his office several days later to lobby him a second time. There was still plenty of background to gather on this man Zani, he told them, plenty of work to do before they again asked Dyson to reach into the police fund for such a trip.

After Ruiz and Martinez left, Miller leaned back in his chair. Dyson, who had a well-known fondness for tinkering with his department's flowchart, was once again in the process of shifting duties and resources, and Miller saw a chance to transfer the troublesome Ruiz and his partner, Martinez, out of special crimes. This whole Zani affair had begun with Bobby Simpson out at OCU, he reasoned. Why not kick it back now? He flipped through his Rolodex, found Simpson's number, and dialed it.

"You see, Miller thought he could dump these two poor old 'Mescan' patrolmen off on me," Simpson later recalled with a smile. "He didn't say that, but I knew that's what he thought. He asked, 'How would you like Robert and Paul?' I hesitated, as if I wasn't quite sure. 'Well, I guess so,' I told him unenthusiastically. Miller just wanted to get rid of them—and, hell, I jumped at the opportunity to have them."

It would take several weeks to complete, but the process had been set in motion.

* * *

Virginia Dinan, president of the Austin Board of Realtors, had been anything but idle since Zani's arrest.

"I knew that he was being held on a bond of only two thousand dollars," she later said, "which meant that while the police were playing 'Starsky and Hutch,' he could have sprung himself and left the country."

On April 1, Dinan flew to Washington, D.C., to attend a national conference of realtors. Before boarding her flight, she phoned the Travis County DA's office and asked to speak to Ronnie Earle. She wanted to see if there was anything that might be done to up the ante on Zani's bond. According to Dinan, Earle told her that the bond had already been raised to $10,000—though, in truth, it remained at the lower figure for another five months.

"Maybe Ronnie told me that just to get me off his back," Dinan later speculated, "but it set my mind at ease enough to go to Washington.

"We were staying at the Mayflower Hotel," she continued, "and I kept calling back to Austin to make sure Zani hadn't been sprung. I even missed a meeting or two because of it. One night I went down to a cocktail party and ran into Maureen Alexander, president of the San Antonio Board of Realtors. She asked me if I was feeling all right. 'You missed a great meeting this afternoon,' she said. 'I thought maybe you were ill.'

"When I explained that we had a problem back in Austin, she looked at me. 'That's just like something that happened in San Antonio last December,' she said. 'Is he a heavy man?'"

Dinan shook her head. But moments later, it dawned on her that Zani had told one of her agents he had lost fifty pounds in the past five weeks. This detail was enough to convince Alexander that he was the same man who had killed one of her agents four months earlier. Dinan went back to her room and placed one more call to the DA's office in Austin, where Earle was working late.

"I know you're sick and tired of hearing about this," she told him, "but something has come up here."

She related the conversation she had just had with Alexander. Earle got very quiet.

"Ms. Dinan," he finally said, after a long pause, "I'm going to hire you."

As the DA and his landlady spoke across the long-distance lines that night, neither was aware that Ruiz and Martinez, having met with John Bustos in San Antonio earlier in the afternoon, were at that very moment speeding to Corpus Christi, hot on a trail that would eventually lead them back to Zani. Yet, except for that chance interplay between two friends in a ballroom of the Mayflower Hotel in Washington, D.C., the case might never have been put together in the end.

Maureen Alexander returned to San Antonio and contacted several of the real estate agents who had been interviewed by the officers from Austin. She also got in touch with Betty Jo Mason, from whom she learned of the family's offer to finance the investigators' trip to Acapulco. But there seemed to be a problem, Mason told her, some legal ramification that prevented APD from accepting private money. Nevertheless, Alexander laid out the dilemma during the next meeting of the San Antonio Board of Realtors, and the members immediately voted an additional $1,000 to continue the investigation into the murder of one of their own.

When word of the board's action reached Ruiz and Martinez, they went straight to Miller's office. They now had two separate offers, they explained: $2,500 from the Dess family and a grand from the San Antonio Board of Realtors. Hell, they told the lieutenant, they were prepared even to use their own accumulated vacation leave if that's what it took. A murder had been committed, after all, and Irma Zani was the key. Miller agreed to approach Dyson again.

The chief, however, was equal to the pressure. A horse breeder and racing enthusiast in his spare time, he knew a great deal about long shots and obstacle courses, and he erected a hurdle for each of Miller's arguments. To take money from the family of a murder victim, Dyson explained, carried with it a distasteful taint of graft. Justice was not supposed to be for sale to those who could afford the price, and certainly not when it came to a crime that had taken place outside his department's jurisdiction.

The Board of Realtors' money was only slightly less problematic, Dyson continued, because it smacked of modern-day bounty hunting. As for Ruiz and Martinez traveling to Mexico on their own time, well, they were free to vacation where they chose—as long as they understood that they went in an unofficial capacity and that nothing they learned there would ever see the light of day in a courtroom.

Miller crept away from Dyson's office, more determined than ever to be rid as soon as possible of the two cops who wouldn't quit.

During the next several days, Ruiz and Martinez spent much of their time at the mule work involved in any murder investigation. They went down a list, supplied by Julius Dess's widow, of every credit card he had in his possession at the time of his disappearance. There were seven, none of which showed any activity since December 3, 1979, the day before the appointment with Ray Thomas and his wife.

From the phone company, Martinez secured a tally of long-distance calls placed by Zani from the motel room in San Antonio, where, the officers noted, he had registered in room 219 as "Dr. Longoria"—a famous family name along the Texas–Mexico border—indicating that "Ray Thomas," the name he had used with Dess, might have been an afterthought. There were six calls, all to realty companies in Austin or Dallas.

About eleven o'clock on the morning of April 4, Good Friday, the APD switchboard operator patched through a phone call to Jimmy Brown. Arkansas State Police investigator Mike Lowe was on the line. He had received Brown's

Teletype, he explained, and noted certain similarities in it to a case of his own.

On July 20, 1978, Lowe told Brown, a real estate broker had disappeared near the city of Magnolia, in southwestern Arkansas. Mary Jimmis Schinn—known to her friends and clients as Bobo—had been contacted by a Texas oilman who said that he was about to be transferred to Magnolia. He wanted to view a home in the city, he said, because he owned some rural property not far from town, and he might be interested in a trade. There was only one problem: His car had developed engine trouble, and he had just dropped it off at a repair shop. He would have to catch a cab to her office.

No problem, Schinn replied. Why didn't she just swing by and pick him up? The oilman demurred. There were some things he needed to pick up at the drugstore. Perhaps she could pick him up at the shopping center across from the repair shop in half an hour or so? Schinn agreed. She had not been seen since.

Early on the morning of April 7, Ruiz and Martinez went to Snooper's Pawn Shop, a few blocks north of the UT campus. They spoke with Bill Triplett, the pawnshop manager, showing him the pawn slip they had confiscated from Zani on the night of the arrest. Triplett had no record of the sale but called his other store, located about a block from police headquarters. Yes, the clerk said after checking his records, the .25-caliber weapon had been purchased by him from the manufacturer and sold to a Mr. Robert Joseph Zani on March 14, 1980, two weeks before the arrest.

Acting on a tip, the officers next went to La Quinta Motor Inn on I-95 in South Austin. After an hour of searching through the registry, they discovered that a man who gave his name as R. R. O'Farrell had checked in on November 1, 1979, and spent the night—in room 219.

Ruiz and Martinez were zeroing in on Zani, though they

didn't always know what to make of the information they gathered. They had no idea, for example, that the name "R. R. O'Farrell" was borrowed from Romulo O'Farrill, Jr., the scion of a wealthy Mexico City family that owned television stations and newspapers, including the English-language daily *Mexico City News*.

In fact, Marilyn Powell, an Austin realtor who dealt with Zani on three occasions, had called Mexico City to verify that the man who gave his name to her as Dr. O'Farrell was indeed associated with the newspaper. He most certainly was, she was told.

"Sometimes a look, a tone of voice, a mannerism, will give you the willies," Powell later recalled. "It makes you stop and think. But I relaxed a bit after I found out that a man by that name really did own a newspaper in Mexico."

If nothing else, Zani was playful when it came to the clues he left behind, even when the humor was lost on his audience.

The officers arrived back at the Twin Towers that morning in time to pick up Brown, and together the three drove out Lamar Boulevard to the offices of the Texas Department of Public Safety for a ten o'clock meeting with Colonel James B. Adams, head of DPS, of which the fabled Texas Rangers are a separate arm. Also present was Adams's chief of criminal law enforcement, Floyd Hacker. The meeting had been arranged by Brown, who had begun teaching photography classes to the forensic staff at DPS, and senior sergeant Jim Beck, Bobby Simpson's point man in OCU.

Adams, a native of the northeast Texas city of Corsicana, was a former assistant county attorney and state representative who had joined J. Edgar Hoover's FBI in 1951. Rising through the ranks of the bureau, he had been named assistant chief of investigative operations under director Clarence M. Kelley and, in 1978, found himself occupying the FBI's number two position. A year later, he left to join the administration of Republican Bill Clements as the executive director of the criminal justice division in the Texas governor's office. A burly, bespectacled fifty-four-year-old whose broad face and receding line of reddish hair gone gray belied a smile more sharklike than friendly, Adams was entering his second month as the director of DPS. He listened impassively as the officers laid out their complaints.

The FBI was withholding information, Ruiz and Martinez said, particularly John Newton in Corpus. They knew the bureau had its own suspects in the Dess murder—a couple who vaguely resembled the description of Robert and Irma Zani—but they wished to impress upon the colonel that their man, the one they had in custody in Austin, was the real culprit. All they needed now was a little cooperation. They had requested help in tracing Irma to Acapulco and had been assured repeatedly that the FBI would have its attachés on the scene track her down. But every time they called to inquire about the progress, Ruiz and Martinez were told, "Things move kind of slow down there in Mexico." It was becoming obvious to the Austin cops that things didn't move at all when a couple of simple patrol officers sought cooperation from the mighty FBI.

"It was a typical RBI deal," Jimmy Brown later recalled. "You know, 'Give us all you have, and *we'll* hold the press conference.' But we didn't necessarily want Adams to crack heads. We just wanted somebody from the Rangers we could work with. They have statewide jurisdiction, whereas we don't. That was the whole idea. I guess Adams cracked heads anyway."

The next thing they knew, the veteran intelligence functionary was on the phone to Norman Stutte of the FBI in San Antonio. Adams, of course, had technically once been Stutte's boss; now he made a "strong personal appeal" for the agent's cooperation in setting up a conference to take place two days hence, on Wednesday, April 9, in San Antonio. He explained that he would make sure a local Texas Ranger, Captain Jack Dean, and his deputy, Gene Powell, were there, as well as Floyd Hacker, Atascosa County sheriff Tommy Williams, and Ruiz, Martinez, and Brown.

Together, Adams added with a touch of sarcasm, all these professionals with so many years of expertise might be able to hammer out a plan to move Julius Dess's murder investigation forward.

On Wednesday morning, Ruiz, Martinez, and Brown strolled into FBI headquarters in San Antonio to find a room filled to capacity with white male faces from the heaviest law enforcement agencies in the region, all waiting expectantly for the Mexican American cops from Austin to brief them. Only John Newton didn't attend.

Stutte and his assistant, Tom Kiley, had set up blackboards and charts along one wall, and the property room had been unlocked so that the three Austin officers could view the backseat and other evidence removed from Dess's Thunderbird. It was a unique experience for the two patrolmen.

"Man, they treated us like we were God," Martinez recalled. " 'Come on in, fellas,' they said. 'Tell us what you've got, and we'll be glad to help you.' Me and Paul are up there drawing diagrams on a blackboard, and we've got half a dozen FBI agents and Rangers listening to us—two shoeshine boys!—telling them what the deal is."

"We presented our case—boom, boom, boom—and made believers out of them" Ruiz agreed. "I don't know what Adams did, but he got results."

Not quite. To be sure, those present at the meeting concurred that the Dess case, to be successful, would have to be worked on a statewide basis, but it didn't take long for the euphoria to wear thin on Ruiz and Martinez. As they drove back to Austin that evening, each heard the other express serious doubts about just how much cooperation they might hope for from the feds. Before long, they understood why.

The previous May, federal judge John H. Wood had been gunned down outside his townhouse in the Alamo Heights section of San Antonio. Known as Maximum John by those who complained of his brutal sentences and blatant bias for the prosecution, Wood was a staunch Republican appointed by Richard Nixon to represent the western district of Texas, a 78,000-square-mile jurisdiction that encompassed El Paso, Austin, San Antonio, and every inch of stark desert scrabble in between. In a matter of weeks, one of the costliest investigations in FBI history was scheduled to have entered a new phase at trial in his courtroom.

Throughout most of the seventies, a war had been waged by federal narcs and agents provocateurs against a loose coalition of suspected drug runners, prison-inmate leaders, Bandidos motorcycle-gang members, and assorted other hoods known as the Dixie Mafia. Among the principal targets in the war was an El Paso criminal attorney and high-rolling gambler named Lee Chagra, who had been murdered five months before Wood. Indeed, Chagra's younger brother, Jimmy, had originally been slated to stand trial before Wood on a variety of drug-related and other criminal charges the very day the judge was blown away. In Wood's court, the odds of anything but a life-without-parole sentence for him were, as Jimmy liked to put it, "about zilch point shit."

Such events had touched off what was said to be the most exhaustive investigation since the assassination of John Kennedy. From right to left, politicians clamored to label Wood's killing "terrorist behavior" and "the crime of the century." President Carter stepped forward, denouncing such "an assault on our very system of justice," while Griffin Bell, Carter's attorney general, assured the nation that the FBI would "leave no stone unturned" in its pursuit of those responsible.

As a result, few law enforcement agencies in Texas could say they had not, at least in some small way, been involved in the search for Wood's killer—including APD. Two days after the murder, Lieutenant Bobby Simpson had provided the FBI with a couple of names. One of his informants, he said, maintained that each person had been approached to carry out the contract on Wood. The bureau chose to ignore him, although Simpson was known to have sources better than most, including the former wife of a Bandido leader who later married one of the lieutenant's own officers. Simpson had long made it his business to keep tabs on those in the Austin area whom he suspected of membership in the Dixie Mafia. Some time back, he had even received a tip that two Bandidos were waiting at that very moment in a van outside the parking lot of the sheriff's office in Corpus Christi; they intended to kill Solomon Ortiz, the informant swore. Simpson phoned his friend to warn him, and the bikers were arrested with a Russian-made AK15 and three hundred rounds of ammunition.

Ruiz and Martinez had often run the traps for their lieutenant, and they knew how many man-hours were being devoted to the Wood investigation. The case would continue to dog Ruiz and Martinez for years to come, even after a hit man named Charles Voyde Harrelson (whose son, Woody, has enjoyed a measure of success playing the dim-witted bartender on the television series *Cheers*) was convicted of Judge Wood's murder. For now, though, the escalating needs of the parallel investigations were entangling Ruiz and Martinez in a frustrating web. Regional FBI resources were stretched to the limit. Jack Lawn, recently appointed to head up the bureau's San Antonio office (and, later, the Drug Enforcement Agency) was under a great deal of pressure from Washington, and any sustained cooperation from him or his agents would be considerably more miss than hit. The murder of a sitting federal judge was serious business, after all. When it came to a drifter named Zani and his involvement in an aging San Antonio realtor's death, the Austin cops were beginning to suspect they were pretty much on their own.

* * *

No sooner had Ruiz and Martinez walked into their office in Twin Towers the morning after the San Antonio meeting than a call came in from real estate agent Marilyn Powell. Virginia Dinan had given her their number, and Powell wondered whether they would mind if she dropped by in about an hour to give them some information. They wouldn't mind at all, they assured her.

Just about ten o'clock, Powell arrived and launched directly into her tale. On November 2, 1979, she said, she had picked up a man named Dr. O'Farrell, who claimed to be interested in the Sutton spread, a house on several acres southwest of town that Powell had been trying to sell for months. They viewed the property, after which Powell dropped him off at La Quinta Motor Inn in South Austin.

Two weeks went by before she heard from the man again. This time he told her that his wife was with him; they were standing in the parking lot outside the Sears store near Powell's office and wished to view the Sutton home again.

As the three were leaving the house on this second visit, Powell continued, the doctor's Mexican wife suddenly remembered that she had forgotten her sunglasses inside. According to Powell, Dr. O'Farrell waited in the car while she accompanied his wife back into the house. Then she drove the couple back to Sears.

" 'We like the house,' " she recalled O'Farrell telling her, as he got out of the car, " 'and we'll call you tomorrow to sign the contract,' " She never heard from the couple again. But that night she received a call from Mrs. Sutton, who had returned from work to find most of her jewelry gone. Despite her protests to the contrary, Powell had evidently let Dr. O'Farrell's wife out of her sight for a few moments.

Ruiz and Martinez showed Powell an impromptu lineup of five photographs. The realtor picked the third one—Irma Zani's passport photo.

* * *

Two days later, the officers received a call from Deborah Burton, a real estate agent in San Antonio, who had been put on to them by Maureen Alexander. Burton recalled that back in November 1979 she had dealt with a client by the name of Ray Thomas. He was in town from Oklahoma, he told her, and wanted to set up an appointment to view a 347-acre ranch advertised by Burton's firm in the local paper.

When Burton picked Thomas up the next day, the first thing he said to her was "You're late." She was startled, she admitted, but relaxed as they spent the morning together. Thomas entertained her with stories of his adventures, speaking fondly of his years at the University of Texas in Austin. Later, she thought it odd that Thomas kept bringing up the subject of Charles Whitman and "the gory details" of the UT Tower incident more than thirteen years earlier. But she finally sensed trouble only after explaining to her client that a small outbuilding on the property was intended as a deer feeder. She remembered his response: "Yeah, they feed them corn all day—and then they blow their heads off."

The next day, a real estate agent named Elena Smith called to say that she, too, had dealt with a strange man, only this one had given her the name "Bob Palasoto." On Saturday, March 15, 1980, Smith said, she received a call from Palasoto, who stated that he had read an ad in the newspaper for a $118,000 house on Hurst View Road, near Lake Travis.

"Do you want to go see it now?" Smith remembered asking him.

No, he explained, he was on his way to Laredo and just wanted to let her know he was interested. He would call early the following day, Sunday, for an appointment, if that was all right. It was, Smith assured him.

About five minutes after eight the next morning, Palasoto

called Smith at her office to tell her he was on his way. An hour later, he was back on the line. His car had broken down, he said, and he asked her to pick him up at the Pancake House on U.S. 183. She complied.

Palasoto climbed into Smith's car, wearing a dirty white shirt, lime green tie, and beige double-knits. On the way to the lake, he told the realtor he was interested only in homes "where the people have either been divorced or deceased." By this, Smith assumed that he hoped to find a distress sale or some widow willing to unload her home fast and cheap. Smith's listing on Hurst View Road pretty much fit the bill.

For the next five hours, Palasoto roamed through the home, peeking into cupboards and rapping the walls with his knuckles, followed by the realtor and the homeowner, an elderly widow who had been enjoying a quiet Sunday morning at home before their arrival. Smith recalled that Palasoto talked incessantly, especially about his family. He said his father owned a mobile-home sales company in Louisiana. His wife had left him and gone home to her mother, he said, and now the two women spent most of their time drinking in bars. Palasoto had even been to a Jesuit priest to work out the emotional trauma of it all.

With Smith and the widow exchanging puzzled glances, Palasoto rambled on. Over the past five weeks, he told them, he had dropped fifty pounds, the result of an incident at his mother-in-law's during which she poisoned his food. Now, every time he sat down to eat, the image of the old crone's face appeared on the plate and he lost his appetite. Smith noted that Palasoto would have to stop and rest after climbing a staircase and that he excused himself a number of times to use the guest bathroom in the hall.

They had finally left Hurst View Road shortly after three that afternoon, stopping at a nearby piece of property owned by state representative Doug McLeod of Galveston, and had then driven a few short miles to the city of Lakeway, where Palasoto insisted in viewing another home. It was there, Smith told the officers, that she phoned her husband to check in, only to learn that he had become concerned enough about her safety to phone the police. It seemed to her that Palasoto derived a curious satisfaction when he heard this news.

She dropped him off that evening at the downtown branch of the Austin Public Library. As he got out of the car, Palasoto told her that he liked the Hurst View Road house and wanted to return the following day for another look. But for now, he had to find a motel room or he would wind up sleeping in the bus station.

Sometime before eight o'clock the next morning, Monday, Smith answered the phone. It was Palasoto. He asked her to swing by the Austin Motel on South Congress so they could drive out to Hurst View Road one more time. Then he launched into an account of the trouble he had experienced the night before when he moved the television set in his motel room and touched off a silent alarm. The next thing he knew, two police officers were knocking on his door.

Smith went by the motel to pick him up, and they headed back to Lake Travis. For several hours, Palasoto inspected the home, asking detailed questions about the water pump and other items that Smith was unqualified to answer. When Harry Montadum, Smith's boss, showed up unexpectedly, Palasoto flew into a rage, beating the walls and stomping his feet on the floors. He recovered enough to inform Smith that he was no longer interested in the home. She drove him back to the Austin Public Library.

Just after five o'clock that evening, however, Palasoto called Smith at her office. He was ready to draw up the contract, he told her, as if nothing had happened earlier in the day. Anxious to close the sale, Smith grabbed a portable typewriter and headed for the library, where the two worked in a quiet corner of the periodicals room until eight-fifteen.

When the time came to cut the earnest-money check, Palasoto said that he had forgotten his checkbook at the motel. Smith then drove him back to his room. After several minutes, he returned to the car and asked her to take him to La Quinta because his things had been moved there without his permission.

Smith was fed up with Palasoto at last. She refused to take him to the other motel and demanded the check he had promised. Palasoto slammed the car door and left, disappearing into the darkness at the back of the parking lot. She didn't see or hear from him again.

Ruiz and Martinez were familiar with such stories by now. They had listened to more realtors than they cared to tally, all of whom described encounters with Zani that really varied in only one important detail from that of J. A. Dess—they had lived to tell about them.

Four days later, however, when two more agents asked to come by and talk, the officers took special notice. The first was Pat Dix, a middle-aged realtor from San Antonio who told Ruiz and Martinez that she had been contacted back in August 1979 by a man who called himself Dr. Pech. Pech told her he was calling long distance from Belize, where he and his wife lived, but expected to be in San Antonio in a couple of days and would like to set up an appointment to view some high-dollar homes.

Two days later, he called Dix and asked her to pick him up in the Montgomery Ward parking lot. Dix wheeled her Cadillac into the lot at the designated time and saw a man in a baggy suit several sizes too large approach the car with his Hispanic wife. It was unusual, Dix recalled, that both of them crawled into the backseat.

As she drove away, Dr. Pech explained that he had just flown into town with the vice president of Montgomery Ward. Then he introduced his wife, who was sitting directly behind Dix, her hair wrapped in a green scarf. The realtor glanced into the rearview mirror and smiled at the woman.

"The only thing I could see in the mirror was her eyes," Dix recalled. "They were the coldest, darkest eyes I had ever seen."

Over the next few weeks, Dix took the couple to a dozen homes, all of them in the $400,000 to $500,000 price range. As they drove around the area, Pech impressed the realtor with his intelligence, entertaining her by reciting the names and dates in office of every U.S. president, from Washington to Carter, and then performing the feat backward. As far as she was concerned, he was one of the most erudite men she had ever encountered.

"We would work one full day, and they would say they intended to call me back the following day for another appointment," she told the officers. "But I wouldn't hear from them for a week or so. Then Dr. Pech would call, saying that his wife had been sick or something like that, and schedule a new appointment."

Though suspicious almost from the beginning, Dix attributed her feelings to exhaustion; she had been working without a break for months. Still, she worried about her safety while with the doctor and his wife. After the second day, she voiced her concerns to her husband, who immediately called a business associate in Belize, only to be told that there was indeed a Dr. Pech in the Central American nation and that he could afford any home Dix might have for sale.

Gradually, they narrowed the list of properties they were interested in until they fixed on a sprawling, multilevel home on secluded Bar-X Trail. Owned by a local clinical psychologist named Skelton, it was built into a bluff overlooking Helotes, just west of San Antonio, a magnificent home with an elaborate security system and all the luxuries a well-to-do buyer would wish. Dix had been trying to sell it for months.

"One day," she continued, "I left the doctor and his wife at the front door of the house and walked down to the garage, where the lockbox was. I went up the dark, enclosed stairwell that led from the garage to the kitchen, walked through the house, and opened the front door to let them in. But they weren't there."

Dix didn't know what to do. She was apprehensive, thinking that the couple might have slipped into the garage behind her to wait by the stairs. Yet, remembering her husband's conversation with his associate in Belize, she still held out some hope of collecting the commission on a $500,000 sale, and she decided to circle around the house and come up behind them.

"So you were obviously suspicious," one of the officers prompted her. "I mean, to go through all of that, you must have sensed danger."

"Yes," Dix replied. "But I still wanted to believe that they really intended to buy a home."

She slipped around the side of the house and reentered the garage. Sure enough, Dr. Pech and his wife were waiting at the foot of the stairwell. Dix, openly alarmed now, tried to get the couple to go up the stairs in front of her so that she could keep her eyes on them. Pech pulled the door open as his wife demurred, insisting that the realtor climb the stairs first. There was an awkward moment. Pech reached the top of the stairs and opened the door to the kitchen, turning back to the others. "Hurry up!" he shouted. "Hurry up!"

"I thought, *This is ridiculous*," Dix recalled, "so I started up the steps with the doctor's wife behind me."

Halfway up, Dix turned to say something to Mrs. Pech. In the darkness, she could see that the woman had taken the green scarf from her head and was holding it above Dix, as if she were about to strangle the realtor from behind.

"The first thing I thought was, *If I push her down the stairs, she'll tumble. Then I can jump over her and scramble out to my car*," Dix later said. "I don't know why I was so sure that she understood what I was thinking. But the next thing I knew, she got this funny look on her face, brought the scarf back down, and pretended to tie it around her neck."

Meanwhile, Pech was looming above Dix, blocking the entrance to the kitchen. Remembering that there was a phone on the wall just inside the door, the realtor lunged forward, picked up the receiver, and dialed her office number. Her secretary answered on the first ring, and while Pech and his wife angrily stared Dix down "about six inches from my face," the realtor blurted out that she was at the Skelton home, that she was with the couple from Belize, and that they planned to leave immediately.

After she hung up the phone, Dix bolted for the front door and ran down the front steps to her car, where she grabbed a mobile phone from under the front seat and pretended to make a call. The unit was inoperable—she had intended to drop it off at a repair shop to have the batteries recharged—but it was enough to convince her clients. As she went through the motions of holding a conversation with someone on the other line, she could see them parting the curtains, watching her from the living room.

"I went back up the steps and stood in the doorway," she recalled. "Pech was just soaked in perspiration, and his eyes were bloodshot. 'I don't feel well,' he said. I drove them back to Montgomery Ward—and never heard from them again."

The second agent that day was Mary Evelyn Lowder. They had meant to interview Lowder before now but, with so many trails to follow, had simply not gotten to it. Her name was familiar to them; they had discovered one of her business cards in Zani's briefcase the night of his arrest, an elaborate fold-over card with a photograph of the agent reproduced inside. But they had no idea what she looked like because, along with the phone numbers and other doodles he had scribbled in the margins, Zani had also inked out her face in the picture with such force that the pen punctured the heavy paper stock. They had a strong feeling that Lowder was luckier than most to be alive. They were right.

Lowder was a fiftyish woman who dressed with the elegant aplomb of an aging film star and carried her exuberance like a sidearm. She specialized in expensive lakefront homes, she told the officers. One of her listings was tagged at $265,000, a luxurious three-bedroom house and separate guest quarters set on five acres with a panoramic view and an intricate stone stairway leading down to a private boat dock.

It was this property that a man identifying himself as Buck Womack called her about on Sunday, March 23. An appointment was scheduled for early Monday, when Womack, who said he was a jeweler from Houston, would swing by her office in his rented car.

The following morning, Womack phoned to say his car had broken down. He had called the rental agency to have it repaired, but in the meantime, would Lowder pick him up in the parking lot of the Highland Mall shopping center? The realtor steered her late-model Chevrolet Caprice to the mall, and Womack climbed in, placing his briefcase gently on the backseat. Then, saying that she had forgotten some papers, Lowder drove back by the office—a common security measure designed to give her co-workers a look at her clients.

Soon Lowder and Womack were headed to Lake Travis. On the way, Womack asked Lowder to stop by a home he had viewed with another agent. "I'm not really interested in it," he told her, "but I'll show you some of the features I am interested in, and we can compare." As long as he didn't intend to buy the house, Lowder had seen nothing wrong with stopping by.

"Let's lock up," Womack said, nodding toward his brief-case as they got out of the car.

Once inside, he paused to admire a collection of antique rifles that hung over the fireplace. "I'd like to have that one," he said.

The comment struck Lowder as unusual. "If I see some-thing in someone's home," she later explained, "I might say, 'Oh, that's nice.' He didn't. He said, 'I'd like to have that one.' "

From there, they drove to the sparsely furnished $265,000 home. Again Womack reminded her to lock the car. The house was owned by a wealthy Houston family but occupied by a caretaker couple who worked elsewhere during the day and returned to the home only at night, along with their teenage daughter, a student at UT.

While she and her client traipsed around the grounds, Lowder tried to make conversation. She mentioned that she had once shown some property to Madalyn Murray O'Hair. "She's not really an atheist, you know," Womack replied curtly. "She just found a good way to make a living."

Lowder pressed on. Her daughter was married to a doctor from Monterrey, Mexico, she said, which prompted Womack to launch into an analysis of the current political situation south of the border. They discussed Lowder's car—was it in good repair? Womack wanted to know—and the jewelry Lowder wore, particularly a gold bracelet with three coins dangling from it, including a $5 American Indian piece. He told her that his mother wore a similar bracelet.

Next Womack regaled her with stories of his travels, telling her about the time in Algiers (or maybe it was South Africa—she couldn't remember) that he was jailed with a machine gun held to his head. Only by convincing his captors to contact a certain diplomat had he been spared. In fact, after purchasing this house, he planned to present it to that same diplomat—as payment for having once saved his life, she surmised.

Womack had previewed the Howard Hunt mansion in South Texas, he continued, but this lovely home on Lake Travis was much more suitable to his needs. Why didn't they return tomorrow to draw up a contract?

"I was living in high cotton," Lowder later recalled. "I always took a seven percent commission, as opposed to the standard six, because I did so much work. I was thinking dollars, no doubt about it."

As they returned to Austin in the early afternoon, Lowder told the officers, she hit the brakes suddenly at a red light and heard Womack's briefcase slide off the backseat to the floorboard. "He almost jumped through the ceiling," she remembered. "I asked, 'Did I break something?' He said, 'Well, I guess not.' "

Lowder dropped Womack at the Travis County court-house, where he said he was working on a research project with a friend. They agreed to meet early the next day.

About eight o'clock on Tuesday morning, Lowder received a call from the wife of the caretaker at the home on Lake Travis, who wanted to warn the realtor that her teenage daughter had stayed home from classes with a cold. Lowder decided not to mention it to her client.

They stopped for coffee at Jim's Restaurant, where Wom-ack paid. Outside, he tried to give her money for gasoline, but she told him it wasn't necessary. As they pulled into the driveway of the lake house, Womack noticed a motorcycle parked in the carport. He stiffened slightly but grabbed his briefcase and walked to the front door, waiting as Lowder fished in her purse for the key to the lockbox. She noted that he must be serious about a contract this time because the day before he had left his briefcase in the car.

In the living room, a young man's jeans and other cloth-ing were strewn across the furniture. Womack seemed in-creasingly uncomfortable. After a cursory glance around, he suggested they sit at the dining-room table and begin ham-mering out the details of the contract. He opened his brief-case and reached inside. Lowder felt a chill and pulled her sweater up around her neck.

Suddenly, a semiclad young woman emerged from a back bedroom. It was the caretakers' daughter, who, far from being ill, had stayed home to dawdle with her boyfriend. Hearing voices, she had climbed out of bed and wandered into the dining room to see what the commotion was, a bath towel hastily draped across her body.

Womack took one look at the teenager and exploded. "I'm not going to do it!" he shouted, angrily slamming down the lid of his briefcase. "I'm not going to do it!"

He stomped out the back door and strode across the grounds, fuming. Lowder sat at the table, staring at his briefcase and wondering how she could manage to salvage the sale. After about twenty minutes, Womack had regained some of his composure. He stepped back inside the house and looked at the realtor.

"I'm going to get a construction engineer out here to see if we can add on to the end of the house," he told her, the edge of anger in his voice subsiding. "Then you and I will come back Friday morning."

They drove back to Austin, stopping again at Jim's Restaurant, where Womack paid for lunch. Afterward, Lowder dropped him off at the Ramada Inn North. He promised to call her later that day or early the next. She spoke to him by phone a number of times on Wednesday and twice on Thursday but couldn't get him to commit to another appointment. She never saw him again.

"It was only later," Lowder concluded, "that I realized he had his eye on my jewelry and my car. He intended to kill me that morning. Someone interfered with his plans, that's all. Otherwise, I'd be dead."

Her voice became dreamy and she stared off into space, as if experiencing the feeling again. She seemed to be trying to answer a question that had remained unanswered too long. "I don't know," she said. "Do you suppose that if he had called back and said, 'I'm ready to buy the house,' I might have been a little bit overanxious? Maybe. It was a flat market, and a lot of agents were throwing caution to the wind."

Lowder's mouth tightened. She stared at the officers with the look of someone who has witnessed a miracle—or survived a disaster. She shifted her shoulders and played with the stone of a rather garish ring on her right hand. The business card with her defaced photograph lay on the desk nearby.

"I *know* he was going to do me in," she said at last, and

her tone left no doubt that she had resolved the issue for herself.

Martinez stood and walked to a file at the other end of the room. He reached for the lineup photographs and arranged them on the table like a Las Vegas croupier. "Do you think you could pick out your Mr. Womack from these?" he asked.

Lowder studied them for several seconds. Ruiz and Martinez watched her eyes, following them with their own as she scanned the faces of the five men—two cops and two inmates from the Travis County jail whose builds were similar to Zani's, and Zani himself.

Then a hint of recognition crossed Lowder's features. She yanked up the sleeve of her dress and pointed to one of the photographs. It was, of course, photo number 3—Robert Joseph Zani.

EIGHT

Interviewing a procession of jittery real estate agents, each of whom told essentially the same story, was all well and good, but Ruiz and Martinez knew they were making little real progress when it came to revealing their suspect's background, something that would allow them to look over his shoulder and get at the truth.

Zani had been transferred to the Travis County jail, a damp and dismal series of cramped cells on the top floor of the courthouse. Though voters had approved bond money for a modern jail, county officials had hopelessly bungled the negotiations with several contractors, and most of the inmates knew they would probably not be around long enough to see the new facility. They awaited their court hearings and sentencing dates in noisy gloom, surrounded by clang and clatter and the sound of aging plumbing as it died away in some distant part of the building.

Zani waited with the others, unable to raise the $200 he needed to free himself. He spent much of his time sitting on the edge of his bunk, staring at the floor in hunched anger. On the few occasions that Ruiz and Martinez visited his cell, hoping to gain a lead on some new piece of information, Zani simply glowered at them, contemptuous and arrogant. Like a loop tape, his words repeated themselves in the officers' heads: *You can find that out.* If they took a certain comfort in knowing he was stuck in the ancient jail, they also realized such luck could not hold indefinitely.

With that in mind, Ruiz and Martinez turned to the temporary driver's permit they had found in the toilet tank on the night of the arrest—the one on which Zani had listed his address as Route 1, Box 101, La Feria, Texas.

Ruiz always more comfortable on the phone than his partner, called the La Feria Police Department. To his surprise, the chief of police himself, Alfred Trevino, answered. Obviously, the tiny town along the Texas-Mexico border between McAllen and Harlingen did not boast the resources to put it on the cutting edge of modern-day law enforcement.

Nevertheless, Chief Trevino agreed to check out the address Ruiz gave him. He called back later in the day to say that he had spoken with a man named Felipe Reyes, who said that he and his wife had lived there alone for the past two years. No, Chief Trevino apologized, he hadn't thought to ask Mr. Reyes if he had ever heard of Robert or Irma Zani.

On April 23, Ruiz, Martinez, and Jimmy Brown headed for La Feria to see for themselves. The Reyeses' small house stood in the middle of a grapefruit orchard, where Felipe worked as the caretaker. Because no one was home, they busied themselves by questioning the three closest neighbors. But after viewing photographs, none could recall ever seeing the Zanis in the area.

When Reyes and his wife drove up, the officers introduced themselves and hauled out the photographs again. Neither recognized the people in the pictures, nor could they explain why their address had been used by some man they had never heard of when he applied for a driver's permit all the way up in Austin. It was all *muy raro,* the Reyeses nervously observed, very strange indeed. There seemed to be little reason to doubt the simple couple, who were almost certainly illegal immigrants frightened by this sudden visit from the police.

Then, just as the officers turned to leave, the postman arrived, and on a hunch, they asked his permission to check through the mail he was delivering. There, among the department-store flyers advertising goods the Reyeses could ill afford, was a laminated permanent driver's license issued to Robert Joseph Zani. Again the bewildered couple could offer no explanation.

"We'll have to confiscate this as evidence then," Ruiz said, pocketing the license. Reyes and his wife shrugged as the officers drove off.

Before leaving South Texas, Ruiz, Martinez, and Brown stopped by the Harlingen Police Department to visit Joey Vasquez, a detective with whom Martinez had once worked a narcotics case. They were piecing together a rough chronology of Zani's moves from the time he left Tulsa in mid-1974 to the night of his Austin arrest in March 1980, they explained, and one of the keys seemed to be the two years or so that their suspect had spent in South Texas. Having had little luck in La Feria, they now asked Vasquez for his help in tracking down the home where Zani had lived or whatever additional information the detective could dig up.

Two days later, Joey Vasquez called Martinez in Austin. He had located Zani's house, he said, adding proudly that he had also checked the property tax rolls at the courthouse. Zani paid $36,000 for the house on March 25, 1975, and sold it for an unknown sum on January 26, 1976, Vasquez reported. The property had since changed hands again. The detective had taken the liberty to ask the current owner for permission to break up a "suspicious" concrete slab behind the house. Unfortunately, he had discovered nothing more than an empty hole about five feet deep. Now he wanted to continue the excavation because he had located five or six other spots in the yard that seemed equally suspicious.

Martinez could just imagine the poor homeowner standing by as Vasquez directed a team of men with shovels to destroy his backyard in a mad search for whatever it was he suspected might be buried there. Thanking the enthusiastic detective for his efforts, Martinez asked him to hold off until they learned a little more—like just what the hell Vasquez expected to find, he thought, hanging up the receiver.

By the first week in May, Ruiz had managed to convince Martinez and Brown that the time was at hand to contact Zani's mother. Zani had told several of the realtors about his years as a student at UT-Austin in the sixties, so the officers subpoenaed a batch of his old college records. From the applications for student loans and other papers in the file, they knew that their suspect's mother was named Gladys Ettamay Zani. They had her last address—218 Xenophon, a quiet, block-long street in the Gilcrease Hills section northwest of downtown Tulsa—and they knew that she was divorced or separated from her husband, an Army corporal named Joseph Peter Zani, who had apparently been stationed in Boston during his son's college days. They also knew they were going to have to tread very delicately when they spoke to Gladys Zani.

They knew all these things, but they didn't know the half of it. A cursory check with directory assistance failed to turn up a listing in Tulsa for anyone named Gladys Zani. Next Ruiz called the Tulsa Police Department, where he was put in touch with a Sergeant Helm, who promised to run a routine trace.

An hour later, Helm called back with startling news: a missing-persons report had been filed with his department in January 1976 by Gladys Zani's sister, Vera Tolbert. The cae had been dropped four months later when an independent examiner verified that Gladys's social security checks bore signatures that appeared to be hers, though no one had actually heard from or seen her since at least July 1974. Helm then gave Ruiz the name of a retired Tulsa PD homicide investigator. Bob Bivens who lived at 216 Xenophon, next door to Gladys. Bivens might be able to help, he said.

Man, you ain't going to believe this!" Ruiz exclaimed,

hanging up the phone and looking at his partner. "Zani's mother is missing!"

"Oh, no," Martinez replied, slipping into the "Amos 'n' Andy" patois he and his partner often used. "You don't suppose . . . ?" He let the question hang in the smoky air of the office and thought of Joey Vasquez, his shovels at the ready down in La Feria.

Bivens, it turned out, had been Gladys Zani's neighbor for twenty-two years. During that time, he had learned a great deal about the family. Robert was an only child whose father had abandoned him when he was too young to remember. As a kid, Robert seemed as sharp as he was troublesome. He and his mother bickered constantly, the arguments sometimes extending into the front yard, where, Bivens hastened to add, he could hardly avoid noticing.

Once Gladys vacationed in Bermuda, the ex-investigator continued, and asked Bivens to pick her up at the airport upon her return. When they got back to the house, they discovered it had been burglarized. Bivens surveyed the scene, noting that the screen on the back door had been sliced from the inside. Both he and Glady suspected Robert, but nothing was ever done about it.

Bivens kept talking, happy to know someone somewhere was again interested in the unexplained disappearance of his neighbor. Gladys, he said, was a friendly sort who had retired from her job in the local office of Sun Oil, a Philadelphia-based petroleum company, and had used her retirement benefits and social security checks to travel as often as she could. As neighbors, they had carried out an informal agreement through the years to pick up the mail, sweep the sidewalk, and generally keep the other's house in order whenever one was gone for an extended period.

On one such occasion in July 1974, Bivens and his wife returned from a ten-day trip to Panama City to find that their mail had stacked up in the box, spilled over the top, and been blown around the porch. Aware that Gladys suffered from cancer—she had had a breast removed some years earlier, Bivens explained—he went next door to check on her. A Cadillac Fleetwood sat in the driveway where Gladys's 1964 Chevrolet Impala was usually parked, and Robert Zani answered the door, greeting him curtly. He and his wife and four children now lived there. Zani told Bivens, before slamming the door in his face.

"I asked him where his mother was," Bivens recalled, "and he said that she was traveling in Arkansas, then Canada, and that she would probably wind up in Fort Myers, Florida, where her doctor had advised her to move for health reasons."

Immediately suspicious, Bivens asked Robert for an address in Fort Myers so that he could write Gladys. Zani jotted something down on a piece of paper. Later, using his contacts at Tulsa PD, Bivens checked out the address and discovered that it was nonexistent. The next day, Vera Tolbert dropped by to inquire about her sister, and Zani gave her the same song and dance about Fort Myers. She phoned Bivens that night to tell him she suspected foul play.

Four to five weeks later, Bivens added, he was puttering in his yard early one morning when a moving van pulled up to the Zani house. He went next door and asked Robert what was going on. "We're moving to Buffalo, Missouri," Zani told him, without further explanation.

Because he had time on his hands, Bivens conducted a little unofficial investigation of his own. Among other things, he learned that Zani had a power-of-attorney letter giving him full rights to Gladys's belongings. He had sold his mother's Impala to someone, then peddled the house at 218 Xenophon to a couple named Epperson. His mother was in Mexico, Robert told the buyers, where she was receiving expensive cancer treatments; that was why he was selling her home. Bivens also learned that Gladys's retirement and social security checks were still being issued, cashed, and spent. Through sources in the local banking community, he discovered that Zani had withdrawn approximately $12,000 from three separate Tulsa bank accounts shortly after his mother's disappearance.

Bivens then summarized for Ruiz his feelings about the case. Two weeks before their Panama City trip, he and his wife overheard a loud argument between Gladys and Robert concerning her refusal to lend him money. In his opinion, Bivens said, Robert Zani was a "very dangerous subject" who had probably killed his mother, burying her body either in the backyard or the basement at 218 Xenophon or on the forty-odd acres of rural property that Gladys owned near Eureka Springs, Arkansas. In fact, Bivens confided, after Robert and his family moved out of the house, he had checked the backyard for unusual signs but found none.

He was sure of one thing, though: Gladys would never have left Tulsa for any length of time without letting some-one know. Hell, Bivens was just her neighbor, yet he re-ceived a postcard from her at least once a week when she traveled. This time, however, neither he nor anyone else he knew—not even her own sister—had heard from Gladys Zani in nearly six years.

If this had been a movie, the script would have called for a jump cut here, probably to Ruiz and Martinez bounding triumphantly down the steps of a courthouse while uni-formed guards in the background of the frame led Zani, the convicted killer, handcuffed and dejected, off to prison.

But this was a murder investigation, not a movie, and the conversation with Bivens had raised more questions than it answered. Instead of closing in on Zani's trail, Ruiz and Martinez realized, they were opening fresh avenues with every inquiry. J. A. Dess in San Antonio, Gladys Zani in Tulsa—how many more names and what other locales would be folded into this case before it was over?

They each sensed an odd foreboding as they left the Twin Towers late that night and stood between their cars in the parking lot to smoke one last cigarette apiece. Even the traffic noise had subsided, as if the avenues of the city were asleep, demanding no notice. Above, the lazy stars adjusted themselves by fractions, exploding now and then in soundless little suicides. Ruiz and Martinez were standing still at the surface of their investigation, like a river frozen to its bed—except that there was an undercurrent rushing below, loud and furious.

The next morning, May 7, 1980, Ruiz placed a call to Sheriff Russell Hill of Dallas County, Missouri, which includes the small town of Buffalo, sitting hard by U.S. 65 some thirty miles northeast of the city of Springfield. If Zani had told Bivens that he and his family were moving there, then Buffalo seemed the next logical step in the investigation.

Sure, he remembered Robert Zani, Hill said in response to Ruiz's first question. The townsfolk considered Zani "weird" and "a real hell-raiser" during the two years or so that he lived in their tight-knit community, and the sheriff had been called in to investigate him on at least four occasions. Hill reached for a file and leafed through its contents as Ruiz took notes.

A local realtor named Glen Hawkins had handled the purchase of the house for Zani, who paid a total of $27,000 on August 6, 1976—$2,000 in cash and the rest in a certified check drawn on a Springfield account. During the transaction, Zani told Hawkins that he expected an adjoining six acres to remain unsold and undeveloped. When Hawkins explained that he had no control over the fate of the other property, Zani became belligerent, telling the realtor, "You're on my shit list." No one had taken the mild threat very seriously at the time, though Hawkins obviously thought enough about it to mention it casually to Sheriff Hill at a church social several days later.

Shortly after Zani moved in, Hill continued, an elderly man named Sid Rucker and his wife walked over to the Zanis' home to get acquainted with their new neighbors. As they approached the gate, the Ruckers saw Zani push a Mexican woman into a storage shed and disappear behind the house. Clearly unwelcome, the couple turned on their heels and left. But they too had called the sheriff to let him know about the incident; it was so untypical of the neighborliness on which Buffalo prided itself.

Not long afterward, the local postmaster dropped by Hill's office to complain about a number of harassing phone calls he had received after a shouting match with Zani concerning his refusal to fill out the necessary paperwork for a post office box. He was a minority, Zani argued, and therefore exempt from providing any personal data. He so resented the invasion of his privacy that he stomped out and drove the thirty miles to Springfield to open a post office box there, presumably completing the paperwork—a standard requirement—without complaint.

Later, Hill said, Zani tried out the same "minority" argument whil applying for food stamps. Nevertheless, as part of her study to determine whether he and his family qualified for the program, the caseworker went to Zani's home the next day. She was thrown off the property. After notifying him that his application was denied, she too reported anonymous late-night phone calls.

Perhaps the strangest story of all concerned the time Zani took out an ad in a Kansas City newspaper and listed a neighboring farmer's thirty-two acres for sale. The two had exchanged harsh words during a dispute over a fence on the property line they shared, Hill said, after which the farmer received calls from people around the state, all of whom expressed great interest in purchasing his land. The problem was, the farmer had never put his property on the market, and certainly not for the ridiculously low price of $5,000.

Sheriff Hill believed Zani was responsible in each instance, but he was never able to uncover enough evidence to file charges.

Hill wasn't alone. Investigators from the U.S. Treasury

Department had once come to Buffalo, still unconvinced of the authenticity of Gladys Zani's signature on her social security checks. Zani refused to let them on his property. Secret Service agents also nosed around for a time. They suspected Zani of writing a letter to Jimmy Carter, in which he threatened the president's life, and a second letter to Carter's young daughter, Amy, containing several obscene references. Both federal investigations had apparently proved inconclusive, Hill said, and had been dropped in February 1979, after Zani abruptly sold the house in Buffalo—at a $7,000 loss—and left town.

"We were all pretty happy to be rid of him," Hill assured the officers.

Throughout the next week, Ruiz and Martinez, overcoming their distaste for telephones, plied the long-distance lines, confirming and reconfirming as much as they could of the information received from Bivens in Tulsa and Sheriff Hill in Missouri. Threading their way by phone through the bureaucracy at Sun Oil, they learned that the company discontinued Gladys Zani's retirement checks in January 1980, in part because none of the checks issued between March and December of the previous year had been cashed. Some of the canceled checks in the company's records bore the endorsement "Pay to the order of R. J. Zani," and most had been mailed to a post office box in Harlingen, Texas—until May 1976, when the address was changed to a box in Springfield, Missouri.

At both the Treasury Department and the Secret Service, Ruiz and Martinez came up against what by now seemed to them to be an endemic inability on the part of the feds to cooperate with local law enforcement. Bureaucrats vacillated, agents failed to return phone calls, administrators gave out partial or misleading information. About all the two police officers were able to get from each agency was confirmation of the existence of a halfhearted investigation, now closed, into the activities of Robert Joseph Zani.

"You might think that everybody in law enforcement is on the same team," OCU's Lieutenant Simpson would later observe. "And you might think that if we're all chasing the same crook, we ought to chase him together. You might think that, but you'd be wrong."

Frustrated by the feds' indifference, Ruiz and Martinez reviewed their suspicions about Zani's possible connections to the intelligence community. It was difficult to judge whether they had stumbled upon some larger cover-up or just another example of Washington's refusal to stoop to the level of a couple of lowly patrol officers. Whatever it was, their gut instincts, always strong, now convinced them that Zani's wife, Irma, represented the single most critical link in the investigative chain they were struggling to forge. They had to locate her, get her to tell what they felt certain she knew, and move their case out of neutral. And they had to do it quickly, before Zani sprung himself or was sprung by someone else.

Simpson suggested that they again contact Captain Lencho Rendon in the Nueces County sheriff's office. Rendon had worked narcotics cases in South Texas for years, maintaining close relationships with many of the authorities on the Mexican side of the border, including Luís Soto Silva, a former Nuevo Laredo police chief who was now a top official in the powerful Federal Judical Police in Mexico City. If anyone could help them pinpoint Irma's whereabouts in Acapulco, they reasoned, it was probably Lencho.

On May 8, Ruiz phoned Rendon in Corpus Christi and explained the situation. As it happened, the chief deputy and his boss, Sheriff Solomon Ortiz, were scheduled to travel to Mexico City on Monday, May 12, to participate in an NBC documentary on the international drug trade. It was a tight deadline, Rendon realized. But he expected the shoot to take about three days, after which he and Ortiz could fly to Acapulco, enlist the local authorities' help in locating Irma, and then meet the Austin officers in the sunny resort, assuming, of course, that Ruiz and Martinez had been able by then to persuade Chief Dyson to okay the trip. It was clearly time to go back to Lieutenant Miller.

After hearing the new evidence the officers had uncovered, Miller was of two minds. If he could manage to nudge the APD bureaucracy, Ruiz and Martinez would be transferred out of his unit and into Bobby Simpson's; then Simpson could deal with the Acapulco trip and whatever other outlandish requests the two renegades came up with. Yet, even Miller had to agree that Zani was probably good for the Dess murder and that there was at least an outside chance that his mother's vanishing act could also be tied to the man who was still sitting in a cell a few blocks away. In addition, they had only a week or so to make arrangements if they hoped to take advantage of Rendon's contacts.

Miller barged past Patsy Moran, the unflappable secretary who had once served old man Miles and had been kept on by Dyson, and sat down in the chief's office. Dyson listened patiently to Miller's third entreaty. Perhaps his resistance was wearing down, the lieutenant thought, as Dyson nodded his assent. There were just two conditions.

First, Ruiz and Martinez were going to have to find some way—some proper way—to pay their expenses. The Austin city council was entering its budget sessions, an annual bloodletting that threatened to be worse than usual in the face of a slumping economy. And though he was willing to pay the salaries for Ruiz and Martinez, Dyson had no intention of asking the council members to pencil in an additional line item to pay for a couple of patrol officers to take a trip to Acapulco. After all, no one in the history of APD had ever gone to a foreign country on an investigation.

The second condition was this: Someone from the DA's office would have to travel with the officers to guarantee that every step they took was legal. If he was going out on a limb for them, the chief damn sure wanted someone else out there with him—and who better than the district attorney, an elected official?

When Miller reported back to Ruiz and Martinez, they were ecstatic. What was more, they knew just who they wanted to take from the DA's office—Frank Maxwell, Ruiz's former partner on the old TAC squad.

A native of De Ridder, Louisiana, Maxwell had moved with his family to Austin when he was still quite young. He grew up in a middle-class neighborhood about as distant as one could get from the humble eastside origins of his ex-partner. Joining the police department in January 1972, he quickly established a reputation at TAC as a solid investigator. The cases were interesting, and his colleagues, especially Ruiz and Martinez, were fun to work with. Even years later, he fondly recalled those days when he "just couldn't wait to get to work in the morning." Still, in 1978, when a slot opened on the newly formed special crimes/public integrity section at the DA's office, he was unable to resist what he considered a good career move.

Now Maxwell found himself summoned into assistant district attorney Allen Hill's office in the late afternoon. He took a seat while Hill completed a phone call. As he listened to Hill's end of the phone conversation, Maxwell tried to guess what his supervisor might have in store. Three weeks earlier, Ruiz had asked him to find out whatever he could on a subject named Robert Joseph Zani. Though Maxwell was unable to come up with anything new, the case was intriguing—obviously much more than what it appeared on the surface—and he asked to be kept informed. In fact, just that morning, while standing at the coffee machine, he had caught a glimpse of Ruiz, Martinez, and a distinguished-looking woman ducking down the back stairs of the DA's office. He wondered if there was some new development and made a note to call Ruiz when he got off work.

Hill hung up and looked across the desk at Maxwell. "That was Bobby Simpson," he said. "The San Antonio

Board of Realtors just voted a thousand dollars to send Paul Ruiz and Robert Martinez to Acapulco."

Maxwell nodded, wondering what any of this had to do with him.

"You're going, too," Hill added matter-of-factly.

Maxwell laughed. Other than a few rowdy evenings across the border in Nuevo Laredo, he had never been to Mexico. *This is probably just another of Hill's practical jokes,* he thought. And if he had to put money on it, he would bet that Ruiz and Martinez were in on the prank, too.

What Maxwell didn't know was that Hill and Ronnie Earle had spoken earlier in the day to Simpson, who explained that Dyson was balking at the prospect of allowing either the Dess family or the Board of Realtors to pay for whatever expenses his officers might incur during the investigation. Cops were paid to do their duty, Dyson argued, and innocent victims of crimes should not be victimized again by being asked to foot the bill.

"Bullshit," Earle had said. "I'll take their money, deposit it in the LEF, and pay the officers out of that."

The LEF, or Law Enforcement Fund, was an account used for, among other things, putting up witnesses who came from out of town to testify at trial, paying informants, or otherwise furthering criminal investigations. It was funded with money seized during drug raids and the like and was strictly monitored by the county auditor in compliance with state statutes. You couldn't draw on the account to paint your office or fund a political campaign, Earle knew, but you could certainly send some cops to Acapulco in connection with an ongoing investigation that now included not one but two potential counts of murder.

The DA immediately called his landlady, Virginia Dinan, who was in the middle of an executive meeting at the Austin Board of Realtors. Dinan excused herself and went to a phone on a small antique table in the hall outside the conference room.

"Ms. Dinan," Earle drawled, "we've come up with some

new information in the Zani case. We know his wife is down in Mexico, and we would like to go get her, but we don't have any money."

Earle explained that Dinan's counterpart, Maureen Alexander in San Antonio, had kicked in expense money for the two APD officers. But now Dyson was insisting that someone from the DA's office go along. "Dyson won't ask anyone for money, but you know that I don't have any compunction," Earl concluded. "Would the Austin board help finance my man's trip?"

"I don't know," Dinan replied, "but I'll walk back in there right now and ask."

Within an hour the board had voted to provide $500 to bolster the $1,000 from San Antonio, and Dinan had personally delivered the check to Earle. Ruiz and Martinez were there to greet Dinan and express their official appreciation when she brought the check by. After the meeting, they had noticed Maxwell getting another cup of coffee down the hall as they walked her to her car. Wait till ol' Frank gets the news, they had said with a chuckle; he won't believe it.

On Monday, May 12, Lencho Rendon called Ruiz at home from Mexico City to say he had spoken to Soto Silva, who assured his old friend that the officers would have the full cooperation of the local Acapulco authorities. They agreed to meet at La Palapa Hotel in Acapulco on Thursday, May 15.

The flight schedule called for Ruiz, Martinez, and Maxwell to catch a 7:35 p.m. Mexicana Airlines milk run from Austin to Harlingen, from Harlingen to the Mexican cities of Monterrey and Tampico, then on to Mexico City, where they were to hop an AeroMexico flight for the last leg down to Acapulco. Early on the day they were to leave, however, a Mexicana representative in Austin left word with the receptionist on the fifth floor of the Twin Towers: The flight from Austin to Harlingen was canceled because of poor weather.

There was a mad scramble to round up a car for the drive to Harlingen for their connecting flight, but the only available one was an old OCU Pontiac. The officers loaded their luggage into the car and, at one o'clock in the afternoon, headed for the border.

As they sped through the highway town of Kyle, about twenty minutes south of Austin, smoke began to spew from the front of the car. The engine sputtered, then quit altogether, and Ruiz steered the car to the shoulder. Martinez climbed out and walked to a small store a couple of hundred yards away, where he tried to place a collect call to Bobby Simpson. The lieutenant was out, so he had the operator buzz Lieutenant Roger Napier and explained the predicament.

"We've got a long way to go, a short time to get there, and we're sitting here by the side of the road because our piece-of-shit OCU unit just broke down," Martinez said. Napier immediately agreed to send Sergeant Jim Beck with another car.

Martinez bought some Cokes and a six-pack of beer and trudged back to the highway. The three officers leaned against the Pontiac, sipping the cool drinks while they waited for Sergeant Beck, who arrived a short time later in a brand-new, unmarked Ford Fairmont.

"We didn't say much to him," Maxwell later recalled, smiling. "We loaded our stuff in the car, pointed to a service station up the road, and left him there. Just took Beck's car and roared off."

They made the border in record time. But as they raced through McAllen, thirty miles west of the airport, with only about fifteen minutes remaining till flight time, they passed a DPS trooper who was parked along the four-lane highway, shooting radar.

"We went by him at, uh . . . Well, let's just say a high rate of speed," Maxwell remembered. "That radar in his unit must have lit up like a Christmas tree. The car jumped, the red lights came on, the dirt started a-flyin', and he took out after us."

While Ruiz kept his foot pressed to the floorboard, Martinez grabbed the Fairmont's radio and dialed in the intercity police radio network. "Sorry about that," he apologized. "This is Austin OCU, and we're trying to catch a flight out of Harlingen Industrial Airpark."

"Ten-four," the trooper's voice crackled.

Glancing behind, the officers saw him cut the overhead cherries and drop back. Then Martinez asked for help in finding their way to the airport. Not only had they blown by a state trooper, he thought, stifling a laugh, but now they had the gall to request assistance. A patient dispatcher at the DPS bay station in Harlingen broke in and guided them through the city to their destination. She even called ahead to hold the flight until they arrived.

The Austinites parked the car and ran through the airport lobby toward the departure gate. Martinez had forgotten his Mexican tourist visa, which an airline employee demanded, but after seeing his APD badge, she took pity on him and thrust a new one into his hands. The officers bustled to their seats on the crowded plane as the other passengers eyed them, wondering who these men were who had held up their flight.

During the hour-long layover in Monterrey, Ruiz, Martinez, and Maxwell wandered the lobby of the airport, where they witnessed their first *mordida,* the system by which Mexican officials regularly supplement their meager incomes. Amazed, the Texans watched as a well-dressed woman, frantic to get on the flight, palmed a wad of pesos to a *federal,* who then slipped behind the Mexicana counter and whispered something in the supervisor's ear.

"Oh, shit!" Ruiz exclaimed, nudging his companions in the ribs. "Look at this!"

The incident seemed to foreshadow what they could expect as they tried to track down Irma Zani in Acapulco. They were jetting into a world of very few rules, a world where almost nothing raised an eyebrow. In Mexico, they had been told, when a law officer asked, "Did you give her the warning?" he was likely to be laughed out of the room. "Warning? Hell, yes, we warned her. We warned her that we were going to kick her ass if she didn't tell us what we wanted to hear!"

NINE

When the plane touched down at Acapulco's Juan Alvarez International Airport about eleven-thirty that night, May 15, the humidity hovered near saturation, as if the skies were having trouble persuading the rainy season not to let loose five weeks early. Following the other passengers down the stairway to the tarmac, Ruiz, Martinez, and Maxwell instantly regretted their coats and ties. Sagging with sweat, their shirts became the angular curves of their torsos as they jockeyed for position in the lines of tourists waiting for *combis* to take them the fourteen miles into town.

The plan called for them to check into La Palapa, an aging hotel in a relatively quiet residential section whose reputation for luxury had long since been eclipsed by the newer resort facilities up along the strip. There they were to wait in the bar for word from Ortiz and Rendon, who would then escort them to see the comandante. No sooner had the sheriff and his chief deputy arrived, however, than the bar manager approached their table with a conspiratorial air.

"Are you gentlemen supposed to meet with Comandante Ricardo Rodea Reyes here tonight?" he asked.

The Texans nodded.

"Well, he just called to say he won't be able to make it," the bar manager continued.

Savoring his role as confidential informant, he fingered

the medallion hanging from his neck and paused for dramatic effect. Then, almost sadly, as if reluctant to give up his final secret, he added, "But he'll be by—*mañana*."

So it was true what Ruiz and Martinez had heard about the way official business is conducted in Mexico. *Mañana, siempre mañana*. Always tomorrow.

While they waited, Ortiz and Rendon filled the officers in on what they could expect from Reyes. The comandante had been sent into the state of Guerrero two years earlier to clean up the pockets of leftist guerrillas believed to be still holed up in the hills near Acapulco. As if to remind himself of the true enemy, Reyes's office walls were hung with posters of Ernesto "Che" Guevara, the Argentine doctor and co-architect of the Cuban revolution. Though Guevara was killed in Bolivia in late 1967, Mexico had been plagued in the intervening years by movements that threatened, in his name, to disrupt the political progress that Mexico's official ruling party claimed to have brought to the country.

One man in particular, a grade-school teacher named Lucio Cabañas Barrientos, had eluded government troops for more than seven years before being gunned down outside the region known as Tecpan de Galeana, near the tiny village where Irma Zani's father once lived. Cabañas focused national political attention on the mountains of Guerrero. Now it was Reyes's responsibility to refocus that attention toward the tourism and good times that visitors were supposed to be able to count on in Acapulco. By most accounts, he had done that part of his job well.

Revolution in Guerrero, however, was being pushed aside in favor of another commodity: illegal drugs. The international demand for marijuana, heroin, and, lately, cocaine, had proved a direct boon for *narcotraficantes* and local officials, and the indirect benefits of the drug business had trickled down to countless farm families in the area. After government officials entered into agreements with Colombian cocaine barons to trampoline their products north of the border, the state of Guerrero emerged as an important staging area for the U.S. market. In Acapulco, Reyes soon learned, the problem was not so much that the system was corrupt as that corruption was the system. No one—least of all Rendon, who knew him best—was willing to offer an opinion as to just where Reyes stood when it came to the enticements offered to local cops by area drug lords.

Just after ten o'clock the following morning, Reyes, true to his word, rushed into the hotel coffee shop. He was a tree stump of a man, thick and squat, with heavy jowls and an entourage of scowling bodyguards and hangers-on who seemed determined to outpace the gringo image of Mexican law enforcement.

Apologizing for the delay, Reyes explained that two of his men had been killed the night before in a shoot-out with drug traffickers on a nearby ranch. He leaned forward and confided a few of the details. Recently, a local campesino had been spotted around town with a great deal more money in the pockets of his Levi's than any amount of subsistence farming could ever produce. Last night Reyes and his men had finally followed the man back into the hills. But they must have hit a trip wire, because all of a sudden shots were exchanged in the blackness.

"So we've just spent the whole night evening up the score," Reyes concluded, stifling a yawn.

"And . . . ?" Rendon smiled at his old friend.

Reyes sighed. "We got ten of theirs, took them up to the mouth of *el pozo* [a volcanic pit north of the city where victims of the police and their paramilitary death squads were said to be dumped], and gave them one last chance to tell the truth. They refused. So I guess you could say we're even—for now."

But there were still loose ends left to be tied and the families of the slain officers to be consoled, Reyes explained. He regretted asking his American law enforcement colleagues—the Texans winced at the association—to be patient, but these things sometimes happened. Maybe he could swing by for them later that evening to take in a floor show at the Acapulco Princess. Surely they didn't plan just to breeze in and out of his city without giving him the pleasure of showing off the most spectacular international playground on earth.

With that, Reyes excused himself and headed for the door. His entourage followed, cradling in their arms several dozen bottles of Carta Blanca beer, which they had secured from the man behind the coffee shop counter.

Faced with a free afternoon to fill, the Texans walked across the street to the beach. Martinez, whose luggage had failed to arrive at the airport the night before, gamely rolled up his sleeves and trudged through the sand in his dress shoes, while the others, clad in slacks and golf shirts, found a table under a straw *palapa*. Before them brooded the ocean, and to their backs the tangle of jungle and fat roots snaked along the ground where Irma's father had spent the best years of his life working like thunder so that a little rain might fall into someone else's garden. They ordered fruity drinks and sat back to eye the tourists.

This was Acapulco, after all, the city of manufactured fun. Everywhere, tourism purred, and the fragrance of flowers and diesel fumes filled the air. Large white birds strutted in the sand with the proprietary gait of hotel managers. American women paraded by, wearing little more than huge sunglasses than lent them the look of aristocratic insects. A muffled, irregular grind drifted in from the motorboats on the bay, indifferent to the sand and foam that wrapped them in the breath of the sea.

Try as they might, the Austinites could not relax. They knew that APD demanded strict justification for out-of-town trips of one hundred miles or more. Now here they sat, running up the taxpayers' tab on a beach in sunny Acapulco, drinks in hand and shoes buried in the sand. They were making little or no progress on the case, just as Dyson and the other department brass had predicted all along. The pressure was on. After about an hour, while Ortiz tried to convince a pair of young ladies from Chicago that he was a photographer on assignment from a high-fashion magazine, Ruiz, Martinez, and Maxwell went back to the hotel.

Late that evening, Rendon phoned their room to say that the comandante was waiting downstairs to take them all out for the promised night on the town. Martinez—whose luggage had finally been rounded up and delivered to the hotel, minus three bottles of expensive cologne—donned clean clothes, and he, Ruiz, and Maxwell headed for the lobby.

The comandante's chauffeur picked them up at the door in a brand-new Good Times van sporting California plates, confiscated, he noted with a smile, from a couple of hippies a few weeks earlier. The Texans climbed into the van with Reyes, who was accompanied by both his wife and his girlfriend—a bleached blonde whose eyelashes fluttered like octopus tentacles—and drove to the Acapulco Princess, followed by a car filled with bodyguards.

To their chagrin, the Texans found that their hosts had also picked up a scruffy suspect, who was being beaten in the back of the van. The teenager knew of a large shipment of marijuana, the comandante explained between advice about what the Texans ought to try from the Princess's menu. Now his men were simply trying to get the kid to come forth with his cohorts' names. Ruiz inched away to avoid getting blood on his shirt, while the comandante's henchmen beat the boy to a pulp, then dropped him off at the municipal jail. (The next morning, they learned that the kid had led Reyes's men to a stash of some five hundred kilos.)

When they finally arrived at the Acapulco Princess, they were stopped by the doorman. Impossible, he apologized. The floor show had just begun, and he wasn't permitted to seat anyone else until intermission. Besides, there was a standing-room-only crowd inside, but he would be happy to make them a reservation for later in the week. Reyes glanced at his chief assistant, who took the doorman aside, and before they knew it, they were led to a ringside table from which a group of tourists had been removed to make way for the comandante and his guests.

Reyes arranged them at the table. Oversolicitous waiters kept the booze flowing while the officers sat back to watch the topless revue. Ruiz, who generally restricted himself to a couple of glasses of white wine, and Martinez and Maxwell, both beer drinkers, found themselves facing an almost endless supply of rum and Cokes. The room seemed filled to capacity with dark men in shades who sat frozen in front of the stage, their stern features sporting the opaque consistency of scar tissue as they anchored their silence in a cove of shot glasses. Except for the tourists, everyone looked as if he had shadows beneath his eyes and tired, creased expressions that no amount of booze could enliven.

At one point, with his wife sitting impassively at his side and his girlfriend down at the end of the table, the comandante turned to the officers and opened his wallet confidentially to show them a picture of his maid. Then, leaning back in a wooden chair too narrow for his girth, he uttered the grand synthesis of a lifetime of reflection: If the man of the house doesn't give the cook a little stir from time to time, there will be no love in the home.

Maxwell spoke no Spanish and found himself wondering why he ever agreed to accompany his friends on such a trip. Ruiz fidgeted, rehearsing in his mind the excuses they would lay out for their superiors when they returned to Austin empty-handed. As for Martinez, each time Reyes saw that his drink had slipped below the halfway mark, he refilled it from the bottle of Bacardi before him on the table. His wide eyes on the stage, Martinez never caught on, and before long, he was hopelessly drunk.

The evening ended in disarray when Reyes, explaining that he wanted to drop his wife at home and then take his girlfriend dancing, asked them to meet him later at a disco. Ruiz and Rendon deposited the others at the hotel and went in search of the comandante. After wandering into a number of gay bars by mistake, they gave up.

To Ruiz's sleepy astonishment, Martinez's hungover dismay, and Maxwell's continuing bewilderment, the comandante sent a state judicial police agent named Humberto Ramírez and his chauffeur around early the next morning, May 17, to take them to interview Irma Zani. They were followed by an old Chevrolet containing a hulking man in filthy clothes whom Ramírez presented as his homicide expert and a fourteen-year-old boy with a rusted carbine slung over his shoulder.

"That's my bodyguard," the homicide expert explained, as if to allay any fears the officers might have about the teenager. "He's real good. All I have to do is point to someone I want him to kill, and boom!"

Thus properly introduced, the Texans piled into the Good Times van with the Chevrolet tailing closely behind. They made their way slowly through the crowded streets of downtown Acapulco, amidst the cries of vendors on corners and ramshackle taxis honking their horns. On a narrow side street, the van and an oncoming pickup locked mirrors.

"*¡Hijo de tu chingada madre!*" shouted the other driver, climbing out of the truck.

The comandante's chauffeur threw open the door to the van and brandished his .45. "Out of the way, *pendejo!*" he hissed. "Federal police!" The driver of the pickup hastily apologized and retreated to his vehicle as the Texans drove on.

They pulled up in front of the offices of Miguel Angel O'Campo Oliveros, the Guerrero state prosecutor, from whom Ramírez had arranged to borrow a portable cassette recorder for the interview. Rendon and Ruiz accompanied the agent into the building as the others waited in the van, eyed suspiciously by the plainclothes *judiciales* who stood on the steps outside, smoking cigarettes and fingering their semiautomatics. Finally, one of the *judiciales* approached the van.

"You can't park here," he told the chauffeur, letting his weapon slip down his arm.

"Federal police," the chauffeur replied, by way of explanation.

"Well, I'm from the state judicial police," the officer insisted, "and I say you can't park here."

The chauffeur reached for his .45 and, without looking at the cop, placed it on the dashboard. "Why don't you just shoot me then?" he taunted the state cop.

Maxwell slid to the floorboard, rehearsing in his mind the improbable headline back home: DA INVESTIGATOR KILLED IN SHOOT-OUT BETWEEN FEDERAL AND STATE POLICE IN GODDAM ACAPULCO. "I can't believe this shit," he moaned. "What are we doing here?"

After trading insults for a couple of minutes more, however, the *judicial* wisely backed off, and the comandante's chauffeur chuckled under his breath.

Inside the building, Rendon and Ruiz learned that O'Campo Oliveros was a distant relative of Irma's. In fact, the state prosecutor said, he had been on duty when Irma and her mother came to denounce Robert Zani on the assault charges back on March 8.

"I told her then that she was crazy," O'Campo Oliveros recalled. "I said, 'Irma, this nice American man marries you and provides for you, and now you want to get him thrown in jail.' But she insisted, and I did what I had to."

With that, he handed them his only recorder—a jam box—and a couple of spare cassettes and wished them luck.

As they headed into the hills west of town, the Texans wondered what they would find when they got to Irma's house. The city soon gave way to a neighborhood of unpaved streets and broken sidewalks with small mountains of refuse littering every corner. Above them, the sky was the color of steel plate streaked gray. Rusted cars lined the street, and little adobe huts lay scattered about in no apparent order. A thunderclap shuddered their weak walls of wattle and mud. By the time the van reached the crest of the hill, gangs of ragged children were chasing it. The officers—except for Maxwell, who opted to stay with the van—walked down a dirt path toward the hut, chasing away the dogs that sniffed restlessly at their heels.

The hut was constructed of mud and stray pieces of wood, with a couple of sheets of corrugated tin serving as the roof. The front door opened without a sound, and in the dirt-floored interior stood Raquel Reyes Ventura, Irma's mother, dressed in black, no less than sixty years of age, her cruel, dark eyes squinting in the morning light and her hair tight to her skull like a silver helmet. She took their hands in hers, less in greeting than in an effort to help them into her home. Irma wasn't there, she said, but she was due back soon and they were welcome to wait.

Inside, the officers spied the two youngest of the Zani brood: twelve-year-old Raquel Carmela, who they knew had been born on March 16, 1968, in Austin's Brackenridge Hospital, and Robert Junior, nine, whose dead eyes, the color of ink on an old agreement, seemed a chilling duplicate of his father's. The kids stared at the officers with the look of tough, miniature bandits, as skinny as vanilla beans. "The pits," Robert Junior sneered when Ruiz casually asked about his father. Then he and his sister disappeared into a back room, as Ruiz caught himself wondering if he or some other officer would one day be forced to deal with the criminal activities of Zani's son.

Just after noon, Irma herself arrived. She was accompanied by her uncle, José Antonio Montes, who introduced himself as her attorney (in fact, he worked for a group of attorneys but was not himself a lawyer). It was the first time Ruiz and Martinez had seen Irma face-to-face, and they noted that her hair was cropped even closer than in the passport photo they had studied for the past seven weeks. She was short and plump, but she swung her hips in a manner still charged with sexual signals. She greeted the officers skeptically, her expression suggesting that of a woman who knows she has made more wrong than right decisions along the way.

Gesturing for them to sit in rickety straw chairs on an open porch outside the front door, Irma lit a cigarette. Her lips left a bright red ring around the filter.

After explaining the nature of their visit, Rendon spoke. "Irma, at this time we would like you to make a comment into the recorder whether you are making this statement under pressure. Are you making it voluntarily because you want to, or are you being forced to make this statement?"

Irma paused, looking at her uncle for a clue. Montes shook his head silently. Neither he nor his client intended to cooperate.

Ramírez, the state judicial police agent, stepped forward. "Come on now, Irma," he said in Spanish. "You know how we work here. You have a house today, tonight it burns down, and tomorrow you have no house. These officers have come a long way to talk to you, and I expect you to help them."

Montes meticulously finger-combed what hair he had across his balding skull and looked away. It was clear that Irma was going to be on her own from here on out.

"I want to answer," she said at last, her English heavily accented. "I want to say it."

"You do want to answer?" Rendon asked again for the sake of the recording.

"Yes."

"There's nobody that is putting pressure on you?" Rendon insisted.

Before she could answer, Sheriff Ortiz cut in. "Or somebody," he began, hesitantly, "anybody that's threatened you to make this statement?"

Irma thought for a moment. "Yeah," she whispered, "in a way. Zani." She had a curious habit of referring to her husband by his last name, as if distancing herself from the surname they shared.

Ruiz opened the last pack from the carton of Carltons he had brought along on the trip. *This is going to be tougher than I expected,* he thought.

Rendon broke into rapid Spanish, explaining to Irma that he wanted her to verify that no one present on the porch at that moment was coercing her.

"No, no, no," Irma said, understanding at last. "No one in the group here is forcing me to make any statements."

"You understand the English language?" Rendon asked, for good measure.

"Yes, I do," Irma replied.

Rendon then introduced Ruiz, who adjusted the volume on the recorder, asked Irma to speak a little louder, and began the questioning.

"Do you remember the day of December 4, 1979?" he asked.

"I wasn't keeping track on anything," she replied.

Ruiz thought for a moment and decided to come at the question from another angle: "When did you first meet a man by the name of Mr. Dess? Do you remember that day?"

"I don't remember."

"Okay," Ruiz pressed on. "Do you remember who you were with when you met this man?"

"With Zani."

"By 'Zani,' do you mean your husband? What's your husband's name?"

"Robert J. Zani."

Irma was beginning to warm to Ruiz. It was usually Martinez who played the good cop during interrogations while Ruiz, aggressive and impatient, tended to badger his suspects into submission. But it was also difficult to resist Ruiz's charm when he poured it on, and he and Irma were establishing a curious relationship that would ebb and flow but remain close throughout the entire investigation.

Over the next half hour, Irma described how she and her husband and four children had moved from Acapulco to the Siesta Motel in San Antonio, where they lived from September 30 to November 26, 1979. Robert spent his time with a number of local realtors, sometimes taking Irma with him and sometimes going alone. She didn't remember why they left the motel on November 26, but she thought they had slept in their brown 1973 pickup with a camper attachment for the next week or so.

On December 3, she continued, they dropped in on José and Bruna Bayardo, casual acquaintances whom the Zanis had met some years earlier when Irma and Bruna shared a hospital room in the South Texas city of Robstown, seventeen miles west of Corpus Christi. About four-thirty the next morning, Robert and Irma told the Bayardos that they were going to Houston to see a doctor. The Bayardos agreed to take care of the children, and Robert and Irma left—for San Antonio. There Robert parked the pickup at La Quinta on the city's south side and called Julius Dess from a pay phone.

Irma then recalled how they waited in the cold for Julius Dess to pick them up that December morning, how they drove south of the city to Atascosa County to look at the thirty-five rural acres listed in the Dess Realty Company catalog and finally to a smaller fifteen-acre tract in nearby Wilson County.

"Let me ask you this," Ruiz broke in. "What were you wearing that day?"

"What?" Irma seemed startled by the abrupt question.

"What were you wearing?" Ruiz repeated.

"I . . . I believe I was wearing my pants," Irma stammered. "I don't know if it was brown or green pants. I just . . ."

Ruiz interrupted her. "Were you wearing anything on your head?" he demanded.

Irma fell silent, looking to her uncle again for guidance. She could tell that Ruiz was driving toward something specific, but she had no idea what it was. Her uncle stared back blankly and shrugged.

"Yes," Irma said at last. A certain resignation had crept into her voice.

"What were you wearing?" Ruiz asked, more gently now.

"A green scarf."

The Texans shifted in their chairs, their questions coming more quickly now.

"So you went to see this thirty-five-acre piece of property?" asked Ruiz.

"Yes," Irma said. "And the man mentioned that he had another piece of property that was like fifteen acres or so with no home on it that was not too far."

"Why did your husband want to see this piece of property, and why did he ask you to go along with him?"

"He wanted to go see the place because he told me that the man had money. And he also mentioned that if I didn't go along with him that I was lost."

"What did he mean by that?"

"I didn't ask him. I just went along with him because I was so afraid. You know, Zani threatened me so many times."

"How did he threaten you, Irma?" Ruiz asked, a hint of sympathy returning to his voice.

"By telling me that if there was anything that he wanted me to do, something that I didn't like, that I was going to be next," Irma replied.

"Did you know what he meant by that?"

"Yes—to kill me."

There was a long pause as Irma lit another cigarette and exhaled the first, deep drag with a shudder of sorrow. Her mother looked on from a chair in the entryway of the house. Though the family lived in bleak austerity, she had tried to teach her child a certain sophistication. Now she could tell that these Texas cops were closing in upon wounds of frustration that no worldliness could salve.

"So he told you he thought Mr. Dess had money?" Ruiz asked, breaking the silence. "What did he want to do? What was his reason for taking him out there?"

Irma was brooding and nostalgic. Then she seemed to return from very far away and very long ago.

"Zani wanted to kill him," she whispered. "He said, 'I got the gun.' No, he said, 'I got something to take care of him.' And I said, 'What do you mean by that?' He said, 'You'll see it. You'll find out.' "

Sheriff Ortiz spoke again. "When did you see a weapon for the first time?"

Irma seemed unsettled. "When?" she stammered. "Well, it was in 1967, right after we got married, because Zani always had this big gun, and he wanted me to learn how to use it, and I was scared to death. I said, 'No, I'm not . . . I don't like . . . I'm not going to play with those things.' He said, 'Don't be a coward. You can do it.' He said, 'If somebody comes along and you just don't like them, you can kill them and nobody's going to touch you.' And I said, I'm not going to do that.' "

Ortiz insisted, "But on this particular day—when you picked up the real estate man by the name of Mr. Dess— when did you see the gun for the first time?"

"Well, I saw it before then," Irma answered, "but I didn't think nothing about it. Zani went by himself to America first, and he bought two guns. He had three in total."

"What caliber?" Ortiz asked. "Can you give a description of the weapons, the color or the names?"

".35, .45, I don't remember," Irma said. "It was something like a .55 or a .45, I think."

".25?" Ortiz prompted her.

".38 or .48," Irma answered, uncertain. She was trying to help, but she obviously knew little about firearms. Ortiz, a former constable and county commissioner and a future U.S. congressman, seemed to have more political savvy than expertise at grilling suspects. He asked a number of leading questions before Martinez, who had been holding his tongue, finally took over.

"Okay, let's go back," Martinez suggested. "What happened afterwards, when he took you to show you the fifteen acres?"

Irma pinched the bridge of her nose as if she were trying to bring what she saw into focus.

"Tell us what happened," Martinez said again.

"The man says, 'I would like to show you where the land ends and where it starts,'" Irma recalled. "He asked me if I was interested in the place. I said, 'My husband is the one.' That's what I said. So then he went to him, and he was just getting smarter and smarter, my husband. And I said, 'Why don't you give him an answer?' Zani said, 'No, you take care of him, you talk to him, you try to make him believe that we're interested in the place.'"

"In Spanish or English?"

"Zani mostly spoke to me in Spanish. He wouldn't speak to me in English."

"Did y'all meet anybody at this place?" Martinez asked.

"In the thirty-five acres, yes, we met somebody," Irma recalled. "Not by name, not by talking to them, but I saw them there, and that's why my husband didn't try to do anything there."

She lit another cigarette and sat back, explaining that Dess had driven them around the fifteen acres for several minutes, glanced to the right front passenger seat to give her the hard-sell pitch. She didn't know how to respond, and Zani wouldn't help. He had just sat silently in the backseat, staring at Dess's head.

While Martinez was questioning Irma, Ruiz had excused himself to check on Maxwell, who, having emptied his pockets of pesos for the neighborhood children, had climbed back into the van and had begun honking the horn impatiently. Ruiz briefed his former partner on the progress so far and went back down the dirt path to the shack.

"The realtor got mad," Irma was saying as Ruiz returned to the porch, "and my husband got mad, too, because the guy was real pushy. He thought we really wanted the place. And Zani said, 'Well, this is pretty high. It's not worth it.' So the man turned to me and said, 'What do you think? Do you like it?' I just couldn't respond, couldn't say a thing. And my husband got mad at me, too. I said, 'Well, let's go then.' "

Martinez leaned forward. "Did you know your husband was going to hurt this man before the argument?" he asked.

"No."

"Did y'all talk about this man having money?"

"Yes. Zani mentioned that the man had money. Every realtor, every doctor—he always said they had money. And I said, 'Let them have it.' "

"Realtors and doctors?"

"Yes."

"What did he want to do to them?"

"He wanted to kill them. He wanted to call for an appointment and get inside and just kill them."

Ruiz reached for the tape recorder, checked to see how much tape remained, and placed it back on the table. "For the money or what?" he asked.

"He said that doctors are thieves and realtors are just a bunch of liars," Irma remembered. " 'I can't stand them,' he would say. 'I can't take them anymore, and I'm going to get rid of some.' 'Besides that,' he said, 'it's an easy way to get money. You can get any kind of credit card you can think of and use them and just . . . nobody knows a thing.' Yes, that's what he said. So he was after money and them credit cards, both ways."

Ramírez and the homicide expert, neither of whom spoke English, were beginning to fidget, but the Texans had inched forward. Irma's mother moved onto the porch in the manner of a disillusioned stowaway sneaking off a ship that never left port. She stood behind her daughter while Montes sat silently sipping a soft drink.

"Okay," Martinez said, choosing his words with care, "what happened after the argument?"

"I said, 'Let's go. It's late,' We didn't have breakfast, and I was getting hungry. So the realtor got inside, and I got in the front, and my husband got in the backseat behind the guy. And the next thing I knew—bang! And I turned around and thought I was going to die."

"By that, do you mean you heard a shot?" Ruiz asked.

"Yes, I heard an explosion. At first, for a few seconds, just one. Then, later on, not very long . . . two more . . . and the car was moving. And I thought . . . I just didn't expect to see anything like that."

It was easy to imagine the scene: Just a cheap pawnshop gun, a little .25, not terribly accurate, but terrible and accurate enough. The bullet ricocheting down the barrel and into the back of Julius Dess's head. the body lurching forward, then slumping over in stiff gymnastics.

Ortiz broke in. "You say the car had already started to move?"

"Yes."

"How did you stop it?"

"Zani told me to pull the key out of the . . ."

"Ignition?"

"Um-hmm. And I couldn't move. I couldn't . . . My husband pushed me. He said, 'Get out! Get out!' And I just . . . When I saw the guy, you know, just bleeding all over . . ."

"Was he bleeding from the face?" Martinez asked.

"Well, on his head," Irma said, her English more halting as she relived the gruesome events. "I didn't look at the side or what. I just saw he was bleeding from his—¿cómo se dice?—forehead. And nose. The blood was just coming out of his nose."

"What happened right after you saw him bleeding?" Ruiz asked. "You took the key out of the car?"

"Yes."

"You stopped the car?"

"Um-hmm."

Ruiz glanced at the tape recorder. "Okay," he said slowly. "What happened after that?"

"Then my husband pulled the body back over the front seat, you know, from the top, over. . . ."

"How did you get him out of the seat belts?"

"Zani cut them."

"Did he have a knife?"

"Yes. Then he pulled the body over."

"Did you help him?"

"I didn't do anything. I just sat in the front seat. Zani grabbed my hair and yelled, 'You better help me or you're next.' But I just couldn't move."

"Okay," Ruiz said in a soothing tone. "So what did your husband do then?"

"Well, he covered the body. He opened the back of the car and took out some insulation and covered the body. Then he took off his—he was wearing a suit, my husband—he took off his coat and put it over the man's head."

"Then what happened?"

"He got in the car, and we drove to Corpus Christi."

Ortiz and Rendon perked up. The story had now moved to their jurisdiction, and they spent the next several minutes trying, without success, to find out what route she and her husband had taken to Corpus. Irma didn't remember. She didn't know what towns they had driven through, whether they had taken the ferry or crossed over the bridge—nothing. She had no idea why her husband had decided to bury Dess's body on the Padre Island National Seashore.

Finally Martinez interrupted, bringing the questioning back to what he considered the core of the case: whether Dess had been robbed in the course of the killing, which, if so, would warrant a capital murder charge. "Irma, after y'all got to Corpus Christi, what happened then?"

"Zani searched through everything," she said, "in his pockets and the whole thing. He took off the man's shirt and T-shirt, I think—I'm not sure he was wearing a T-shirt—but he took off everything."

"Did he take his wallet, his money?"

"Yes, he did. And he only found three dollars."

"Three dollars?" It wasn't much, but it was sufficient to ask a jury for the death penalty.

"Yes, and a check," Irma said. The hint of a smile played across her face but never quite made it to her mouth. "He had a check already filled out. I think he was going to get money out of the bank."

"Did your husband keep the check?"

"No, he burned everything."

Irma went on to describe how she and Zani used a stray board and some driftwood to dig a shallow grave and cover the body with sand. Afterward, she said, they gathered up Dess's clothing, identification, and other belongings and carried them about fifty feet down the beach, where they burned them.

"What else was taken?" Ruiz wanted to know.

"Some credit cards. Then my husband took a rag and wiped the car. He didn't think he could clean the buckle of the seat belt so he cut it off with a knife and threw it in the ocean. He also took off the man's watch and rings and threw them in the water."

"He didn't want to keep them?"

"No, he didn't want nothing. Just the money and the credit cards."

Irma related how they climbed back into the Thunderbird and drove north along the water for about three miles until the car got stuck in the sand just south of a park ranger outpost. Ever arrogant, Zani trudged to the building and demanded help. Norm Bonneau, the Nueces County park ranger on duty that night, explained that park policy prohibited him from pulling cars from the sand—a frequent request—but Zani was welcome to use the phone to call for assistance. Bonneau even tried to supply him with the name of a nearby wrecker company.

Zani's notorious temper flared, and he stormed out of the station. Halfway back to the car, however, he encountered D. R. Ross, a forty-five-year-old carpenter from Kansas who was in the habit of driving his multicolored converted school bus to Padre Island each year, where he spent the months of November and December camped out on the beach, pursuing a young woman who worked in the Nueces County courthouse.

"Is that your blue T-Bird stuck in the sand?" Ross asked, explaining that he had a tow chain in his bus and would be happy to help.

Zani immediately softened, and after they had hauled the car out of the sand, he offered to pay Ross for his trouble.

"Hell, it was no trouble," the good-natured Ross protested. "But you can buy me a beer if you like." He pointed through the mist to a weatherworn cafe called the Sand Dollar, perched on stilts at the dune line about two hundred feet up the beach. Zani ordered a beer and two Cokes from the owners, Earl and Cora Allen, who would later remember the trio because Ross, whom they knew, joked that he had finally brought them some customers to perk up their off-season business.

According to Irma, she and her husband then drove back to San Antonio, stopping somewhere along the highway to burn several articles of their own clothing that had been splashed with Dess's blood. Later, they stopped again, this time to toss the T-Bird's spare tire in the brush beside the road—Irma couldn't explain why. Finally, they had pulled into the San Antonio airport, parked the car, and once more wiped it clean of prints. They then hailed a cab back to La Quinta, where they had parked their pickup, and hit the road again. It must have been about one-thirty in the morning, Irma guessed.

"Where'd y'all leave to?" Martinez asked, recalling that she had told them earlier about leaving the children in Robstown with the Bayardos.

"I believe we went to Harlingen," Irma said, hesitating.

"Do you remember where you stayed there in Harlingen?"

"Uh . . . I can't remember dates and days. I don't know."

"Was it a hotel that you stayed in?"

"Yes."

"Was it Harlingen or La Feria?" Martinez asked, testing her with yet another locale, which he remembered from the address noted on the temporary driver's license floating in the toilet tank on the night of Zani's arrest and, later, the permanent license that had arrived by chance in the mail on the day he and Ruiz visited La Feria.

"No, it wasn't Harlingen. I think it was McAllen or . . . I don't remember. West . . . some areas around there. I just— if I saw the hotel, I could recognize it, but I don't remember."

She was hedging now, but the officers couldn't tell whom she might be trying to protect. Later, they would confirm that Robert and Irma had driven through the night to Robstown, where they were again put up by José and Bruna Bayardo.

"We stayed probably two or three days at the most," Irma continued. "Then, we left and we came to . . ."

Side one of the ninety-minute cassette tape clicked off, triggering a blast of American rock and roll from the local station to which the prosecutor evidently tuned his jam box when he wasn't lending it to police officers visiting from foreign countries. Someone jumped to turn down the volume, knocking over several empty soft-drink bottles on the table.

Irma continued to talk. She recounted how her husband had read a report in the morning newspaper of December 10 describing a body discovered by authorities in the dunes of Padre Island two days earlier. It had been turned over to the Nueces County medical examiner, whose preliminary findings suggested that it was probably the body of missing San Antonio realtor J. A. Dess. A complete report was expected in a couple of days, the article concluded.

The newspaper report scared them, Irma said. They hadn't planned on the body's being discovered so quickly, and they hadn't expected coverage of the murder in the press. It was time to make a run for it, get the hell out of the area as soon as possible. After a brief discussion, they decided to drive to Acapulco, where they hoped to stay with Irma's mother until things cooled off. The trip would take three or four days, they calculated, and they would save money by sleeping in the pickup along the highway.

At a roadside park outside Eagle Pass, just before crossing the border into Mexico, the fugitives stopped to burn Dess's credit cards. Zani lit a match, watching the sparks ignite and grow until flames melted the plastic liner and licked at the inside walls of the metal garbage can. There they were, fleeing in the wake of a murder that had netted them a grand total of $3 and a batch of credit cards they hadn't even had a chance to use. It wasn't supposed to have turned out this way.

Suddenly Zani tore off his suit coat, Irma recalled, and tossed it on top of the flames. Even with the heat of the fire on his face, he told her, a chill had climbed his spine beneath the thin cotton shirt. He had worn the coat almost constantly for the past six days—although it was encrusted with the blood of a real estate agent whose only mistake was his somewhat pushy attempt to unload fifteen acres of undeveloped property in the barren stretches of Wilson County, Texas.

TEN

Ruiz bummed a Marlboro from Martinez and glanced at his watch. It was just past one-thirty in the afternoon—still plenty of time and tape left. He thought of Gladys Zani. Almost six years had come and gone since the last time anyone had heard from her. To Ruiz, a man who grew uneasy when more than a few days went by without a visit to his own mother, it just didn't figure. Irma had been more forthcoming than they could have hoped for thus far; maybe she would now be willing to discuss her mother-in-law's whereabouts as well. He turned the cassette over and pushed the record button.

"There are no more questions from this particular case," Ruiz began. "You've been very helpful, Irma."

He paused, searching for a way to ease into the next subject. "Uh . . . can you tell me . . . uh, who else . . . uh . . ."

Martinez knew where his partner was leading and came to his rescue. "Can you tell us who else your husband has killed?" he asked bluntly.

"Yes," Irma immediately replied. "He told me that he killed a guy in Austin."

"Austin, Texas?" Martinez asked, his voice rising as the others moved closer to the edges of their chairs. Here was a completely unanticipated development.

"Yes. In Austin, Texas. Someplace around the university."

"Do you know what year that was?" Ruiz cut in.

"Uh, no," Irma replied. "I didn't know Zani then."

"How old was your husband?"

"Well, he's what—thirty-six now? He probably was nineteen or twenty. I don't know."

Ruiz scooted forward in his seat. "Irma," he asked gently, reaching out to touch her forearm, "when did he tell you this?"

"After he killed his mother."

"After?"

"After he killed his mother, yes—because he said it was not the first time. He said he was kind of getting used to it."

The Texans were quiet. Their combined experience at interrogating suspects totaled dozens of years. They were accustomed to all kinds of investigations—from stopping young punks on the street, shaking them down, and finding their pockets filled with merchandise that had been in the family for all of ten minutes to developing intricate surveillance schemes that sometimes took months to unfold in the soft underbelly of modern society's criminal cartel. But this interview with an ex-whore in a shack gone to seed on a hillside above Acapulco was now veering down at least two distinct paths, and none of the men knew just how to proceed.

"So what happened when he killed his mother?" Martinez asked at last, breaking the silence. "Did they have a fight, or why did he do it?"

"Well, it was awful, awful."

"Where did this happen?" Martinez insisted. "What state?"

"In Oklahoma," Irma said. "Tulsa, Oklahoma."

Ortiz was up and pacing now. "Were you there when his mother was killed?" he asked from behind her shoulder.

"Yes, I was there. We went out to Arkansas to see the land that she had over there. I believe it's about forty acres, I don't know. It was just a Sunday, and we wanted, you know, to picnic. He had the gun, and he told me that he wanted to use it on her head. I told him it wasn't right. I said, 'Zani, don't do this. If you want to do this, do it by yourself, alone.' He said sooner or later it was going to get done."

"Why would he want to kill his own mother?" Ruiz asked.

"They always fought so bad, so ugly, so dirty. And I was in the middle, and I just . . . I didn't take sides because I always lost."

"Okay, then what happened?"

"Then we came back from Arkansas, and we stopped in a small town to have something to eat. And they started fighting."

"Do you know what it was about?"

"Everything was all about me because she never cared for me, didn't like me or nothing. That's why. One of the biggest reasons."

"What were the other reasons?"

"Uh . . . It's dirty, ugly."

"I know it is," Ruiz whispered, though he really didn't know.

"You'll feel better," Ortiz added sympathetically. "You'll get it off your chest."

Irma averted her eyes, shaking her head from one side to the other in little slow-motion whiplashes of resistance.

"It's important," Ruiz said, still touching her arm.

"Well, he said that his mother treated him just like . . . maybe worse than a husband. And he said that his mother had touched him and played with his peter and all that. What he told me was, his mother kept wanting his body ever since he was . . . he started changing into a man. And once he started going to college, he started to understand things about women and studying, you know, problems about women, and he understood why his mother was doing those dirty things to him. She never did make love to him, but she was real close to it. And he started to hate her."

"It bothered him a lot then?" Ruiz prompted.

"Yeah. And when we got married, she didn't help him.

She refused to help him, and because of his dumb mother . . ."

Irma was sobbing quietly, gulping for breath in the muggy air of her mother's front porch. "He told me these things way too late," she continued. "But I still tried to . . . for him, you know, because she's my mother-in-law whether she likes it or not. I always try to do my best. And he didn't like for me to give her attention, to help her and all, nothing. And that's why he's down on me. He said, 'I'm going to tell you this, but don't repeat it to anybody. It's dirty and you're not going to like it. I can't stand her anymore. I can't see her like a mother. It's not here in my heart. It's not in my mind. It's just in . . .' And I said, 'You just go ahead and tell me why you make me suffer, too. I don't like to suffer for somebody else's problem.' "

"What happened after that?" Ruiz asked.

"Well, he drove back to Tulsa. It was kind of rainy."

"Do you know what month it was? What year?"

"God, those things . . ."

"Was it in 1974?"

"I would say so."

"Okay. What happened after that, after y'all got back?"

"Well, the kids were in the car, and Zani told them to wait there, not to move. And he said, 'You come along with me.' I said, 'No, you just go ahead. Whatever you have to do, just do it.' "

"If you can face this way," Ortiz interrupted, motioning to Irma to direct her words toward the tape recorder.

"So I got out of the car," she continued, her voice louder now. "And he said, 'Bring the towel out,' because we took towels to the river in Arkansas, you know. It was so many lightnings and thunders and all that nobody heard anything. Zani turned on the television real loud, then the radio. The next thing I knew, I turned around . . . and then I heard a scream, and he hit—he hit his mother with a hammer."

"A hammer?" asked Martinez.

"Yes."

"Now, be very, very sure about this," Ruiz cautioned her. "Did you see him actually hit his mother with the hammer?"

Irma hesitated.

"If you saw it, we need to know that you saw it," Ruiz insisted. "It's hard, Irma, but I know that you've got to . . . got to . . ."

"You need to get it off your system and off your chest, really," Ortiz broke in again. "It will help you, I mean . . . just . . ."

"Yes, I saw him."

"Did he hit her from the back?" Ruiz asked.

"Yes, the back, yes."

"How many times did he hit her?"

"I believe one time, when she was going to have a drink of water."

Gladys Zani had been standing at the kitchen sink, Irma said, still agitated by the argument with her son and his wife. She took a drink of water and, as was her habit, immediately washed the glass, wiped it dry, and returned it to the cupboard. Suddenly, she heard Robert moving quickly behind her; then the world went black as the towel was thrown over her head.

Thick trickles of blood dripped from her shoulders in that first instant before she crumpled to the linoleum floor. Her muscles tensed and her fingers went rigid, pointing like thin red fish. She fell at her son's feet, and a dark stain inched out from her head into a deepening pool, like octopus ink. More blood bubbled noiselessly at her mouth as she looked up at her son.

"All she said was, 'Why?' " Irma continued. "She asked, 'Why?' "

"Then what happened?" Martinez asked.

"Then, she fell to the ground, uh . . . on the floor, and then he . . . he still hit her in the face."

"With what?" Ruiz insisted.

"With a hammer." The impact, Irma said, embedded shards from her glasses into Gladys's eyes. "And he said,

'She's still alive, that old bitch.' That's what he said. 'That old bitch is still alive.' He said, 'You grab a knife wherever you can find it. Wherever you can find it, grab it.' And I just couldn't move. I was just looking and just watching what he was doing. And then he said, 'Are you going to do it or not? Because you're going to be next.' I couldn't even grab a knife. I was just shaking. I dropped two or three knives on the floor. I just couldn't hold it."

Irma continued. "Then he said, 'One of these knives is going to end up in your head if you don't do anything.' So, yes, I got the knife. And he said, 'You just put it there. Stick it to her.' "

"Put it where?"

"In the heart, because he said that the witch was not dead yet. He said, 'If you don't do it, you're going to be next.' What could I do? My children were outside waiting, and it was raining. So he said, 'You better do what I tell you.' I said, 'I don't have to.' I couldn't move, and I just sort of . . . Oh, it was awful, awful."

"So then what did you do?" Martinez asked.

"He got real close to me with a hammer in his hand. And I said, 'My God, I don't want to be next.' So, yes, I did it. He forced me. He made me do it."

"How many times did you put the knife in her?"

"Once."

"One time?"

"Uh-huh. When I stuck the knife, it . . . He pushed it real hard, finished the whole thing."

"Okay, what happened after that?" Ruiz asked. "What did you do?"

"He started rummaging in the basement to find a place to put the body," Irma recalled. "He told me to get moving. I said, 'You did it. I didn't do it.' And he said, 'Irma, I'm not kidding. It's not the first time I'm doing this. I've done it before, and it's nothing. It's nothing to me to do it again, to you.' So I helped him drag the body to the basement.

"Then he made me clean the kitchen," she continued. "I

cleaned everything. It was awful, bloody, and then I got sick. I started throwing up."

"What did you do with the kids?" Ruiz wanted to know.

"They were waiting in the car."

"They stayed in the car?" he asked incredulously.

"Yes, they stayed in the car, maybe thirty minutes."

There was a long pause. "Okay, so what happened after y'all took the body down the stairs and cleaned up the kitchen?" Ruiz said at last, shaking his head at the brutality of it all.

"Then he went to open up the car and let the kids out. They came into the house and went to bed."

"Did they miss their grandmother?"

"They didn't notice anything."

"They didn't say anything at all?" Ruiz asked.

Irma shook her head slowly and lit another cigarette.

During the interview, conducted almost entirely in English, Irma's mother had entered and left the porch several times, uncertain what was being said or what role she should play. Now Irma motioned for her to sit next to her on the arm of the cheap straw chair, as she continued the story of her bad investment of faith.

They spent that night in Gladys's house, Irma told the officers. In the early drizzle of the following morning, she and her husband packed the children off to the first day of a new school week. Then Robert Zani drove to a nearby hardware store and bought a large electric saw. Meanwhile, Irma was to haul down two suitcases from a hall closet and take them to the basement. When her husband returned, they went down to the basement and laid the corpse over a small drain in the concrete floor.

"He began cutting up the body," Irma recalled, "and he stuck the arms and legs in one suitcase and this part"—she put a hand at her neck and another at her waist—"in the other."

"The torso?" asked Martinez.

"The torso, yes. I just stood there watching."

"You were watching this at all times?" asked Ruiz.

"Yes. He wouldn't let me go."

"Were y'all talking to each other?" Martinez wanted to know.

"No. He was laughing. I don't know why he started laughing, but I was afraid. I thought, you know, *This guy is going to kill me, too.* I had to stay there because I knew something would happen to my children."

According to Irma, Zani stashed the suitcases in a corner while she cleaned the basement, sweeping the blood and flesh and small slivers of bone matter down the drain with several buckets of water. By that evening, the body had begun to stink, and Zani knew he had to get it out of the house. They put the children to bed, and the next thing Irma knew, Zani said, 'We're going down to Arkansas.'"

Irma then described how she and her husband loaded the two suitcases filled with body parts onto the backseat of the car. The skull, too large to fit in either suitcase, was wedged between them on the seat, its lifeless eyes clinched in the grip of death.

With Irma sitting beside the suitcases in the back, they headed east on Oklahoma Highway 33, crossed into Arkansas at Siloam Springs, and angled on the back roads that wind north of the Ozark National Forest toward Gladys's property at Beaver Lake, a piney area just south of the Missouri state line, near Eureka Springs.

"Zani said, 'Now, here's what you're going to do,'" Irma continued. "He said, 'You throw them piece by piece wherever I stop. Do it—and be fast.'"

"Did you throw the entire suitcase?" Ortiz asked.

"No, he told me to throw them piece by piece wherever he stopped," Irma repeated.

"And each time he stopped, you threw one piece and moved farther along and threw another piece?" Ortiz insisted.

"That's right, yes."

"When the body was mutilated, did she have any earrings or anything he took off the body?"

"She was wearing a ring, and he took it off."

"What did he do with it?" Rendon asked.

"He threw it in the lake."

"Did he throw anything else in Beaver Lake?" Ruiz asked.

"Yes, I believe so. There's a big bridge there, and we threw those suitcases. He tore them up and threw them in the water."

"He threw the suitcases?"

"And he also threw the hammer and her watch there, over the bridge. The ring, the watch, the hammer, the suitcases . . . and clothes, I think. Because he left the body without anything on."

"What did he do with the head?" Rendon asked.

"Well, that I don't know, because he said, 'I'll take care of this by myself.' He told me that he was just going to hang the head on a tree or something. I tell you, I went crazy. I wasn't listening to what he was saying. I thought the whole thing was sickening."

"You don't know what he did with the head?" Martinez repeated Rendon's question.

"He said he buried it there on the property."

"But you were with him, Irma," Ruiz broke in. "You just didn't see him bury it?"

"Yes. I didn't get to see where he buried it, because I was waiting in the car. It was real late, and he dug a small hole and put the head down in there. But then he wasn't satisfied. He thought somebody would find it or something would happen to it.

"Then, that night," she continued, "when we got home, he said, 'I'm not sure I should leave that thing out there. I think I'll go back tomorrow morning real early and take care of it.' "

"Did he go by himself? Or did you accompany him?"

"No, he went alone. He said, 'Now I don't have to worry

about it.' That's all he said. He didn't mention anything else."

"Did he have any remorse after this happened?" Ortiz wanted to know. "Was he sorry that he did this?"

"He never did tell me."

"What about his expression, his facial expression?"

Irma took a deep breath and looked at her mother, who was still sitting on the arm of the chair, her hand on her daughter's shoulder. "All he said to me, twice, was that he hoped for me to do the same thing with my mother," she said, fighting back tears, "because he didn't like the idea that I was writing to her. He didn't like that. And that's what he wanted for me to do, also. And he tried . . ."

Irma's words dissolved into sobs. She lowered her head while her mother put her arms around her heaving shoulders and stared uncomprehendingly at the Texans.

"All right, Irma," Ruiz said at last, "I'm going to ask you one thing. I want to know if, at any time, you ever talked to anyone about these things. Did you ever write home and tell your mother this is what he did?"

"No."

Ruiz pressed on. "In your opinion, knowing your husband, how many people do you think he killed? Your mother-in-law and Mr. Dess—do you think he killed more than these two people?"

"No, I have no idea. I couldn't . . . I wouldn't say things that I don't know."

"He didn't mention killing anybody else?" Martinez asked. He looked at the note he had written on his pad forty-five minutes earlier when his partner had hesitantly tried to lead her into a discussion of Gladys Zani's disappearance and Irma had unexpectedly mentioned a murder in Austin, "someplace around the university."

"No," Irma said.

"Did he ever mention mutilating or cutting up any other bodies?" Ortiz tried his hand at the question. He also remembered the reference to Austin.

"He only said that some people didn't get away with what they did," Irma said.

Rendon stood up and turned his back on Irma. With his rumpled blue *guayabera* stretched across his waist and his handlebar mustache curling above a couple of unshaven chins, he seemed only slightly less menacing than the "homicide expert" who sat impassively in a corner of the porch throughout the interview session. Suddenly, Rendon wheeled around and put his face close to Irma's. "Did he ever tell you that he killed someone else?" he asked, his even tone implying the cold message that, try as she may to duck the others' questions, he expected an answer—now.

"Yes," Irma replied, after a long pause, "he said that he killed, uh . . . a young guy in Austin."

"In Austin?" Rendon persisted.

"In Austin, yes."

"Did he say when?"

"No," Irma answered. She had already mentioned what she knew of the incident, which was very little. Why were they bringing it up again?

Martinez caught on. "We've gone through that," he said quickly.

"We've gone through that?" Rendon asked, looking at his colleagues. "I'm sorry. I just . . ."

"Yeah, we've gone through it," Ruiz said.

"Are we pretty well satisfied then?" Rendon asked, looking around at his colleagues.

Ruiz checked the tape. "I'm satisfied," he said. "I think everyone else is satisfied. Do you have anything else?"

The others shook their heads. Ramírez, the young bodyguard, and the homicide expert stared at the floor blankly. Montes, the attorney, widened his eyes. He appeared to have been dozing. But at the tone of a question fired in his general direction, he perked up, though he didn't understand the words.

"Okay, this will end the interview with Irma Zani," Ruiz said, ignoring him and speaking into the recorder. "I do want to ask, though, before we complete it, would you be willing to come back to the United States to testify in regard to this case?"

"Yes, I will go," Irma said, "as long as I don't get hung. I'm not guilty of anything."

She uncrossed her legs, shifted her weight in the chair, and crossed her legs again. "If I did things," she continued, "it was because of him. He threatened me. He told me that I was going to die. He told me that I was going to be next, and that's one of the reasons that I couldn't speak. I couldn't say anything to anyone. But I said to myself, 'Someday, somehow, he's going to pay for it.' "

Irma raised her head and looked from one officer to the other. "I don't wish anything to him," she said, quietly, "nothing bad at all. But he looked for it, and he kept looking for it to the last."

PART

3

ELEVEN

Cops—the good ones—have a way of becoming obsessed with their murder investigations. They eat, drink, and shit them, trying to balance their home lives with the intrigue of tracking down a man who has dared take another's life. Wives say their husbands lie awake in the dark of night with the suspect's name on their lips, thrusting themselves up out of the covers, drenched in sweat. They lunge for the phone when it rings at all hours but forget to call home when they plan to be late. While playing with the kids in the backyard, they catch a glimpse of the murder as they believe it unfolded, imagining their own family's faces where the true victim's should be. The violence and fear woven so deeply into the fabric of their work reproduce themselves in the cops' own lives.

The job, after all, runs counter to every good impulse. Citizens don't summon the police when all is well, so cops come to see society at its most vulnerable, broken-down moments. A gradual erosion process begins the moment a cadet leaves the police academy, and all but the most nerdish—"career rookies," to their colleagues—become masters of compromise. They learn to crack the unwritten code: that there are right wrongs and wrong wrongs. Shift after shift, they negotiate their way through complex human dilemmas the law cannot hope to solve. And after a couple of years on the street, every one of them has seen people quite literally get away with murder.

In the end, cops, like other bureaucrats, grow enormously resistant to change, automatically suspicious of any challenge to the department's insularity, self-protection, and, in some cases, systemic corruption or racism. A murder investigation takes on a life of its own, and the officers assigned to the case are sometimes viewed as prima donnas, affecting elitist attitudes as they swagger down the halls, savoring the high excitement of their work while their colleagues immerse themselves in the minutiae of accident reports and citizen complaints.

Even by these standards, Ruiz and Martinez were driven men. During their careers, they had seen APD grow into a full-service organization, open twenty-four hours a day, seven days a week. Someone had to answer when the phone rang, whether the person on the other end of the line wished to report a real emergency or simply feel a little less lonely in the middle of the night. Every member of the force knew he was expected to pitch in, but no cop worth his commission wanted to be the one stuck on the desk.

It had taken a leap of faith for Ruiz and Martinez to get permission for the Acapulco jaunt in the first place, and now they wanted desperately to prove themselves to the brass back home.

As the comandante's chauffeur bounced the van down the dirt streets to the pavement that signaled the start of the face Acapulco showed the tourists of the world, the officers worked the controls of the state prosecutor's jam box. They rewound and forwarded the tapes of Irma's startling interview to hear again the sections that strengthened their case and justified their trip. They listened to the voice on the recording recall the shooting of Julius Dess in a field south of San Antonio, the bludgeoning of Gladys Zani in her Tulsa kitchen, and the murder of a UT student in Austin back in the sixties.

Texas law prohibited Irma from testifying against her estranged husband, but the tapes nevertheless represented powerful testimony. Ruiz and Martinez knew that if they would get Irma back to Texas to help them verify her claims, Robert Zani would be hard-pressed to wriggle free in a court of law. If they could also recover the weapons the Mexican authorities had confiscated from Zani five months earlier, they could run ballistics on them at the DPS offices back in Austin. It would be a long shot, they agreed, but if one of the weapons happened to be the .25 Browning automatic that killed Dess, the case would be very nearly clinched.

The main problem was going to be Irma's uncle, José Antonio Montes. Dull and plodding as he may have seemed, he had demonstrated at least enough legal savvy to consult with the lawyers in his firm, who suggested he demand a letter of immunity from prosecution for his niece before allowing her to accompany the officers.

Suddenly, Irma's recorded voice whirred and sputtered, dropping into a sickly lower register before wobbling to a complete stop.

"This damn thing just ate the tape!" Ruiz exclaimed, banging the jam box on the dash.

The chauffeur pulled the van to the curb as the others, seeing their investigation weakening in a tangle of magnetic tape, carefully tried to extract the cheap cassette from the machine's recording heads. They pulled several inches of twisted tape out, but it was no use.

Ortiz suggested they drop by an electronics shop to see if a technician could salvage the tape before giving up on it. Sure, the chauffeur said, he knew just the place. He swung the van in the wrong direction down a one-way street, and the officers piled out in front of a tiny store crammed with cheap blenders, table fans, and the dusty carcasses of television sets in mid-repair. The shop owner greeted the chauffeur and his gringo companions as if they were all old friends, leading them to the back room. There he cleared a space on his grimy workbench and got started.

They watched the man hunched over the cassette and discussed their next move. It was imperative, they argued, that someone return immediately to Austin for the letter of immunity Montes had requested. They could no more afford to leave Acapulco without Irma, allowing her the opportunity to change her mind and vanish, than they could sit around the expensive resort waiting for a draft of the letter to arrive by mail. The bills were mounting around them daily, and Ortiz and Rendon, their point men with the local authorities, were under pressure to get back to Corpus Christi. The obvious solution was to send Maxwell, who would be much more valuable back on his home turf than he was in the wild terrain of Mexican law enforcement. Maxwell readily agreed to leave that night.

Meanwhile, the shop owner had managed at last to disentangle most of the tape and splice it back together. They tested a few seconds of it on the jam box and thanked the man, who refused their offers to pay him for restoring the single most important piece of evidence they had come by thus far.

With the late-afternoon sun now beginning to fade, there was little time left to catch a flight, much less to call ahead for a reservation. The chauffeur sped to the hotel and kept the engine running as Maxwell sprinted up to the room, threw his belongings into a bag, and hurried back down to the van. On the way to the airport, Ruiz and Martinez reminded their friend of what they needed him to do when he got to Austin. He should alert APD that Irma had talked, they said, and that she had mentioned two possible cases other than the Dess murder. Then he should draft a letter of immunity and get it to them right away—tomorrow, if possible.

Oh, and by the way, maybe he could wire them some money while he was at it, because the $1,500 from the realtors had been rapidly depleted in a flurry of pesos.

Maxwell smiled, assuring them that he would kick the DA's office into high gear.

At the airline ticket counter, a harried clerk stopped the officers. There were no more flights to Austin that night, she explained. All that remained was a direct flight to Dallas, leaving in ten minutes, and even that one was overbooked. Without a reservation, there was simply no way to get Maxwell a seat. Besides, it was too late to arrange a connecting flight to Austin at the other end. She shrugged her shoulders in apology and turned to the other passengers waiting in line.

Quietly, the comandante's chauffeur slipped behind the counter and disappeared into a small office. After a few moments, he stuck his head out and beckoned to Maxwell, who grabbed his bag and headed off toward the loading gate. They weren't sure, but the payoff Ruiz and Martinez had witnessed in the Monterrey airport on the trip down seemed to have just been reenacted. By now, however, they had stopped fighting the vagaries of official Mexico, especially when those vagaries worked in their favor.

Maxwell's flight touched down in Dallas just after midnight. The airport was largely deserted at that hour, and even the car rental counters had closed for the night. Walking outside, Maxwell spotted a Hertz courtesy van parked several feet away. He flashed his badge and persuaded the driver to take him to the agency's office at the opposite end of the airport complex, where he was able to charge a vehicle to his personal credit card and take off for Austin, some two hundred miles south.

Along the way, he pulled into an all-night truck stop for a soft drink and a bottle of Pepto-Bismol to calm the stomach cramps he had brought with him from Mexico. Sometime after four o'clock in the morning, he crawled into bed next to his startled wife.

"Wake me in three hours," he mumbled, falling asleep without further explanation.

When the sun came up, Maxwell phoned Ronnie Earle at home, who asked him to come straight out to the house. After a recent murder in the other half of the duplex he rented from Virginia Dinan, Earle had moved his family to a rural spread just beyond the city limits, where his kids were able to keep horses and assorted barnyard animals. The move occasioned snickers from courthouse regulars, who remarked that when crime touched too close to home, their DA dealt with the problem very simply—he left town.

Maxwell arrived to find Earle out back, tossing handfuls of corn to a gaggle of scrawny chickens in a coop behind the house. Though tired, ill, and pressed for time, Maxwell couldn't help chuckling at the sight of his boss as gentleman farmer. Earle hooked his thumbs in the front pockets of his overalls and leaned against the coop as Maxwell related the details of the Acapulco trip.

"This sounds like a B-movie or something," the DA said, laughing.

Indeed, Maxwell replied, and now it was over budget. Ruiz and Martinez needed cash to pay their bills and the bribes necessary to recover the .25, he explained. Then, of course, there was the matter of Irma Zani. Not only was she talking, but she was also saying the right things, and she was willing to repeat them all on Texas soil. But her legal representative in Acapulco had demanded a letter of immunity. Maxwell didn't want to seem impertinent, he said in apology, but they needed that letter now, before she changed her mind.

Earle stopped laughing. He knew he was out on a long political limb, and in an election year at that. What with a couple of APD officers, the Nueces County sheriff and chief deputy, and even one of his own investigators running around a foreign country in pursuit of a possible murder case, the potential fallout was obvious. Some Travis County residents already believed their DA spent too many resources on too few results. If he squandered time and money on a

Mexican wild-goose chase, Earle's Republican opponent would be sure to hang him with the charge during the upcoming campaign.

Nevertheless, Earle immediately authorized a wire transfer of $1,000 from the LEF to an Acapulco bank. While Maxwell handled that, Earle said, he would get dressed and drive into the office to begin the process of drawing up the immunity letter. It would take some time, he cautioned, because the letter was going to have to come from the office of Atascosa County DA Alger Kendall, in whose jurisdiction Dess's murder was believed to have taken place. Earle had no authority over Kendall; still, he would try to impress upon his colleague the urgency of the situation.

Because it was still too early for the banks to open, Maxwell headed home to bide his time and wait for a prearranged phone call from Ruiz and Martinez in Acapulco. The collect call came about eight-thirty, and Maxwell answered it in his dining room. Yes, he assured his friends, the arrangements were under way. He would be wiring them money shortly, and he suggested they call back around noon to find out which Acapulco bank would be holding their funds. As for the immunity letter, that too would be ready soon, though he couldn't guarantee when. If they called back again in the late afternoon, he would tell them what arrangements he had made, if any, to get the letter to them. Eventually, Maxwell's phone bill would reflect collect calls totaling more than $200 from the coastal resort that day, as Ruiz and Martinez, with nothing more pressing to occupy their time, repeatedly phoned for updates.

By midafternoon on May 20, the hungry Austin officers were able to get themselves out of hock after driving their rented VW Safari (known as the Thing during its brief life span in the United States) along Avenida Miguel Alemán, the bay-front boulevard, to a Banco Nacional office where they watched a teller count out the peso equivalent of $1,000. Then they pumped a few liters of fuel into the empty gasoline tank and went off in search of something to eat.

Meanwhile, Ronnie Earle called Texas Ranger Jack Dean, whose base of operations corresponded roughly with Kendall's jurisdiction. Earle discussed a number of points he hoped would wind up in the letter of immunity and asked Dean to get together with Kendall as soon as possible. Instead, Dean called his second-in-command, Gene Powell, and ordered him to drive straight to the DA's main office in Karnes City, about fifty miles southeast of San Antonio. Powell was to phone him when the letter was ready, Dean instructed, so he could make arrangements with Ronnie Earle to get it to him.

Kendall listened to Powell's version of the events surrounding the case and sat down to draft the letter. With no real knowledge of who Robert and Irma Zani were, he could envision Irma's immunity demands as a trap. All she had to do, Kendall realized, was return to Texas under the immunity grant, testify that she, not her husband, had killed Dess, and then both of them would walk. In less than an hour, Kendall typed up a letter he hoped would be broad enough to guard against such a possibility.

Late the next morning, May 21, Ruiz and Martinez went to the Acapulco airport to retrieve the immunity letter, which Maxwell had picked up from Powell only hours earlier and personally delivered to a Braniff Airlines pilot waiting for takeoff on the runway in San Antonio. No doubt about it, they agreed, ol' Frank had really humped it. In a day and a half, he had been able to secure $1,000 and a letter of immunity and ship it all a couple of thousand miles to the edge of the Mexican jungle.

As it turned out, Kendall had prepared two drafts of the letter, which, although he had misspelled Irma's maiden name, were wily examples of the DA's expertise. The first read in part:

I, Alger H. Kendall, Jr., District Attorney of the 81st Judicial District, including Atascosa County, do hereby make the following statement and agreement with Irma Sevano [*sic*] Reyes de Zani:

It is my understanding that Irma Sevano Reyes de Zani has some information as to the death of Julius Alfred Dess, which possibly occurred in Atascosa County, Texas; that Irma Sevano Reyes de Zani is an accomplice in said death, and is subject to indictment and prosecution.

I do hereby agree as District Attorney for the State of Texas for Atascosa County, Texas, to not seek an indictment and to not prosecute Irma Sevano Reyes de Zani and she does the following:

(1) Return to Texas.

(2) Gives a complete statement of the events of Julius Alfred Dess' death.

(3) Cooperate with all investigators of all agencies investigating the death of Julius Alfred Dess.

(4) Turn over all evidence, pieces of evidence and all information known to her about the death of Julius Alfred Dess.

(5) Give a complete statement to officers regarding all criminal violations of the State of Texas or any other State of the United States known to her, committed by Robert Zani.

(6) Testify in any Court of Law in the State of Texas, the United States, or any State in the United States.

This agreement of non prosecution entered and signed this 20th day of May, 1980.

The second draft was identical—except for paragraph three, which contained twelve words not included in the first draft. This version read: "I do hereby agree as District Attorney for the State of Texas for Atascosa County, Texas, to not seek an indictment and to not prosecute Irma Sevano

Reyes de Zani if she did not directly cause the death of Julius Alfred Dess and she does the following."

Clearly, Kendall's second draft was intended to keep open the option of limited immunity—the small-town DA's rather cagey attempt to preserve a case that, after all, he might conceivably be called on to prosecute. As for Ruiz and Martinez, they were experienced enough to recognize Kendall's motives. If they could convince Irma and her uncle to accept the second version, they would have more room to maneuver during the rest of their investigation. They decided to keep secret the existence of the first letter—the one that granted her total immunity—and pull it from the briefcase only as a last resort.

While Ruiz and Martinez manned the long-distance lines to Austin, Ortiz and Rendon were busy trying to recover the .25 from the Acapulco authorities. Rendon especially was well versed in the language of his Mexican counterparts, a combination of leisurely persistence and tough understanding designed to back them to the wall just far enough to permit them a measure of dignity while he got what he wanted. "We need that gun," he told them, shrugging as if to apologize for the strict rules of U.S. law enforcement, which allowed a cop only so much leeway. Then, repeating his essential message—"we need that gun"—he leaned back in his chair, laughed at their jokes, and bought another round of drinks.

Both Rendon and Ortiz realized that the gun had probably been sold and resold countless times in the five months that had passed since the comandante and his men confiscated it from Zani. Weapons were not easy to come by in Mexico, where law enforcement officials were expected to purchase their badges and come by their equipment any way they could. A .25 Browning automatic was not likely to be readily surrendered.

About noon, the comandante's chauffeur again came by

the hotel to drive the Texans to Irma's house in the hills west of town. On the way, they asked him to stop at O'Campo Oliveros's office, where Rendon and the chauffeur went inside to check on the state prosecutor's progress in tracking down the .25, while the others sweltered in the van. After about thirty minutes, Rendon emerged, his shoulders slumped and his mustache drooping. He pulled open the sliding door of the van, looked at Ruiz and Martinez, and shook his head in dismay.

"No gun?" Martinez asked.

Ortiz shifted in the front seat to look at his chief deputy. Rendon winked at his boss ever so slightly, reached under his *guayabera,* and, letting a slow grin spread across his face, tossed the .25 onto the backseat where Ruiz and Martinez sat.

"Sonuvabitch!" Ruiz cried, grabbing the revolver. He glanced at the serial number to check for the sequence he had memorized—439381.

With the murder weapon in hand, the Texans made their way to Irma's house, where they placed the second immunity letter on the table for Irma and her uncle to review. Irma corrected the spelling of her name, scratching out each reference to "Sevano" and writing "Serrano" in the space above. Montes studied the pages, asking for an occasional translation, while Rendon explained that Irma would probably be given a polygraph test at some point to verify the truth of her assertions. When Montes was satisfied that all was in order, he advised Irma to initial the changes she had made and then sign the letter.

The officers stood to leave, urging Irma to be packed and ready for them to pick her up on the way to the airport shortly after noon the following day. Turning to Raquel, they assured her that they would have her daughter back in Acapulco "in a couple of weeks." They already had a return ticket, they said, dated June 4. There was some question whether Raquel fully understood what was happening, but she nodded her consent, adding that she would watch the children until their mother got back from Texas.

No one knew it at the time, but it would be nearly six years before Irma saw Acapulco or her family again.

The flight arrived in Harlingen at seven-thirty on the evening of May 22, 1980. They wondered if the unmarked Ford Fairmont might still be where they had left it seven days earlier, but they decided that Lieutenant Napier had probably already sent Jim Beck or some other hapless homicide cop to retrieve it. They rented a car instead and drove directly to Corpus Christi, where the officers booked two rooms in the Hilton, just down the hall from Irma. There was no charge, because Rendon served as the hotel's chief of security in his off-duty hours.

The next morning, after a light breakfast in the hotel cafeteria, the four officers and Sharon Trayler, another of Ortiz's investigators, loaded Irma into the car and headed for Padre Island National Seashore. For the next several hours, the diminutive former prostitute directed them around the beach. She took them first to the burial site and showed them how her husband had dug Julius Dess's grave with a piece of driftwood, covering the body with sand. Next she led them about fifty feet south, where she said they had burned the realtor's clothes, business papers, and other belongings. Then she directed them two miles farther down the shore to where Zani had run the T-Bird up on a dune in the dark. Finally she led them two hundred feet through the thick sand to the Sand Dollar, where they had taken D. R. Ross, the Kansas carpenter in the converted school bus, and bought him a round.

About midafternoon the group drove back to the Hilton for a quick lunch, after which Ruiz and Martinez packed their bags, thanked Ortiz, Rendon, and Trayler for their help, and then drove back to Austin with Irma.

The weather had turned cool by the time they arrived at

the Ramada Inn North at nine o'clock that night, May 23, and parked outside the office. Once more, they went over the terms of their agreement with Irma. She was a witness, they reminded her, not a suspect; as such, she was not in custody and was free to come and go at will. In return, she would cooperate with the local law enforcement agencies that were picking up her tab, and she would do so truthfully. Irma assured them she understood.

The hotel desk clerk was the same young woman who had been on duty two months earlier when Ruiz and Martinez arrested Robert Zani. Two rooms were available, she told them, a unit at the north end of the hotel's first floor—and room 219.

Ruiz and Martinez looked at each other. From time to time in a murder investigation, there were moments that fairly begged for a brief time-out to savor the irony. But it had been a long day, and the partners resisted the temptation. Martinez hoisted Irma's suitcase and trudged off across the parking lot while Ruiz registered her in the ground-floor unit.

TWELVE

During the next twelve days, representatives of law enforcement agencies with an interest in Irma Zani and her husband converged on Austin, anxious for the opportunity to interview a cooperative witness about the unsolved crimes that cluttered their files. In the quiet moments when she was left to herself in her room, Irma dozed on top of the bedspread, watched television, and ordered meals from the motel cafeteria, scrawling her initials—I.S.Z.—across the bottom of the receipts, which were being sent to APD for payment. She rang up a sizable long-distance phone bill as well. Several times each day, she placed calls to the only phone that existed in her mother's Acapulco neighborhood, asking the woman who lived there to run down the block and tell her children that their *mami* wanted to speak to them.

One afternoon, Ruiz and his wife, Crispin, dropped by to take Irma shopping. For more than an hour, she walked up and down the aisles of a K mart, expressing fascination with the wide range of merchandise, as if she had never been allowed a leisurely visit to a department store during all the years she lived with Zani. Crispin encouraged her to select a few items to take back to her family, courtesy of Mr. and Mrs. Ruiz. Irma chose clothes for the children and an inexpensive perfume for her mother.

When she had signed the immunity letter, however, Irma

had accepted the responsibility of assisting law officers in their investigations, and her schedule was about to become quite a bit busier. A woman who seemed to gain control over her life only by becoming a victim, she was eager to put it all behind her and return to Acapulco.

On Monday, May 26, a meeting was held at the Travis County DA's office to discuss the evidence Ruiz and Martinez had gathered so far in the Dess case. The two Austin officers were joined by Frank Maxwell, Lencho Rendon and Sharon Trayler from Corpus Christi, Norman Stutte and Joe Riley from the FBI's San Antonio office, Atascosa County sheriff Tommy Williams, and Texas Ranger Gene Powell. After listening to the tape of Irma's Acapulco interview, the group agreed that Williams and Powell would take Irma to Atascosa County that night, and that Ruiz and Martinez would drive down the next day to help the group try to determine the spot where, according to Irma, her husband had shot the realtor.

About six-thirty Tuesday morning, Ruiz and Martinez left for Pleasanton, the largest city in Atascosa County, a drowsy town of some seven thousand whose hopeful name did little to disguise the fact that it had never seen better days. Williams and Powell had checked Irma into the local motel the night before, after trying without success to find the murder scene in the dark. Ruiz, and Martinez hoped the group would have better luck in the daylight.

Williams and Powell drove to the motel to pick up Irma, then headed for the Horwedel property near Poteet, about six miles away, with Ruiz and Martinez following in their own car. Irma recognized the land. Dess had brought her and Zani there, she said, though she insisted that the killing had taken place on a second property. It was about a thirty-minute drive away, she thought, but she had no idea in which direction. For several hours the two-car caravan wandered aimlessly along the farm-to-market roads and narrow lanes that crisscrossed the area, pointing out landmarks as Irma shook her head. Some of the area looked familiar, she said in apology, but it didn't match the description she had already given them. Finally, Ruiz and Martinez flagged down the lead car and suggested that they regroup at the municipal offices in nearby Poteet.

There Williams called Betty Jo Mason in San Antonio and went over the situation. They were having trouble locating the murder scene, he told her. If she would look through her father's records to see if there was some indication that he had planned to show Ray Thomas and his wife another property on December 4, 1979, it would be helpful. Mason called back within minutes. She'd found a listing for fifty acres in Wilson County, some twenty-five miles east of Poteet. There were even a few directions scribbled on a piece of paper, pinpointing a spot just off Texas Highway 97 to Floresville. Williams jotted down the location, thanked Mason, and beckoning to the others, headed for the door.

Still in two cars, the group headed east, angling down a series of dirt roads toward the fifty acres Dess had described in his notes. As they pulled up to the gate, Irma studied the landscape. Suddenly she sat up straight. "This is it," she said. "I remember that big oak tree next to the road."

Williams eased the lead car down the rutted trail while Irma stared intently out the window. She kneaded her hands into the folds of her slacks, and the officers noticed that she had begun to perspire heavily.

"This is it. This is it," she repeated, as the car inched along. "There's that shack. And over there next to that small pecan tree is where he had his car parked. And right there is where Zani shot him."

Williams hit the brakes, and they all piled out of the cars. Irma tried to stand, but her legs shook. She said she felt faint. Then she crumpled to the ground and began to sob uncontrollably. The officers fumbled around, trying to comfort their only witness in the midst of the scrub brush and yellowing grass that already was wilting in the heat of the early South Texas summer.

In time, however, Irma calmed down sufficiently to repeat her version of what happened that day nearly six months earlier. When they left the Horwedel property, she recalled, Dess told them about another property. The owner, who lived in California, had been trying for some time to sell all fifty acres and had only recently decided to let it go in fifteen-acre parcels. Dess would be happy to take them there, but they would have to hurry; it was getting late, and he still needed to run by his bank in San Antonio to cash a check.

The three spent about an hour walking around the property, Irma recalled, after which Robert told the realtor that they wanted to "sleep on it" and would get back to him the next day. They climbed into the car—Dess in the driver's seat, Irma beside him, and Zani in the back.

Then Irma recounted how her husband had suddenly shot Dess and how they had pulled his body into the back of the car, covered it with insulation, and driven to Padre Island. She again walked them through the details of how they buried the corpse, got stuck in the sand, bought "the man in the multicolored bus" a beer, and drove back to the San Antonio airport. They had then hopped a cab to retrieve their pickup at LaQuinta, she repeated, then stayed a few days with the Bayardos in Robstown before fleeing to Mexico.

By the time she was finished, Irma was exhausted. They had spent a long day driving down dusty roads and traipsing through underbrush in the sun. But Williams and Powell seemed satisfied and, thanking her for her cooperation, drove off toward Williams's office in Jourdanton, the Atascosa County seat. Ruiz and Martinez bundled Irma into their car and headed back to Austin. She slept the entire way, rousing herself at last when Ruiz steered the car into the parking lot of the Ramada Inn.

Irma didn't know it, but precisely twenty-four hours before she and the officers stopped by the city hall in Poteet to call Betty Jo Mason, her husband had been at the court-house down the road in Jourdanton to testify before an Atascosa County grand jury hearing the Dess case. Zani had refused to cooperate after being sworn in, and he had been transported back to his jail cell in Austin that night, where he found that his bond had suddenly been raised to $10,000.

At 3:35 on the afternoon of May 28, two Tulsa police officers sat down with Irma in an interrogation room off the main hallway of the special-crimes section on the fifth floor of the Twin Towers.

Ruiz listened in on the session. Back on May 6, he recalled, he had spoken to a man named David Freiberger, a former police officer who had since gone to work for Bell Telephone in Tulsa. Freiberger told him about a case in which a fifty-four-year-old Tulsa real estate saleswoman had been found dead in a home where she had taken a prospec-tive buyer. He didn't remember the exact date, but he knew it was a rainy Friday afternoon about four or five years ago. The realtor and her client, a white male, had arrived at the house about four-thirty. Half an hour later, the owner had come home from work to find the realtor's car in the drive. She had waited to allow the agent time to wind up the visit but had finally grown impatient and gone inside.

She discovered the realtor on the floor of the master bedroom. Her slacks had been pulled off and neatly folded on the bed. What was even stranger, Freiberger said, was that the victim had still been wearing her shoes, panty hose, blouse, and bra. There were nine stab wounds in her stom-ach, and she had taken at least three strong blows to the head after having apparently been strangled. Her purse was discovered in the living room, its contents—minus about $450 in cash and several major credit cards—scattered on the floor. As far as Freiberger knew, the only lead in the case was that the suspect drove a green 1962 Rambler station wagon with no hubcaps.

Ruiz wrote a report after the conversation, though he was troubled by the sexual implications of the scene and by the Rambler, neither of which was characteristic of what was known so far about Zani. Nevertheless, when Freiberger suggested that a friend might be able to provide an update on the case, Ruiz jotted down the name—Sergeant Roy Hunt, Tulsa PD.

Ruiz phoned Hunt the next day. Hunt could add nothing further to Freiberger's account, though he did have two additional murders in which he suspected Robert Zani. One was a liquor-store manager who had been found bludgeoned to death a couple of blocks from the Dover Corporation, where Zani was employed at the time. The other was a junior-college student whose mutilated body had been dumped in a Tulsa apartment complex a short time later. Hunt requested a set of Zani's fingerprints for comparison with the latent prints lifted from both murder scenes, and the officers had stayed in touch over the next three weeks.

Now Hunt and his partner, Sergeant Fred Parke, had flown to Austin to see if Irma Zani might help them clear up these crimes, as well as the matter of Glady Zani's disappearance. Ruiz and Martinez had met them at the airport, given them a quick briefing on the case, and then driven to the Ramada to pick up Irma. Martinez, however, had taken an instant dislike to the Tulsa cops, detecting in them an attitude similar to that of the cadre of veteran rednecks that still infested the Austin police force, so he excused himself to run some errands. And as Hunt read Irma her rights and fumbled to learn a little background on the suspect, Ruiz couldn't help thinking that his partner might have been right.

"Were you married to Robert Zani in the early part of 1974?" Hunt began. "Or when did you marry Mr. Zani?"

"I was married in 1967," Irma replied.

"You were married in 1967," Hunt repeated. "And where were you married darling?"

Ruiz cringed at the obsequious tone. He looked at Irma, who also seemed uncomfortable.

"Mexico," she said, sullenly.

"And are there any children from this marriage?" Hunt wanted to know.

"Yes."

"How many?"

"Two," Irma responded, clearly unnerved at having to supply answers for a couple of cops who hadn't bothered to read the reports already on file.

"You have two children from this marriage?" Hunt pressed on.

"From this marriage, right," Irma answered. "I have two more girls, but they're not his."

"That's from a previous marriage of yours?" Hunt asked.

"I wasn't married, actually," Irma replied, looking away.

"Okay," Hunt continued, "you just had two nice young girls . . ."

"Yes," Irma cut him off.

After several minutes of clumsy questions designed to establish when Irma and Robert lived in Tulsa, Hunt and Parke tried to lead her into a discussion of her husband and his relationship with her mother-in-law. "Did anything unusual occur between Robert and his mother?" Hunt asked.

"During that time, yes, there had been some funny things there in her house between them."

"Like what?"

"Well, like she did not, she didn't care much for me. There's that one. Lots of times she gave me the impression that she was kind of interested in her own son."

"Interested in her own son," Hunt repeated slowly. The interview was creeping toward an unexpected topic. "You talking other than motherly interest?" he asked hesitantly.

"Other than motherly, yes," Irma replied.

"You say you felt like that there was something other than

Zani, class of 1962, Lamar High School, Houston.

Zani, running for UT student body president on the Mickey Mouse platform. From the front page of the *Daily Texan*, March 17, 1966.

Texas driver's license with Zani's picture that arrived in the mail when Ruiz and Martinez were in La Feria, Texas.

Original sketch of the suspect, drawn by Sergeant Robert Kelton on July 30, 1967, during the meeting of those who had been in the Town and Country on the morning of Vizard's murder one week earlier.

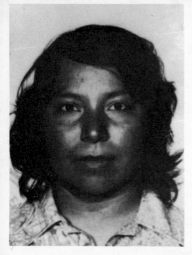

Irma Serrano Zani on June 4, 1980, the day Texas Ranger Gene Powell spirited her off to Atascosa County under arrest.

Raquel Reyes Ventura's Acapulco home, May 1980. Note the Guerrero state prosecutor's jam box on the floor of the porch where the interview with Irma was recorded. Left to right: a curious neighborhood boy, a state judicial police officer, and Paul Ruiz. *Photo by Robert Martinez.*

Gladys Zani in the driveway of the Houston home where she and Robert lived during his years at Lamar High School. The Chevrolet is the one Robert later sold after killing his mother in Tulsa.

The business card of Mary Evelyn Lowder, an Austin realtor who narrowly missed becoming Zani's victim. The card was discovered in Zani's briefcase on the night of his arrest in March 1980. Note the obliteration of her face in the photograph and other notes in Zani's hand.

George Vizard (third from right), with other SDS members at an Austin rally in early 1967.

Vizard, listening to political activists' speeches on the UT-Austin campus in late 1966 or early 1967. Mariann Vizard is at right, wearing a plaid skirt.

Snapshot taken by a roving photographer in Acapulco on May 16, 1980, during the only two hours the officers had free to spend on the beach. Left to right: Robert Martinez (still in his street clothes), Nueces County sheriff Solomon Ortiz, Paul Ruiz, Travis County DA's investigator Frank Maxwell, and Nueces County chief deputy Florencio "Lencho" Rendon.

Outside the Hyatt Regency in Austin in late 1981, during an informal reunion several months after the Zani trial. Left to right: Paul Ruiz, then a Travis County DA's investigator and the chief of security at the Hyatt Regency; Solomon Ortiz, about to kick off his successful campaign for U.S. congressman; Lencho Rendon, who would go to Washington as his boss's chief legislative aide; Robert Martinez, still in OCU and sporting a moustache and longer hair for an undercover operation. *Photo by Crispin Ruiz.*

The .38 special (top) and the .357 magnum brought back from Acapulco. The .357 had killed George Vizard in Austin nearly fourteen years earlier. The .38 was never connected to a crime.

Robert Joseph Zani on March 28, 1980, the night of his arrest in Austin on charges of credit card theft.

Joe Turner, Travis County assistant district attorney. Turner's prosecution of Robert Zani set a national precedent for admissibility of hypnotically-induced testimony in the courtroom. *Photo by Zack Ryall.*

motherly interest in Robert by Mrs. Zani," Hunt continued. "Did you observe anything that made you feel this way, any physical thing that made you think that?"

"It's not simple," Irma stammered. "I tell you . . . . She told me . . . She asked me is Zani, who was really good at making up, is Zani . . . I didn't know what's the matter with her unless she wanted to live with him and make him feel better. That's how she would talk. Even though Zani, he wouldn't even mention her name . . . But she would come out with it."

"She would come out with the statement that if she slept with him, he would feel better?" Hunt asked, finding it difficult to follow Irma's halting acount.

"Yes, yes. That's what she meant at the time," Irma responded.

"Did he ever indicate to you at that time, or any other time, that he had a relationship with his mother?"

"No. What he told me was, his mother kept wanting his body ever since he was . . . he started changing into a man, you know?"

"Sure."

"And he was living at home up until he was like fifteen or sixteen, because she would baby him and just treat him like a little boy. She would just, you know, want his body . . ."

"Okay."

". . . and he didn't know what was going on. He didn't know anything. He said, 'That's just, you know, maybe that's a mother's way of taking care of her son,' or something like that."

"Did he ever indicate to you that he realized that maybe this was not the proper way or proper relationship between a mother and son?"

"He told me that it wasn't right. He told me not to let the kids get close to her."

"You were aware that she had, for lack of a better word, molested your children, also?" Hunt asked.

"Yes, yes."

Irma held her head in her hands, and her voice choked off in an incoherent babble. Parke gave her a Kleenex while Hunt scratched down the words he could make out: ". . . horrible woman . . . kicked me . . . mistreated . . . such awful things . . . not because she's gone . . . never did her harm . . ."

Her shoulders heaved as she gulped for breath between sobs. Finally she raised her head and looked straight at Hunt, as if to indicate that she had regained her composure and was ready to proceed. Her eyes were puffy and her face streaked, but her features had taken on a tough, hardened quality.

"You mentioned something just a moment ago," Hunt continued, studying his notes with some embarrassment. "You said, 'Now that she is gone.' Do you have any knowledge about that—about her being gone?"

"Yes, I do," Irma whispered.

"Would you relate to Investigator Parke and I what that is?"

"I know she is dead."

"She is dead?"

"Yes."

"And you know of your own knowledge that she is dead?"

"Yes, I do. Zani killed her with a hammer."

Now that an actual confession was being captured on the recorder, Hunt and Parke came alive. They spent the rest of the tape asking Irma to reiterate what she had already told the Texas officers, delving with greater detail into Tulsa street names and locales than had Ruiz and Martinez on the porch of the Acapulco shack. Despite their clumsiness, they were able to elicit several new pieces of information from Irma, some of which provided a glimpse into the twisted workings of Robert Zani's mind.

She told them, for example, that she and her husband and children had lived in the house at 218 Xenophon for about five months after Gladys's murder. During that time, Zani sold his mother's car, jewelry, coin collection, and furniture to supplement the income they were receiving by cashing her social security and Sun Oil pension checks each month. With the money from the sale of the house, they moved to La Feria, Texas, and were relatively happy for a couple of years.

She didn't know why, but they eventually moved again—this time to Buffalo, Missouri, where they continued to live on the monthly checks until the Secret Service began nosing around. That was when Zani got nervous, she said, and packed the family off for a three-month stay in Acapulco, where he rented a sprawling home on the beach with a swimming pool in the back courtyard. She recalled how impressed she was when her husband paid the $850-per-month rent all in advance, handing the landlord $2,550 from the wad of cash he carried in the pocket of his tan slacks.

It was only a matter of days, though, before Zani got restless. He told her he was flying to Washington, D.C., leaving her with the four children in Mexico. There he planned to apply for a passport and travel to a number of foreign countries, where he would try to sell information to their intelligence agencies. Just what secrets he possessed that might interest other governments he didn't say. But he did tell her that if this latest money-making scheme failed, the family was going to return to the States and get rich by killing real estate agents, lawyers, and doctors.

The Tulsa investigators had gone through two tapes by the time Parke ended the conversation at 5:03. "Currently, at this time, are you still legally married to Robert Zani?" he asked.

"Yes, unfortunately," Irma replied wearily.

"Are you contemplating filing for a divorce?" Parke wanted to know. "Are you going to start divorce proceedings against Mr. Zani?"

Irma looked away. "I don't really want to talk about it right now," she sighed.

The next morning, May 29, Ruiz and Martinez again brought Irma to the Twin Towers. Cecil Calvin, a special agent with the Secret Service in Austin, wanted to interview her regarding her husband's forgery of Gladys's signature on the social security checks over the period from August 1974 to December 1979. Irma repeated that Zani had used the money to support the family, though this time she added that he never gave her money to spend on herself or the children.

Calvin also questioned her about the threatening letters to Jimmy Carter and his daughter, Amy, which the Secret Service suspected Zani of mailing. According to Irma, her husband had dismantled the typewriter used to compose the letters and had buried it—she didn't know where. However, she recalled that Zani had boasted about having written them in such a way that the Ku Klux Klan would be blamed. Beyond that, he never elaborated.

Later that same day, Texas Ranger Gene Powell dropped by the Twin Towers to take an official statement from Irma concerning the events surrounding the murder of J. A. Dess, which she had described during the long Monday they had spent in South Texas two days earlier.

To Ruiz and Martinez, who had become somewhat protective of their witness, it was clear that Powell believed Irma was far more involved in Dess's death than she was letting on. The ranger seemed irritated when Irma retold her version for the umpteenth time, refusing to vary the details of how her husband fired all three shots into the realtor's skull from the backseat of the T-Bird as they began to leave the property in Wilson County. After about thirty minutes, Powell cut the session short and left.

On June 3, Lieutenant Frank Brady of the Oklahoma State Police and Leighton Stanley, a lieutenant with the police department in Moore, a town of about fifty thousand along I-35 just south of Oklahoma City, drove to Austin to question Irma regarding the 1978 murder of a real estate agent named Bobby Gene Thomas. The victim had disappeared while showing property to a client, and his nude body had been found the next day in the trunk of his car. He had been shot execution-style, a single bullet from a Yugoslav small-caliber automatic lodged deep inside his skull. Police had lifted a complete handprint from the outside surface of the trunk.

Irma was brought to the Twin Towers yet again, where she told the Oklahoma officers that Zani frequently left home for weeks at a time and that it was possible he was involved in their homicide, though she claimed to have no specific knowledge about the Thomas case. By now, she seemed to be confused about which officers were investigating which murder. She repeated her story of Gladys's death for Brady and Stanley, who, though fascinated, had no jurisdiction in the case.

Ruiz and Martinez, noting that the Moore victim's last name and the alias Zani had used with Dess were the same, encouraged her to continue, hoping she might reveal something new. For the first time Irma mentioned that the electric saw her husband had used to cut his mother's body into pieces was hidden in the Tulsa parsonage where she and Robert lived just before and after the murder.

Ruiz excused himself to phone this latest bit of information to Sergeant Hunt in Tulsa, while Martinez accompanied Brady and Stanley, armed with photographs and fingerprints of Robert Zani to check with their evidence in Moore, down to their car in the APD parking lot.

Meanwhile, the Central Texas press began to pay attention to the case. The first report, by *Austin American-Statesman* writer Jim Berry, had appeared on April 2 under the headline AUSTIN ARREST LEADS TO MURDER PROBE. Sergeant Jimmy Brown and Lieutenant Gilbert Miller each offered opinions, their interest in the investigation evidently renewed in light of the reporter's questions.

"The man we arrested here last Friday and charged with credit card theft fits the description [of the San Antonio murder suspect] and there is a strange parallel in the method of operation involved in the events leading to the slaying," Brown was quoted, somewhat enigmatically.

Five paragraphs later, Miller chimed in, confirming that "the suspect was arrested here last Friday at a North Interregional motel where he was found in a room that . . . was occupied by a man who checked in with a stolen credit card."

On May 23, the day after the Texans returned from Acapulco, reporter Lucius Lomax, who had replaced Crispin Ruiz on the *American-Statesman*'s police beat, gave readers their first hint that the investigation was widening beyond the scope of Dess's murder with a story headlined POLICE QUESTION SUSPECT'S WIFE IN MEXICO. Ronnie Earle and Jimmy Brown were quoted as saying that an unnamed drifter "might be implicated in five slayings, including that of his own mother . . . a San Antonio real estate agent . . . real estate agents in Moore, Okla., and Magnolia, Ark., in the late 1970s [and] a University of Texas student in 1968 or 1969 [*sic*]."

The next day, *Corpus Christi Caller-Times* reporter Jay Jorden filed a story entitled POLICE QUESTION SUSPECT IN MURDER OF REAL ESTATE AGENT. Again, the main source for the story was Jimmy Brown, who seemed to be enjoying the prospect of seeing his name in print.

Six days later, the *Austin Citizen,* a weekday newspaper that has since folded, published essentially the same story. Headlined WIFE MAY BE KEY TO FOUR KILLINGS, the article contained a number of quotes from Lencho Rendon, who was said to have been "contacted by APD and asked to fly to Acapulco to talk the woman into returning to the U.S."

The same day, a story ran on the UPI wires. Written by Ann Arnold (soon to become the press secretary for newly elected Texas governor Mark White), the story contained unattributed quotes from APD's Lieutenant Gilbert Miller, who, like Brown, had found a renewed stake in the case even though he was still working behind the scenes to transfer Ruiz and Martinez out of his unit:

> Travis County authorities said Wednesday Tulsa police have questioned the wife of a man suspected of at least three murders—including the dismembering of his own mother.
>
> Austin police located the suspect's wife in Acapulco, Mexico, and with the help of Nueces County Sheriff Solomon Ortiz and Captain F. H. Rendon of Corpus Christi convinced her to come to the United States to aid the investigation.
>
> The Atascosa County grand jury took up the Dess murder briefly Wednesday but deferred action. Authorities indicated they have evidence the crime occurred in a nearby county rather than outside Jourdanton where Dess had taken the couple.

The San Antonio press also got wind that the police had brought a witness in the Dess murder back from Mexico. Though there had been routine coverage back in December of the realtor's disappearance and the discovery of his body four days later, the Alamo City's notoriously servile media had been silent ever since.

All of that changed with the publication that week of a bizarre story in the *San Antonio Light*. In an article headlined DESS CASE WITNESS IN HIDING, a young staff writer named Juan Montoya displayed a knack for being taken in by dissembling cops.

> Austin detectives have convinced the Mexican wife of a 36-year-old drifter to leave Acapulco and testify in an investigation that may shed light on five murders, in-

cluding those of her mother-in-law and of Castle Hills real estate agent Julius A. Dess.

Two members of the Austin Police Department Special Crimes Division and a representative of the Travis County district attorney's office returned Friday from Mexico where they had spent nine days attempting to persuade the woman to come to Texas and testify in the investigation. . . .

Detectives Paul Ruiz and Richard [sic] Martinez were the officers who returned the woman but details of her arrival and whereabouts were kept secret by police. . . . Sources close to the investigation say the woman has also told police her husband is implicated in the 1968 [sic] death of a University of Texas male student. A spokesman said authorities are now combing decade-old files to ascertain the identity of the alleged murder victim. . . .

Sergeant Jim Beck of the APD Organized Crime Division said investigators "are looking into possibly five murders," including the suspect's mother, who disappeared from her Tulsa, Okla., home in January 1976 [sic]. It has been alleged, police said, that the 64-year-old woman was killed with a hammer, chopped into pieces and spread along the highway from Tulsa to Eureka Springs, Ark. . . . Also, her Social Security checks reportedly have been cashed since her disappearance and La Feria officers, at the request of Austin police, fruitlessly dug up a back yard where the suspect formerly lived in a search for her remains. . . .

Authorities say they have received inquiries from as far away as South Dakota because of similarities in the method in which Dess was lured to his death and the murder of a realtor there. Police also said the man in custody is a suspect in the disappearances of two other real estate agents in Moore, Okla., and Magnolia, Ark., in the late 1970s.

The suspect went before the Atascosa County grand

jury on Monday but reportedly refused to answer any questions concerning the Dess murder. "He's not saying anything to anybody," Texas Ranger Gene Powell said. "We got him out of jail on a bench warrant to testify before the grand jury. We're not sure when he'll be returned to Austin, but he isn't due to come up on the credit card charge until the latter part of June. He'll be staying in Atascosa County for a while," he said.

Police refused to divulge any specific details concerning the woman's return to testify. "All I can say is that we have had telephone communications with her at her mother's house in Acapulco. The two officers and the person from the DA's office have returned with the woman and she is somewhere on the continent," APD's Beck said.

Atascosa County District Attorney Alger H. Kendall said new evidence emanating from the wife's testimony might prompt his office to issue a capital murder indictment against the man but he said immunity for the woman in return for her testimony has not been discussed.

Although all of the reporters had erred with names, dates, ages, and other minor points, Montoya's story was particularly distressing to anyone familiar with the case. Powell, for example, claimed that Zani was still in Atascosa County when, in fact, he had already been returned to Austin. Kendall assured the reporter that Irma had not been granted immunity for her testimony when, in fact, she carried in her purse at all times a copy of the letter presented to her in Acapulco. And Beck now injected himself into the investigation with the outlandish tip that Irma was "somewhere on the continent."

Ruiz and Martinez had just settled into their office on the morning of Wednesday, June 4, when the phone rang. Irma was scheduled to leave Austin's Robert Mueller Airport on the first leg of her flight back to Acapulco at two o'clock that afternoon, and the officers were studying the field notes and files they had all but memorized to make sure no significant avenue was left unexplored before they let her go. Martinez reached for the phone on the second ring.

"This is Gene Powell," the voice said, dispensing with any niceties to get straight to the point. "Do you guys mind if I give Irma a polygraph on the Dess deal?"

Martinez signaled Ruiz, who quietly picked up the extension. Martinez had been unable to overcome his initial distaste of the Texas Ranger, and he cringed now as he listened to Powell explain how he was still unconvinced of Irma's innocence in the realtor's death and wanted to give her the lie-detector test they themselves had warned her about when they brought her back to Texas.

"Yeah, no problem," Martinez said at last, "but remember that her flight leaves in five hours."

Powell agreed to bide his time for an hour while Ruiz and Martinez went to pick up Irma at the Ramada. At ten o'clock he would drop by the Twin Towers to take Irma the mile and a half to DPS headquarters, where polygraph operator Ron Rogers would strap his wires and sensors to her to determine, Powell snickered, just how much she really knew.

By one o'clock that afternoon, with only an hour left before flight time, Ruiz and Martinez were worried. They still needed to get Irma back to the hotel so she could pack her bags and catch the plane. Ruiz called DPS but was asked to leave a message because Powell was unavailable.

"Fuck this," Martinez spat, already heading for the door. Ruiz followed his partner down to the parking lot, where they hopped into the Duster and headed for the sprawling DPS complex. There they found Powell and Irma in an office, initialing the final corrections on the statement she had just given.

"Man, she's dirty as hell," Powell said, as the officers burst into the room. "She failed the polygraph. She admits that she fired one shot into Dess, and I'm going to take her to Floresville and put her ass in jail."

Ruiz and Martinez were livid. They had brought Irma back from Acapulco under the terms of an express agreement, guaranteeing her she wouldn't be prosecuted if she was truthful. Sure, she probably knew more than what she claimed so far. Perhaps she really did fire one of the three shots, but it was almost certainly under threat from her husband. Zani was the dangerous one, not Irma.

The officers called Powell out into the hall. "We're checking into getting her a divorce from Zani," Ruiz tried to explain, as Martinez seethed by his side. "That way, she can testify against the sonuvabitch."

He couldn't care less, Powell informed them. The officers argued that what he didn't understand was that the court would appoint Irma an attorney if Powell filed charges; any further cooperation from her would be hopeless after that. Powell was intransigent.

As they stepped back into the office, Irma glared at them. It was clear she regarded their conversation with Powell as the ultimate betrayal. There was no way for Ruiz and Martinez to let her know that the criminal justice system had been bogged down with interagency rivalries and technicalities of the law.

"She says that she shot Dess one time," Powell said with glowering finality. "In my book, that makes her a murderer."

"Fuck you," Martinez hissed under his breath, unable to control his anger. He and his partner had been outflanked by the state's premier law enforcement agency. As a result, their principal witness was about to be charged with a murder they were certain her husband had actually committed.

Powell shrugged, turning his back on the officers and placing a set of cuffs around Irma's pudgy wrists. Ruiz and Martinez watched helplessly as the ranger led her to his car and buckled her in for the trip down to Wilson County. Martinez glanced at his watch as Powell's car pulled out of the parking lot. It was sixteen minutes till Irma's flight was scheduled to leave.

The next day, they learned that state district judge Robert Eschenburg had entered a writ of attachment, holding Irma Zani as a material witness in the grand jury probe of Julius Dess's murder.

THIRTEEN

Ruiz and Martinez knew the investigation into the murder of J. A. Dess was slipping their grasp, a casualty of the maddening turf battles that raged incessantly within the Texas criminal justice system. There were more than 2,500 police jurisdictions and an equal number of courts in the state, all vying for primacy in the arrests-and-convictions sweepstakes. When you added the FBI and other federal agencies to the mix, the wonder was that anyone ever managed to wriggle free from the law enforcement overkill. Yet, they did—in growing numbers. And now, with the FBI's haughty lack of cooperation and the Texas Rangers' rush to judgment, Ruiz and Martinez faced the possibility that Zani too would skate the only real charge they had him on: credit card theft.

Over the next few weeks, Ruiz and Martinez ran traces on the .25-caliber Browning automatic they had brought back from Mexico. It was their leg up, they reasoned, the major bit of evidence Powell and the others did not possess in the Dess case. If they could connect it to Zani, there might still be a chance to make a case against him.

A check with the National Crime Information Center scored an immediate hit. The weapon was registered, though the responsibility of doing the grunt work to establish its history now lay with Ruiz and Martinez. After a series of phone calls, they learned that the weapon had been purchased directly from the manufacturer in 1968 by Oshman's Sporting Goods in the South Texas town of Bay City. It had remained in the store's inventory until the following year, when it was sold to a man named Gerald Conway Barr, a local car salesman.

They tracked down Barr to Prentiss, Mississippi, where he had taken a job as foreman with a rural electric company. Sure, Barr said, he had bought the weapon in Bay City. He and his wife had split shortly thereafter, though, and Barr had rented a U-Haul trailer, thrown his belongings inside, and hightailed it to Houston. It wasn't until after he unpacked at his new home that he discovered the gun was missing. As far as he was concerned, the two black men he had hired to help him move probably stole it.

With the help of the Alcohol, Tobacco and Firearms Bureau, Ruiz and Martinez picked up the trail again. A retired Lockheed employee named Clifton Turman had been mugged on an Atlanta, Georgia, street sometime during the night of August 30, 1973. Among the items stolen was a .25-caliber Browning, which Turman had bought in July 1972 from an Atlanta pawnshop to protect himself from his estranged son, who had recently threatened his life in a family squabble.

Obtaining a listing for C. E. Turman from directory assistance in Atlanta, Ruiz dialed the number. Florence Turman answered. Her husband had died the year before, she explained, but she remembered quite clearly the details of the mugging. He was attacked by four black men on the sidewalk near a mechanic's shop where he had taken his car for repairs. In the scuffle, the gun fell to the ground, but when she returned with her husband to the scene the next day, it was gone. What she couldn't remember was just which pawnshop had sold the weapon to her husband.

Ruiz and Martinez had reconstructed a remarkable history of the gun, but then the trail went cold. Many Atlanta pawnshops had since gone out of business, and among those that remained, a surprising number regretted having to tell the officers that all but their most recent records had been "destroyed in a fire." From the night of August 30, 1973, when Turman pulled it from his pocket to protect himself on an Atlanta sidewalk, until December 4, 1979, when it had been used to discharge three quick bullets into Dess's head in a field south of San Antonio, there was no telling what route the .25 had traveled. Ruiz and Martinez had plenty of circumstantial evidence, but they would have felt better had they been able to establish a direct link between the weapon and Robert Zani.

On June 13, Ruiz called the motor vehicle theft division at DPS, where George Hetzel—known to one and all as Skeeter—answered the phone. Ruiz wanted him to run a check on Gladys's 1964 Impala.

"What's the VIN?" Skeeter asked.

Ruiz recited the digits of the vehicle identification number—418695-170103. Three minutes later, Skeeter called back to give him the last known license-plate number on the car, which had not been registered since 1976. Ruiz then asked him to send Teletypes to Oklahoma and Missouri to get an update.

"Already been done," Skeeter assured him.

At four-thirty that afternoon, Skeeter called back with the update. The car was registered to a man named Jim Abercrombie, who had bought it in December 1976—in Buffalo, Missouri, he said.

Ruiz obtained Abercrombie's phone number from information and immediately called. Vita Abercrombie answered from the kitchen of the couple's Buffalo home. Yes, her husband had bought a 1964 Impala from a man who lived just outside town. They paid $250, she recalled, after reading an ad in the local paper. She gave the man a check but was surprised to receive a call at her office only minutes later from a bank teller, who had become suspicious when the man tried to cash it. In the background, Abercrombie heard him arguing and "causing a bit of fuss."

"He was a quick talker," Abercrombie remembered, "the type who thought he knew it all." His name was Robert Zani.

Lieutenant Roger Napier and Sergeant J. M. Beck (not to be confused with the officer named Jim Beck, who had been left beside the road in Kyle, only to resurface with a cryptic quote in the pages of the *San Antonio Light*) had been searching through the file cards in APD's stack of unsolved murders ever since Frank Maxwell returned from Acapulco with word that Zani, according to his wife, boasted of killing a UT student in the late 1960s.

It was a laborious task. The three-by-five-inch cards, written by hand, were often illegible. To make matters worse, many of the cases were still tagged as unsolved in one file but subsequently cleared in a record stored elsewhere. In an age before widespread computerization, there were few cross-references to speed the job. Gradually, though, after studying every Austin homicide between 1965 and 1969, they narrowed the list to offense number A69421—the 1967 murder of a clerk and sometime UT student named George John Vizard in the Town and Country convenience store at 3310 Northland Drive.

The case rang a faint bell with Napier; he recalled being on duty that Sunday morning thirteen years earlier. The lanky lieutenant, who had joined the force in 1960 and headed up the homicide unit once before his current stint, recognized some of the details as belonging to one of the handful of unsolved murders he had occasionally reviewed through the years. Now he ordered Beck to pull together whatever records existed.

Beck returned with mixed notices. Even after combining the paper copies of the original offense reports with newer microfilmed records, large gaps remained. It was impossible to follow the sequence of events in the investigation, which was littered with names of potential suspects and leads that might or might not have been explored. Other than that, Beck said, about all they had was a report from Fred Rymer at DPS that the murder weapon was either a .38 special or a .357 magnum. The weapon, he added, had never been recovered.

Napier ran his fingers through his graying hair, mulling over the lack of evidence. After more than a decade, there were few clues left. Still, the case was the only one in their files that bore enough similarity to Irma's story to be even a possibility.

Napier looked at his sergeant. "Any prints?" he asked hopefully.

Beck rifled through the pages in front of him. Well, yes, he said, squinting to decipher the blurred streaks on the microfilm copy. John Williamson, APD's fingerprint expert, had reported recovering a batch of latents at the scene. But, hell, that was thirteen years ago.

"Get him on the phone," Napier ordered.

Celebrated for his uncanny memory and brilliant eye, Williamson had been known to clear crimes while routinely sorting through fingerprint cards in his cluttered office, catching a familiar pattern or a contour he recognized and then searching his files till he found its match. Napier had a hunch that if anyone could be counted on to have squirreled away records from some unsolved murder case, it was Williamson.

On June 16, Williamson called Napier. He had rummaged through his garage, where he stored dusty stacks of boxes and folders that no longer fit in his APD office, found what the lieutenant was looking for, and compared it with the prints taken from Zani at the time of his arrest.

"And?" Napier asked.

"Well, according to my records from that day, I lifted a left index and a left middle-finger latent from a one-pound loaf of Mrs Baird's bread that was on the counter," Williamson began.

"And?" Napier asked again.

"I took a left middle-finger latent from a package of Baker Boy fudge brownies," Williamson continued.

"And?" Napier insisted.

"A left thumbprint from a package of butter-rum Life Savers, which was also on the counter by the cash register," Williamson recited from his notes.

"And?" Napier prompted him again, louder now.

"They all belong to the subject identified by APD number 116298," Williamson concluded, the slight smile on his lips evident even over the phone.

"A name, goddammit!" Napier shouted into the receiver. The lieutenant had already decided that Williamson's reputation as a dry, humorless man was ill deserved.

"Oh, I'm sorry," said Williamson, feigning an apology and pretending to shuffle through his notes. "Let's see. Yeah, here it is. Robert Joseph Zani."

Ruiz and Martinez were astounded when they heard the news. In the shriveling heat of a summer that had not yet officially arrived, they rushed to APD headquarters, where Napier and Beck awaited them in the lieutenant's office. He was reopening the Vizard investigation, Napier informed them, and assigning it to them. He had already cleared it with Simpson. Beck would be their sergeant.

The investigators listened as Napier mapped out the plan of attack he wanted them to follow. There wasn't much to go on, he explained, but despite the age of the murder, a successful prosecution was still possible if Vizard and Zani could be tied through class rosters, common acquaintances, or affiliations in the same campus groups.

Beck had already spent a day on campus checking with the UT campus police and confirming that both Vizard and Zani were students at or near the time of the murder. This elicited gibes from Ruiz and Martinez, who were aware of Beck's well-deserved reputation around the department for unsurpassed contacts within Austin's black community. If you needed information on crimes committed by or against blacks, they knew, you went to Beck, who operated a barbecue joint on East Twelfth Street, in the heart of Austin's ghetto. But campus affairs were another matter.

"Everyone knows there ain't no blacks at UT," Martinez said with a laugh, referring to the university's infamous performance in the arena of minority student recruitment. "Why's Beck involved?"

Beck gave Martinez a mock look of insult. In Zani's case, he proceeded, records indicated that he had enrolled on September 21, 1962. With the exception of a few weeks during the fall semester of 1965, he remained in school until June 3, 1967, studying English, French, Latin, and Greek. On the registration form, he listed Houston's Lamar High School as his alma mater and his mother's Houston address as his permanent residence.

Houston? Ruiz and Martinez tried to disguise their surprise. They had been unaware till then that Gladys Zani and her son had ever lived together in Texas.

"I want you to get every damn UT record you can on Vizard and Zani," Napier told them, aware that the powerful university's arrogance toward local law enforcement and the community at large might be difficult to overcome. "Subpoena the shit if you have to, but I want to know every class they took and anything they may have had in common—anything at all."

Back in their office at the Twin Towers that afternoon, Ruiz and Martinez switched gears from the Dess case to the Vizard murder investigation. If the Rangers and their cronies at the FBI wanted the San Antonio realtor's affair to themselves, then so be it.

Ruiz hoisted the horn and called David McClintock, associate dean of students at UT. Forgoing all pleasantries, he advised McClintock's secretary that she should begin gathering any records she could find on George Vizard and Robert Zani because he planned to drop by the next day with a subpoena. She quickly complied.

Across the room, Martinez was reading through the copy of the case file Beck had given him. Napier hadn't been kidding when he said there wasn't much to go on. Entire sections of the original report were missing, and what little there was seemed useless. Only a few details merited further checking, in his judgment, and he penciled notes in the margins of the pages to remind himself to pursue them when he had time. Basically, it looked like he and his partner were going to be starting from scratch on this one.

Then Fred Rymer's supplement of August 2, 1967, caught Martinez's eye. Napier hadn't mentioned it. "We have completed our examination and wish to report that it is our opinion that the bullet is either a .38-caliber or possibly a .357-caliber bullet," the report read, "and was fired from a firearm having eight lands and grooves with rifling inclined to the right."

Martinez immediately thought of the other two guns that he and Ruiz had been told were confiscated from Zani by Acapulco authorities. He had made a mental note of them— a .38 and a .357—even though there was nothing to tie the weapons to at the time.

Skipping over the technical details in the rest of the report, Martinez scanned the page, searching for the last sentence that experience had taught him Rymer always affixed to the end of his expert reports: "We are retaining the evidence until advised by you of a disposition."

Was it possible Rymer had saved the bullets recovered from the scene of Vizard's murder in 1967? Even more incredible, had Zani kept the murder weapon all those years only to have it taken from him by a bunch of avaricious Mexican cops? It stretched credulity to think they might have both a murder weapon and fingerprints in a case that was so old.

Martinez dialed Rymer's number at DPS and, somewhat

embarrassed, asked the firearms expert if he would mind checking his files to see whether he still had a couple of bullet fragments from a thirteen-year-old murder. No need to check, Rymer replied. He never discarded any evidence in an unsolved murder. "I've got the slugs right here," he assured his friend. "Just get me the gun, and we'll test-fire it to see if they match."

Martinez looked at Ruiz. His partner was on the phone, the receiver cradled on his shoulder as he scrawled notes on a pad balanced between his knees.

"Holy shit!" Ruiz was yelling at whoever had been unfortunate enough to pick up the phone at the other end. "You mean I can't even get a DOB on the deceased in this piece-of-shit report?" He glanced across the room at Martinez and rolled his eyes to the ceiling while someone—probably a poor clerk in the ID section, Martinez guessed—went to scour the records. No doubt about it, Martinez thought, the original Vizard investigation was one of the worst examples of police work he had ever seen. Even the victim's date of birth had failed to make it into the original report.

As soon as his partner got off the phone, though, Martinez planned to tell him that they had just been handed a chance to make it right. All it was going to require was one more little trip to the sunny coast of Mexico.

At precisely 11:45 on Saturday morning, June 21, Braniff flight 33 out of San Antonio lurched to a stop on the tarmac in Acapulco. Among the 173 passengers were Ruiz, Martinez, and Lencho Rendon. This time the Texans had no intention of spending a single day longer than necessary hanging around the expensive resort. They had come for two items—the .38 and the .357. Hopping a cab, they made their way directly to La Palapa, where, according to Rendon, Comandante Reyes and an aide were scheduled to meet them. To their surprise, the comandante was already there when they walked in; apparently, no *marijuanos* had interfered with his obligations this time.

After preliminary pleasantries over a beer for Reyes and coffee for the others, Rendon got to the point. Last month, he reminded the comandante, Ruiz and Martinez had recovered a U.S.-made .25. Now, it was *muy importante* that they recover the other guns Reyes's men had confiscated from Robert Zani back in January. Ballistics had already proved that the .25 was the one used in the murder they were checking into during their first trip to Acapulco. They were sure the other two weapons could be tied to murders as well.

"*¿Claro que si!*" Reyes replied agreeably, motioning toward the waiter to bring another beer. "But it might take a little time."

Reyes went on to say that Miguel Angel O'Campo Oliveros, the Guerrero state prosecutor who had lent them the jam box on their previous trip, was in Mexico City for the weekend. They would have to wait till he returned on Monday, he apologized. If O'Campo Oliveros was delayed beyond then, Reyes himself would assist them in obtaining the evidence.

"Why doesn't he just 'assist' us now?" Martinez whispered between clenched teeth.

Rendon ignored him. The comandante was engaged in a classic bob-and-weave, stalling in the hope of being offered an incentive greater than the simple satisfaction of carrying out his professional duties. But Rendon had some moves of his own.

"We're going to book our return flight for Tuesday, then," he told Reyes, gracing the comandante with a smile that was as broad as it was devoid of warmth. "By that time, I'm sure you will have given us what we need."

On Monday morning, O'Campo Oliveros returned to his office to find the Texans camped outside the door. Rendon explained the nature of their visit. Not only were his two *amigos americanos* hoping to obtain the weapons, but they wanted to take statements from him and the officer who had arrested Zani in Acapulco—a legal requirement, he said, to show the potential jury an unbroken chain of custody on the weapons.

"No problem," O'Campo Oliveros replied knowingly, as if to demonstrate his familiarity with the legal system in the United States. Then he nodded toward a slight, middle-aged man who had leaned inconspicuously against a wall across the room throughout the meeting thus far. The Texans assumed he was O'Campo Oliveros's bodyguard.

"Let me introduce you to Rufino Salas García," the state prosecutor said as the officer came forward to shake their hands, "from the state judicial police. He's the one who made the arrest." The Texans masked smiles at their first sight of the meek man who had arrested their big, bad suspect.

It was agreed they would return to O'Campo Oliveros's office at nine o'clock that night to take the statements and, they hoped, pick up the weapons. They arrived about eight minutes late and were told that the state prosecutor had waited for them and then gone home. But he had left a message: They should return at ten o'clock the next morning, Tuesday, June 24.

"Eight minutes late and the guy gives up," Martinez said, disgusted. He was not the only one beginning to suspect that they were getting the runaround.

Determined not to miss him this time, Ruiz, Martinez, and Rendon showed up half an hour early the following day to wait for O'Campo Oliveros. Ten o'clock came and went, and none of the dozen or so plainclothes officers hanging around the offices would venture a guess where he was or when he might be expected. Finally, Rendon excused himself to find an unoccupied room from which to call Reyes, but the comandante was unavailable.

In frustration, Rendon pulled out his address book and looked up the Mexico City phone number of Florentino Ventura Gutiérrez. As first commander of Mexico's federal judicial police and the resident agent-in-charge of Interpol, the Paris-based international police agency, Ventura's authority was roughly equivalent to that of the FBI and CIA directors combined—in part because he had no bothersome restrictions imposed on him by a timorous Congress. In fact, Ventura was widely regarded as the most powerful cop in Latin America. Rendon had met him in the early seventies when he worked drug cases along the Texas-Mexico border with then Neuvo Laredo police chief, Luís Soto Silva, who was now Ventura's second-in-command. The three had remained friends through the years.

As he waited for him to come on the line, Rendon considered the legendary career of the man he was about to ask for help. Tall, thick, and full of himself, Ventura had risen from a modest background to become head of an elite investigative unit in the late sixties known as El Grupo Especial. He answered directly to the Mexican attorney general in those days, working high-priority cases involving national security, narcotics, and politically sensitive matters the president wished handled discreetly and efficiently. Almost single-handedly, it was whispered, Ventura had eliminated Mexico's vocal student movement by "disappearing" more than five hundred key leaders.

Rendon's recollections were interrupted by the sound of his old friend's voice crackling in his ear. "¿Como estás cabrón?" Ventura yelled.

After a few moments of greetings, gossip, and good-natured ribbing about their past exploits, Rendon explained the reason for his call. He hated to bother Ventura with such a minor problem, he apologized, but this stonewalling from the local Acapulco authorities had gone on long enough. Ventura grunted his concern, and Rendon imagined the old man's powerful Aztec features locked in grim dismay at the lack of professionalism his agents in the field were showing his old friend from Texas.

"I understand, compadre," Ventura said at last. "Please, can you give me two hours?"

Rendon glanced at his watch. It was just past ten-thirty.

He slipped his address book back into his jacket and rejoined the others outside the state prosecutor's office, where he whispered a shorthand version of his conversation with Ventura.

Ruiz and Martinez smiled at each other. They had the distinct impression that the premier comandante's request for two hours had been less a plea than a promise.

At twelve forty-five O'Campo Oliveros rushed into the building, carrying a paper bag beneath one arm. He was flushed and agitated, as though events had all of a sudden escalated beyond the reach of his control. Letting the officers into his office, he offered a lame apology for being late and placed the paper bag on his desk. Then, after pausing to catch his breath, he invited them to open it.

Tearing the paper away, they found the two guns wrapped in a greasy green cloth that looked like it had been yanked from the top of a pool table. Ruiz unwrapped the weapons, and Martinez studied them in the light streaming through a window—a .38 Rossi Special bearing the serial number D341906 and a .357 Magnum Ruger Blackhawk, number 78283.

Instinctively, they knew it was the .37, now encrusted with dirt and lead buildup, that had been used in the execution of George Vizard in the Town and Country thirteen years earlier.

FOURTEEN

Travis County assistant district attorney Joseph Andrew Turner had two passions in life—criminology and country-and-western dancing. When he wasn't in his office, he could usually be found at the Broken Spoke or some other local dance dive, tripping the two-step until all hours. Dancing, he liked to say, was a vertical expression of a horizontal feeling.

At twenty-five, Turner was so intense he looked more like a balled-up fist with legs than what he really was: the youngest assistant DA in the history of Ronnie Earle's operation. Born in Spokane, Washington, in 1954, the fourth of six children of a career military man and his wife, he had spent his early years moving from state to state in the manner of most Air Force brats. Though his mother thought he should become a priest, young Joe had other plans. He had seen the drama of criminal law on TV, watching eagerly as Raymond Burr's Perry Mason defended the innocent and exposed the guilty. During a two-year stint at Incirlik Air Force Base in Adana, Turkey, the Turner family had compensated for the lack of television entertainment by gathering around the radio to listen to an evening program called "Points of Law," in which the announcer described hypothetical legal disputes while audiences tried to anticipate the proper rulings. The criminal problems never failed to get Turner's attention.

By the time Master Sergeant Rush Turner was assigned to Bergstrom, a Tactical Air Command base on the southeast edge of Austin, on June 4, 1968, he had taken his family halfway around the world a number of times. That first night back in the States, thirteen-year-old Joe and his family gathered before a cheap black-and-white television in a motel room across the highway from Bergstrom and watched as Senator Robert Kennedy laid claim to victory in the California Democratic presidential primary.

"I think we can end the divisions within the United States, the violence," they heard the candidate tell supporters in a Los Angeles hotel. Moments later, the Turners sat stunned as Kennedy was gunned down while trying to make his exit through a dark kitchen passageway. No doubt about it, they decided, the country had changed dramatically in their absence.

Turner soon enrolled in Austin's John H. Reagan High School, where he fell into the habit of scanning the newspaper for interesting criminal trials. He frequently skipped classes to go down to the Travis County courthouse and watch the action. He was fascinated by the live drama, particularly when local lawyer Roy Minton, one of Texas' premier defense attorneys, had the floor. The rotund Minton seemed the personification of Perry Mason. Turner found himself increasingly driven to try criminal cases.

The truth was, Turner had always pushed himself. While his father was in Vietnam and Joe was still in high school, he opened a business on the side to help pay for his eventual college education. With money saved from a part-time job at a local discount store, he bought fifteen saltwater aquariums ranging in size from twenty gallons to forty-five gallons. He worked out a wholesale agreement with a Houston-based distributor of exotic tropical fish. Turner leased the tanks and fish to local banks, medical clinics, and other businesses that wanted to spruce up their lobbies. The deal called for Turner to set up the tanks, service them periodically, and replace any fish that floated to the surface during the length of the contract.

While cleaning one of his tanks in a neurology clinic one day, the doctor offered Turner a job as a bill collector. Thus, the slender, somewhat frail youth added another unlikely business to his growing income base.

When Turner entered the University of Texas in 1972, he loaded his course schedule with government classes. Richard Nixon was about to be returned to the Oval Office, employing dirty tricks and illegal tactics that would come to light only after the election. Turner set his sights on a law degree, which he then planned to use in going after such politicians and their corrupt consultants.

He transferred to Sam Houston State University for his second year. The school was in the East Texas city of Huntsville, the headquarters of the state prison system, and boasted one of the best criminology departments in the nation. Turner earned spending money and extra credits by working as a prison guard in the Texas Department of Corrections' Ferguson Unit, an experience that hardened his resolve, he later said, "to put away the crooks." Three months after his twentieth birthday, Turner graduated summa cum laude, having completed the four-year degree program in just twenty-seven months.

In the summer of 1975, Turner entered the University of Texas school of law and was immediately hired to clerk in the powerful local firm of Minton, Burton and Fitzgerald, whose main partner remembered the aggressive young teenager who used to sit in the courtroom when he was supposed to be in school. In August 1977, Turner received his degree.

One month earlier, at the age of twenty-two, he had gone to work for Travis County attorney Jim McMurtry, where he was soon put in charge of the fifteen lawyers who made up the trial section—even though he did not become licensed to practice law in Texas, according to records, until November 11 of that year. Nevertheless, Turner soon earned a nickname—"Mad Dog Turner"—and a reputation as a tough, junkyard fighter who did his legal homework and rarely lost a case. Though he hadn't forgotten his ambition to nail corrupt public officials, Turner believed that the place to learn how to try cases was in the misdemeanor court, where the dockets were filled with DWI, hot check, and other relatively low-profile offenses.

"In those days, before public attitudes about drunk driving shifted, the jury was usually looking for a way to acquit," he would later recall. "There was a strong feeling among them of 'there but for the grace of God go I.' So you really had to polish your persuasive skills to get them to convict some poor soul on the opinion testimony of a single police officer."

In early 1980, Turner was looking for a change. A friend, local attorney Juan Gallardo (later a state district judge), had asked him to go into private practice. The two had even rented an office, bought furniture, and installed telephone lines when an assistant to Ronnie Earle called to say that the DA wanted Turner to come to work in the district attorney's office. Turner was flattered, but after explaining that he had already made other plans, he turned down the offer.

The next morning, Earle himself called. "Have lunch with me before making your decision," he pleaded.

Over lunch, the DA was at his best. He trotted out the standard arguments designed to impress a young attorney. Here was Joe's opportunity to do right, to serve justice and the community, to try felony cases. For his part, Turner knew that the special crimes/public integrity unit of the office, under the able administration of Allen Hill, was Earle's pet project. Even its plush digs in a separate building funded by the state legislature signaled the unique place the unit enjoyed in the DA's organizational chart. And though Earle was only offering him a position in the trial section for the time being, Turner figured that if he proved himself, he might soon win a transfer into the more prestigious unit.

"He dangled the hook, and I bit," Turner later said, summing up the conversation. In February 1980, one month before Robert Zani's arrest on the charge of credit card theft, Joe Turner became an assistant district attorney of Travis County.

By early summer the Zani case was the talk of the DA's office as word spread of the extraordinary efforts by Ruiz and Martinez to move the investigation toward an indictment and eventual murder trial. It was a sexy case, one that came along only rarely in a public prosecutor's career. Even Earle's critics conceded that his interest seemed both genuine and sustained on this one. Maxwell had regaled the attorneys with stories about his trip to Acapulco on the Dess investigation. And after Ruiz and Martinez returned a second time with the probable murder weapon in an entirely different case, many of the attorneys, including Turner, openly lusted for a chance to get involved.

In April, Turner's decision over lunch two months earlier to accept Earle's job offer paid off; he was asked to join the special crimes/public integrity unit. Hill wanted him to take a look into allegations against small-time businessman Guadalupe Chapa, whose indictment on gambling charges and connections to certain county politicians assured that there would be more than the usual amount of publicity. One glance at the case, however, and Turner guessed it would never see the light of day in a courtroom. Still, he agreed to take it on, knowing it was his entrée into the special crimes/public integrity unit. Once there, he would recommend that the Chapa affair be settled quietly. Then he would be positioned to leap into the Zani case at the earliest opportunity.

Turner today denies he had inside knowledge that just such an opportunity was about to present itself. But the fact is that John Dietz, the assistant DA in charge of the Zani investigation, announced plans in late July to go into private practice—with none other than Juan Gallardo. Dietz inherited Turner's slot in private practice (he even kept the phone number Turner had originally reserved), while Turner was given Dietz's caseload and a promise that he would be free to choose whichever cases he wanted. He chose Zani's.

To Robert Zani, of course, it was all just so much legal maneuvering. He looked down his nose at the system, believing, in the opinion of one jailer, that he was "miles above the rest of us." He tried to smother his insecurities with intellectual bluster. And though he was obviously bright, his efforts usually came off more as misplaced arrogance than strength.

Zani was struggling to control the rush of events, grasping at emotional strings that had been cut and left dangling since he was a child. All the hurts and resentments and disappointments of his life were knotted up inside like a fist in the gut. He kept to himself most of the time, sleeping long hours and snoring out the hieroglyphics of his dreams. Alone in his cell, he had no real inkling of the kind of case Ruiz and Martinez, and now Turner, were building against him. He had heard little from them since the lineup with Donald Wilkey on the night of April 2, though he had read in the press that the two officers had managed to bring Irma back from Mexico. It was an impressive feat, he had to admit, and he wondered what his wife might be telling those grand jurors down in Atascosa County.

Now and then, as if to distract himself, Zani lingered at the edges of a group of fellow inmates. He listened to their complaints about everything from jail food to incompetent lawyers to wives or girlfriends who never visited. Sometimes he joined in, entertaining the men with stories of the international adventures he claimed as his own. He started his stories slowly, feeling his way along, searching for some kind of gimmick to get them interested. A mysterious boat, say, sailing in the dead of night with its hold full of gunpowder disguised as sacks of coffee. Then, not knowing how to proceed, he would stall for time by imitating the foghorn— "*hooo, hooo, hooo*"—cupping his hands round his mouth and blowing through them as he invented the rest of the plot. Eventually, a tale filled with unexpected twists and turns would emerge, becoming more and more impetuous and hard to follow, leaving little inconsistencies and loose ends his listeners never thought to question till later.

But when the talk turned to their legal dilemmas, Zani was contrite. In Travis County, he reminded them, the only charge against him was number 60,000—the credit-card-theft rap. And that, he repeatedly hinted, was a matter he would clear up as soon as he got his day in court.

In fact, on June 30, Zani was arraigned on the credit-card-theft charge before state district judge Jim Dear, though he apparently didn't consider the occasion his "day in court." During the proceedings, David Wahlberg, the court-appointed attorney assigned to Zani when Alberto Garcia begged off following the April lineup, approached the bench, gesturing toward Dietz to join him.

"Your Honor," Wahlberg began, "my client has a statement which he wishes to make for the record. I would like to say that I have advised Mr. Zani that making this statement is probably not in his best interest, and I have strongly advised him against it. He wishes to proceed, however, and since I believe a defendant has a right to make his own decisions, I am going to allow him to make a statement if the court wishes to hear it."

Dear peered over the bench. "I assume you have gone over with him the nature of the statement?" he asked Wahlberg.

"I have strongly counseled him against making any incriminating statement," the attorney assured him.

Turning his attention to Zani, Dear asked the defendant if his rights had been explained to him.

"No, sir they have been *read* to me," Zani replied, giving the judge a preview of an argumentative nature that would become all too familiar in the months ahead.

Dear tried again. "And do you understand that the reason the right to remain silent exists is because any statement you make, anything you say, anything you do or write down, can be used, no matter how innocent-seeming it is to you, by the state to prove you guilty of whatever they are accusing you—or what they may not have yet accused you of?" he asked.

"Yes."

"Knowing that, do you still wish to make a statement?"

Zani immediately began to backpedal, another characteristic with which courtoom observers would soon become well acquainted. He tended to make sweeping statements filled with ominous innuendo, then shut down the moment he was challenged. Now he addressed the judge in a facetious tone, yet another maddening habit that failed to endear him to many.

"Your Honor, I would like to make a statement prior to trial," Zani patiently explained, as if teaching the legal facts of life to a child. "In other words, you set the trial for the fourteenth. I would like to make one prior to that—not right at this moment but prior to that."

"I see," Dear said, sighing. "July the fourteenth for a jury trial, ten-thirty in the morning."

It figured to be a tiresome day.

On Monday, July 21, Robert Zani was indicted by a federal grand jury in Corpus Christi on charges of murder in connection with the Dess case. Zani's fears about his wife's testimony had not been unfounded.

Early the next day, the defendant appeared before Dear for the promised hearing on the credit-card-theft charge, which the judge had found an excuse to delay till July 22.

The defendant's first order of business was to relieve David Wahlberg of his duties.

"You wish to discuss the matter of firing your attorney. Is that correct?" Dear asked.

"I don't wish to discuss it," Zani snapped. "I want him fired, period."

"Without any kind of reason?"

"How many reasons would you like?"

"I would like to hear them so I can know if they're proper or not."

"Would it be okay if I read a statement, and in that statement would be included the reasons?"

After being warned of his rights once again, Zani stood up and arranged several sheets from a yellow legal tablet on which he had composed his rambling statement. "I have been immured in the Travis County Jail for nearly four months," he began. "During that time I have been denied access to the courthouse or any other law library. My written requests have either been ignored or unjustly denied. My right to competently assist counsel in my defense and my right to due process has been denied. It is as foolhearted to continue with these proceedings as it would be to begin a long journey without a road map. Law books are road maps in legal proceedings, and I have been denied access to them.

"Number two: During my incarceration I have twice been denied access to medical attention, in spite of written requests. During this same period, I have had my life threatened by an inmate. Incidentally, this only substantiates my opinion that my life is no safer in the hands of the state than it is in that of David Ruiz [an Austin convict whose handwritten petition in 1972 had triggered a massive, ongoing reform of the Texas penal system].

"Number three: During my incarceration in the Travis County roach-infested gulag, I have been unjustly victimized by venomous, malevolent, scurrilous attacks released to the news media, most probably by the alchemist district attorney and his office and/or the Austin Police Department.

Such attacks read like a *National Enquirer* copy. Said statements are unprofessional slop at best, and vicious, malicious garbage intended to damage reputations and destroy personal lives at worst. Such fictional statements have negated my right to a fair and impartial trial. In fact, such harassment, adverse exposure, and extensive pretrial publicity is an insurmountable impairment to impartial legal proceedings of any nature."

Zani read three more points, further protesting his handling by the local media and the failure of anyone in law enforcement to administer a polygraph test to him. Pausing to sip from a water glass, he continued: "Point number seven: Why have my repeated requests starting May 21st of this year for an interview with an FBI agent been ignored, procrastinated into oblivion, and therefore denied? I might insert here that I understood the news media to say I had been indicted by a federal grand jury in Corpus Christi for murder. So point number seven, I think, will take care of itself."

Those assembled in the courtroom exchanged puzzled looks as Zani read on. "Number eight: Why was I removed from the Travis County Jail and 'taken for a ride' down a lonely desolate dirt road and then threatened?" Zani wanted to know. He was apparently referring to his May trip with Gene Powell and Tommy Williams to Atascosa County, but even those intimately involved in the case were now having trouble following his comments.

"Point number nine," Zani continued. "What happened to the clothes I was wearing when I entered the Travis County Jail? I have been informed that they were 'misplaced.'"

"Point number ten: Why for no reason whatsoever was I locked in solitary confinement for twelve days, much of the time in total darkness, during which time I was subjected to questioning and harassment without the benefit of any attorney's presence?" Again, Zani was evidently referring to the Atascosa trip.

"Such cruel and unusual punishment of those innocent until proven guilty is an apex of Gestapo-like tactics," he continued, his voice rising. "Such uncalled-for and unjustified treatment is a violation of all of my constitutional rights. In fact, anyone in such a position has had their legal and human rights or privileges, if you will, negated.

"Point number eleven: What about the illegal seizure perpetrated by the Austin Police Department in my case, and why haven't I been given the result of my competency examination or copies of any other documents filed in this court supposedly on my behalf?" Five days earlier, Austin psychiatrist George Parker had examined Zani and found him competent to stand trial.

"Point number twelve," Zani read. "I would like to ask the court for strict observance of the Speedy Trial Act, and I would remind this court that I was in custody forty-six days before counsel was appointed to me.

"Lastly, since most defendants—other than Cullen Davis [the Fort Worth millionaire whose trial, retrial, and eventual acquittal on capital-murder charges had been played out on the front pages of newspapers across the state]—don't have enough money to fight prosecutors, then the courts of Travis County allude [sic] justice and due process only to the wealthy. Thus, policy is set above conscience in Travis County. Therefore, as a layman I ask the Court for, number one, access to my court records; number two, access to a law library; number three, access to proper medical attention; number four, access to an FBI agent; number five, access to the news media."

Zani placed the yellow sheets on the table and took another sip from the water glass. Dietz shifted in his chair, thinking that the defendant was about to wrap things up. He was wrong.

"Number-six," Zani continued, picking up the papers again, "I would like access to a representative of Amnesty International. Number seven, I would like access to the grand jury now in session in Travis County and the nearest federal grand jury.

"Also, point number eight, I would like the appointment of motivated counsel to me concerning the pending accusation of credit-card abuse. The counsel which was appointed by the court has in no wise been reasonably effective. Pseudo delays, procrastination, the facade of a competency hearing, and wholesale deceit, among other things, indicate that it would be an honest statement to say that I have had virtually no legal counsel whatsoever in this matter. It is my opinion that this attorney has acted as a friend of the court. If the court continues to deny me the right of 'reasonably effective counsel,' then at this moment I am giving notice that I am putting this case on appeal."

Wahlberg stared at a point midway between his seat and the bench, quietly seething, while his client turned another page and continued to read.

"Point number nine: Even though it is my understanding that this court has an excellent reputation for impartiality, due to the harshness of the adverse publicity I have received here, I request a change of venue to beyond an adjoining county."

Dear had been expecting this request, and he was tempted to grant it immediately just to be rid of the sanctimonious Zani. Instead, he adjusted his robe and kept quiet as Zani droned on, demanding reimbursement for the clothing he insisted had been lost by jailers and asking to be placed in a safe cell.

"Furthermore," the defendant read, "I am convinced that the malignant, concerted smear effort perpetrated against me is politically motivated . . . not because of anything I have done or anything I am suspected of doing, but because of where I have been and the company I have kept. It is my contention that no one in recent Travis County history has been subjected to such horrendous fictitious publicity, libeled beyond belief, had all of their personal, civil, and human rights violated while being innocent and while being held on one felony charge and a ten-thousand-dollar bond.

"Here in Rasputinish Ronnie Earle's bailiwick of sophistry, convicted child molesters and rapists receive much better treatment than I have. Why? It is my contention, again, that such devious, demonic motivation for a smear of character assassination is political.

"Furthermore, it is my suspicion that two Austin Police Department detectives are involved in the disappearance and probable death of two small children and are in violation of two serious federal obstruction-of-justice crimes. It is also my opinion that at least two Texas Rangers, two county sheriffs, one Secret Service agent, and the district attorney are, among others, also guilty of two extremely serious federal obstruction-of-justice crimes, including one of national consequence.

"The words of Mammon may be false, but the words of a judge pronounce justice," Zani concluded. "All I am asking for is due process and justice—and a new attorney."

It had been a bewildering display, and after pausing several moments to gather his thoughts, Judge Dear attempted to sort through the hyperbole of Zani's statement and to rule on his legitimate legal requests. First, Dear dismissed Wahlberg, who expressed his relief and headed for the door. Then, while deferring a ruling on the change-of-venue request, he granted Zani's access to a law library, agreed to inform the two grand juries that the defendant wished "to avail himself of their ear," and instructed the bailiff to escort Zani to the jury room, where several members of the local media were waiting to talk to him.

"I assume you will be on your best behavior back here and not attempt to climb out the ventilator shaft or something like that," Dear chided him, unable to resist the temptation to tweak Zani with a little facetiousness of his own.

"I came downstairs uncuffed," Zani retorted.

* * *

During the impromptu press conference in the jury room, Zani refused to be photographed because he was wearing what he called "guilty clothes"—a jail-issue jumpsuit. Sporting black horn-rimmed glasses, he leafed through the pages of the statement he had just read in the courtroom to make sure he didn't forget to repeat his best lines.

He denied the charges, again calling them "slop." He accused prosecutors of employing a "smear effect" and said that he had been "libeled beyond belief," both in court and in the media. Then he attacked what he termed the "Ronnie Earle aristocracy" in the district attorney's office and blasted the jail once more as "roach-infested."

Though reporters found it easy to agree with him on the last point, they had considerably more difficulty accepting Zani's broad hints that he was being held against his will because of "certain information" the authorities wanted kept secret. When pressed, he became belligerent, refusing to elaborate. He again insisted that he was in trouble not for anything he had done but for whom he had seen. He claimed to have been granted partial immunity from the Texas Rangers in connection with activities between April and June 1979, when he had traveled to South America on some unspecified mission.

"I have no guilt," he declared, adding that he intended to make a statement when and if he got his day in open court, implying, again, that the just-completed hearing before Judge Dear did not qualify as such a day. What was said then would be so explosive that he "would expect charges to be filed against other persons," he assured them.

Back in his cell, Zani quickly became a classic example of the jailhouse writ writer. With nothing but time on his hands, he pored over lawbooks, filling page after yellow legal page with his painstaking scrawl. Brighter than the average con, he was soon writing Judge Dear every few days, filing motions on his own behalf as well as for fellow inmates, who presumably paid him for the service in whatever cellblock currency Zani deemed acceptable.

In one motion, Zani complained that he had been denied access to a pen during his entire incarceration; it was unclear how he explained the hundreds of pages that constituted his missives to Dear, all written with a fine-point Bic. In another, he requested the right to a quiet place for preparation of his case. In all, he sent some three dozen motions, letters, and personal diatribes to Dear over the next few weeks. "Petitioner is a layman," the motions invariably began, "untrained in formal legal proceedings and unlettered in the legal nomenclature and complicated, complex, and hypertechnical science of jurisprudence and as such should not be held to the strict standards required of an attorney.

Guided by models provided in the books he was now able to consult, Zani peppered his motions with his own highfalutin prose. "After such callous disregard for defendant and his rights, state should not be permitted a second bite of the apple, or a third bite for that matter," he wrote in one. "In accordance with due process and fair treatment, defendant should not be compelled to languish for months on end in a 'correctional' facility, deprived of his freedom, while innocent (what is innocent defendant being 'corrected' for?) and then having to go through the same sadistic deprivation, and the same sheer saturated horror *again*, due to harassment on the part of the state whereby defendant becomes an unwilling victim of the malestrom [*sic*] of injustice."

Dear tucked each new motion away in a file drawer marked "Z" for Zani. If nothing else, the judge thought, the defendant had succeeded in raising the entertainment quotient of his inmate mail by several notches.

FIFTEEN

While Judge Jim Dear played legal pat-a-cake with Zani, and while assistant DA Joe Turner prepared to take over the case from the departing John Dietz, Ruiz and Martinez continued their efforts to prove true the only thing Zani had said since his arrest that they believed: "You can find that out."

The Dess case had been all but yanked from them, and Irma was in Floresville with Gene Powell and the feds; there was little left for Ruiz and Martinez to contribute there. As for the Gladys Zani case, the officers had handed over their files to Tulsa detectives Hunt and Parke, who were still trying to nail down the evidence needed to indict Zani for his mother's death. Moore, Oklahoma. Magnolia, Arkansas. These and other police departments had been furnished Zani's prints and photograph to check against similar crimes in their cities, and now they were on their own.

So Ruiz and Martinez turned their full attention to the thirteen-year-old murder of George Vizard. They proposed to reconstruct everything about the atmosphere of those times, everything about the pudgy student radical and convenience store clerk, everything, especially, about Robert Joseph Zani.

Acting on information given them by Bivens, the former Tulsa PD officer who had lived next door to Gladys Zani, they contacted Vera Tolbert, Gladys's sister. Tolbert recalled a number of interesting things about her nephew. She remembered, for example, that Gladys had bought him a sky-blue VW Bug while he was attending UT-Austin. During this time, she said, Robert had been employed as a researcher in the university's archives, work he particularly enjoyed because of the sensitive material he was able to gather on "bigwig politicians"—enough, he boasted, to put them in jail. He said he supplemented his income by informing to the FBI on suspected drug dealers.

"He was very political," Tolbert told the officers, agreeing to send them a copy of Robert's high school graduation photo. "He griped a lot and always wanted to do things to correct the government." The comment reminded Ruiz and Martinez of a recent press account in which Zani told the reporter that he was "apolitical in college."

Next they contacted Virginia Warner, an old friend of Gladys's. Speaking from the kitchen phone in her home in Westminster, Colorado, a suburb of Denver, Warner suggested that Gladys and her son were uneasy blood relatives. Asking the officers to hold a moment, she put the receiver down and rummaged through a desk drawer for a letter she had received from Gladys back in February 1970.

"Dear Virginia," she read, skipping through the gossip about common acquaintances till she found the section she had in mind. "My grandbaby's name is Raquel (named for her grandmother on her mother's side). Raquel Carmela (I think Raquel is the Spanish name for Rachel but am not sure). I sure miss that little squirt since I was down there. She says about anything she wants to and—like Robert—is too smart for her age. She will be two years old a month from today (March 16). She is so big for her age I have to use a size-five pattern to make her dresses—so chesty and hippy! Of course, I have the other two grandchildren that Robert adopted and they have me, but it's very hard for me not to be partial. Anna Marie was six years old on February 12, and Patricia will be five years old on May 1. Raquel thinks she can do anything they can, and she just about can."

Warner told the officers that she concurred with Tolbert's opinion that Robert was a political junkie. In fact, she recalled how impressed he was by the publicity surrounding a friend of his—Charles Whitman, the UT Tower sniper who had put Austin on the map as the site of the worst mass slaying in U.S. history. Zani talked about being trapped in the Student Union Building next to the tower when the shooting began and even contacted a Tulsa reporter to give an interview for the local paper, Warner said. She had kept a copy of the article, headlined TULSAN TELLS OF SNIPER'S TERRORISM, which she agreed to send to the officers.

Martinez took note. Like other Austinites, he remembered vividly the Whitman affair; it had still been a frequent topic of conversation when he joined the police force seventeen months afterward. In the years since, Martinez had made something of a study of the sniper incident. He knew that Coleman DeChenar, the same man who performed the autopsy on Vizard, had worked on Whitman. There was even a controversy, Martinez recalled, over whether Houston McCoy or Ramiro Martinez (no relation) had been the APD cop who finally took the sniper out. It had been Burt Gerding, the ranking officer on duty that day, who had bounded up the steps of the tower in the first few seconds after Whitman was felled and who had declared McCoy the hero.

APD had blown that investigation, too. Only later was a document discovered in the files of the student health center indicating that Whitman visited a psychiatrist four months earlier and admitted to having "overwhelming periods of hostility" during which he thought about "going up on the tower with a deer rifle to start shooting people." If nothing else, Ruiz and Martinez agreed, they had better scour APD's files for the missing portions of the Vizard offense report. They didn't want it said at some future date that they had overlooked a key piece of evidence.

With the help of Zani family members like Vera Tolbert

and friends like Virginia Warner, they had already learned that Zani's relationship with his mother was a good deal less loving than that which he enjoyed with his grandparents, F.L. and Mamie Plumley of Tulsa. On September 27, 1966, for instance, Zani wrote his grandparents to complain that Gladys had cut off his funds. Scrawling on university stationery pilfered from a supply cabinet in the archives, he wrote:

This is not going to be an easy letter to begin or end, but I am going to do my best to say this so that it may be understood. I don't know if you'll understand just how much I dislike writing this, but at this time I have utterly no choice.

Mom wrote me a day ago saying that she could not send me any money. To me, this was a last-minute thing and one for which I was totally unprepared. In a short time it has placed me at my wits [sic] end and at my rope's end. I have, of course, only eight months to go, until the last of May, and then it will be over. I'm in desperate need and looking everywhere possible for help. If something does not turn up I will be forced to quit the second week of October for lack of funds. So this is my letter to you, and Grandpa, and I hope you will give it some consideration.

I have a job here at the archives, and it's a fairly good one. Still, it does not nearly pay my expenses. To make a long story short, in order to finish and get my degree I need approximately $1,000. I know that is a lot of money and I cannot promise an exact date of payment. All I can say is that I would start payment next October, if that would be all right. I can only add that at that time I should be a Marine officer. There is little else I can say except that I am sorry to have to write this letter. And I can assure you that I would not do so

unless I felt it was absolute necessary. I hope that you
and Grandpa will consider this.

Love, Robert

P.S. I hope you enjoyed your trip to Colorado.

Exactly one week before Vizard was murdered, Zani wrote
again, thanking his grandparents for the loan the previous
fall. The letter was thick with the obsequious tone and
teenage self-importance he never outgrew, and he failed to
mention that he and Irma had been married just eighteen
days earlier. Filling another piece of university letterhead,
he wrote:

Somewhat late, but at least a letter to say how things
are here and inquire as to how things are there. As for
myself, I didn't return to the U.S. [from Mexico] until
July. Not only did I encounter many more problems and
delays than I expected, but I became very ill the second
week there and never got much better. I still am sick
but so much better. Stomach trouble beyond anything
I have ever known. So 5 days ended up as 3 weeks. The
government down there caused me so much worry I
almost gave up—being sick to boot—but I finally made
it.

Returning, I'm kept working, but the job is more than
I can handle. My boss likes my work and has asked me
to stay on in September—and I may, but it is difficult. I
never took Spanish here, and to speak it is one thing, to
read it as it was written 250 years ago is something
else. However, if my boss is satisfied—he pays for it—I
guess for now that is the important thing.

For the record, I am a Marine now. It is as official as
the fact that the war is to get bigger—by at least
100,000 troops. I'm taking several big steps now—but
I'm taking them, so in the end it's my baby, right or
wrong. Again, I thank you so much for helping me with
one of them.

When I returned in July, I found a letter from Mom
. . . but haven't heard any more. I guess I'll write
although it is extremely hard to know what to say. I
said what is in my heart and that got jeered down. What
else is there? Well, you know the story—and somehow
I think I know a little more how you feel about all that
has passed. And you know exactly how I feel now. I
cannot deny my own blood—in this the fruit has ex-
celled the tree. For me to deny your own blood is to
deny life itself—but fewer and fewer believe that nowa-
days.

Do drop me a line and say how things are with you
all. It has been so hot and dry here that I can't imagine
heat being any worse—anywhere.

I do hope that you are feeling better than when I last
saw you and that a *calmness* is beginning to set in.
Eventually rain stops. *Eventually* the drought ends. So
it is in nature. So it is with people. Let us pray that
eventually becomes *rapidly*.

Love, Robert

Peering into Zani's personal life often put Ruiz and Martinez into bad moods. There was no denying he was an
asshole, they told one another, and Martinez especially
broke away as often as he could to concentrate on the more
standard police work that always seemed to make him feel
better. He called Strum and Ruger Firearms in Southport,
Connecticut, the manufacturer of the .357 they had brought
back from Mexico, and asked for information on a weapon
with the serial number 78283. He was told that the gun had
been shipped from the factory on June 16, 1966, to the main
warehouse of J. S. Oshman's Sporting Goods in Houston.
From there, the gun had been shipped to its Austin store on
July 5.

Ruiz and Martinez rushed to the store on North I-35,
across from the Ramada Inn, where the manager checked

his records. Sure, he told them, the weapon had remained in the store's inventory for a couple of weeks, and then it had been sold on July 23, 1966.

The cops looked at each other. July 23, 1966—exactly one year to the day before Vizard's murder. At a time before it was required by law, store policy had been to keep detailed records.

"And who bought it?" Martinez asked.

"Guy named Robert Joseph Zani," the manager replied. "Gave his address as 1012 West Twenty-second Street."

After weeks of trying to trace the .25 that had killed J. A. Dess, Ruiz and Martinez had hit pay dirt, connecting Zani to the murder weapon used on Vizard in less than a morning. Sometimes, they joked as they left the store, it was incredible how easy their job seemed. Not often, but often enough.

On July 22, the day of Zani's press conference, APD released its own statement to the media, requesting information to help the police finally solve the murder of George Vizard. The department was taking its case directly to the public the day before the thirteenth anniversary of the killing on that early Sunday morning at 3310 Northland.

It was the perfect news hook, and the coverage was heavy. A story appeared on the front page of the *Daily Texan*, the UT student newspaper. The *Austin Citizen* asked, "Did you know these men?" above photographs of Vizard and Zani as they looked near the time of the murder. Radio and television broadcasts ran to several minutes, featuring clips of Zani's press conference, interviews with APD officers, and, in his swan song as a prosecutor, John Dietz.

The public gambit unleashed a torrent of tips and phone calls from an Austin populace for whom interest in the unsolved murder was, to the officers' surprise, very much alive. The first came from Ken Moyer, who had seen a TV report and wanted to let the officers know that he had been acquainted with Vizard. The two had gone to San Antonio together for preinduction physicals after receiving their draft notices in 1966, Moyer said. He recalled that federal authorities kept George for further questioning when the session ended, while Moyer returned to Austin alone. He didn't know why.

The next call was from Bob Henderson. He remembered both Vizard and Zani because of their unusual names, he said, indicating that he had kept up with campus politics while attending UT in the sixties. Zani listed himself under absurdist names in the student directories of the time— Robespierre Xenophobia Zani and Mustapha Mahatma Zani were two that Henderson recalled—and gave his address as Brenda Lee Avenue in Gene Autry, Oklahoma. In 1966 Zani even ran for student-body president on the Mickey Mouse platform, clad in giant mouse ears and a fake mustache. He placed last in a field of three, though at least 924 voters had evidently agreed with his platform to abolish student government. "We don't govern anyone," Zani wrote in his campaign flyers, "and one can only logically infer that the best organization to do nothing is a nonexistent one. We have a myriad of organizations filled with fraternal rodents gnawing at the cheese of egotism at the expense of actual student representation." Such attempts to poke fun at student politics had not won the admiration of those in the self-serious SDS, Henderson added.

George McClellan, too, had known Vizard and others associated with the SDS movement and the political scene that revolved around the Chuck Wagon back in the sixties. Ruiz and Martinez smiled when McClellan suggested that the first person they should contact was a former cop—Burt Gerding. Beyond that, however, McClellan offered several names the officers had not heard thus far. They began writing them down to compare with a list of SDS members they had obtained from APD intelligence files.

Late in the afternoon, Russ Roberts phoned. He had attended high school with Vizard in San Antonio, Roberts said, and had been his roommate at UT from September 1963 through May 1964. They attended a couple of SDS meetings together in late 1963 but had gradually grown apart as George pursued his politics and, later, Mariann. Roberts didn't remember Zani, but he gave the officers a few more names to add to their list.

The phone continued to ring. One man said he used to work in Hemphill's Bookstore, across the Drag from campus, and knew Vizard as a regular customer. Another had dated Vizard's former girlfriend while attending junior college in San Antonio. Someone else urged them to call Court of Criminal Appeals judge Sam Houston Clinton, whose daughter, he asserted, had been heavily involved with the SDS.

Other callers suggested that the officers contact Ed Guinn, a black musician, songwriter, and record producer; Jim Franklin, the poster artist from the Armadillo World Headquarters; Kathy London, whose parents owned a well-known Austin fabrics store; local reporters Ed Bennett and Cleveland Moore; county judges Steve Russell and Guy Herman; and a variety of other people—all of whom, the officers were assured, could tell them what they needed to know. By the end of the day, Ruiz and Martinez were beginning to see why the original investigation into George Vizard's murder had run aground in a thicket of names and associations and vague political fears.

Even Vizard's widow chimed in. Mariann, who had married a local community activist named Larry Waterhouse, issued a press release that attempted to walk a fine line between the pressures she felt to exalt her ex-husband's political legacy and the need to accept the realities of the police investigation:

My family and I are gratified to learn that, thirteen years after our terrible loss, a suspect has been found in the brutal slaying of George John Vizard IV. We have been made aware of evidence which would seem to point to Robert Joseph Zani as the killer. Many questions remain in my own mind as to whether, if Zani killed my former husband, he acted alone or in concert with others, and what his motives may have been. Some evidence would seem to indicate a political motive.

However, George's dedication to peace and equal rights remains as an inspiration to hundreds who knew him or knew of him, and in that sense his killer or killers failed utterly in their destructive aims. That has been my solace in the years since George's murder and will continue to be so in the years ahead.

I would like to urge all of George's and my friends to examine and carefully weigh the evidence which will be presented in the hope that many of our questions will at last be answered.

I would also like to commend the investigators' energy and dedication and can only wish that similar zeal had been shown by investigators at the time of George's death. Perhaps we would then have been spared the pain, disruption, and opening of old wounds which the renewed publicity already seems to promise.

If George Vizard's life and death meant anything, it was that truth and justice are more powerful than lies and oppression. I am confident that eventually the truth will prevail.

On July 27, Gilbert Miller called Ruiz and Martinez into his office. Handing them each an official-looking sheet of paper, he explained that they had been transferred out of special crimes and into the organized crime unit. From now on, he said, as he lit a cigarette and placed it next to another that was still lit in the ashtray, they would report to Bobby Simpson. He wished them luck.

Throughout the rest of July and the first two weeks of August, Ruiz and Martinez, working in tandem with Joe Turner, revisited the sixties. They interviewed as many former SDS members as they could find and scoured old newspapers and UT files to reconstruct a fascinating portrait of 1967 Austin—a time when the city seemed about to be wrenched from its historical moorings as the local chapter of the SDS became one of the strongest in the nation.

They remembered the times, of course, because they too had lived them. It had been an age of unprecedented prosperity and rebellion, the war in Vietnam uniting a generation in anger and disgust—from the barricades of Paris and Prague to the mass demonstrations in Madrid, Mexico City, and beyond; from the breaking of segregation's back in the South to the exploration of sexual freedom in all those places and more. A student generation in revolt had searched for a new political place and the theories to give it substance.

The Austin SDS, they learned, had boasted about one hundred paid members adept at incurring the wrath not only of university officials but also of state lawmakers. During the 1967 legislative session, state senator Grady Hazlewood of Canyon introduced a bill permitting investigations into "campus drugs, sex, and leftists." Representative Delwin Jones of Lubbock authored a "beatnik bill" allowing authorities to dictate dress codes in state-funded institutions, and Representative Burke Musgrove of Breckenridge called for an end to SDS's status as a student organization, asserting that members were "rude" to him when they opposed his bill to make LSD an illegal drug.

An oft-repeated story in SDS circles described the DPS officers who were ordered to bust a group of activists at an early demonstration. "But we're anticommunists," the students pleaded.

"We don't care what kind of communists you are. You're under arrest," one of the troopers supposedly snapped.

Some of those with whom Ruiz and Martinez spoke had not liked cops then and weren't about to cozy up to them now. B. J. Combs, for example, tried to make them believe that his political involvement had been minimal in the sixties; the SDS crowd, he said, had been a bit too radical for his taste. Those who remembered Combs, known by the nickname "Trap" in those days, would have barely recognized the self-portrait he provided Ruiz and Martinez. Not only had Combs lived in the same dorm as Zani, but he had also attended the Vizards' wedding, escorted Mariann to her husband's funeral, and generally been regarded as one of the grunt soldiers in the student movement's battle against the establishment, according to APD and FBI intelligence. Even in 1980 Combs was in the thick of liberal precinct politics in Austin.

Others, like Jeff Shero, wanted to downplay their politics to protect the business interests they had acquired in recent years. Shero had been president of the local SDS chapter and, after his enforced withdrawal from UT in June 1966, went to work in the organization's Chicago headquarters. Later, he returned to Austin with a new name—Jeff Nightbyrd—and a new interest: building the weekly publication he edited, the *Austin Sun,* into a respected underground paper. But in 1980 Shero/Nightbyrd was entertaining thoughts of assembling an expensive cable television system, and the last thing he wanted was to tip potential investors off to his radical past. (Nightbyrd resurfaced in the late 1980s, peddling pure urine samples to employees of companies caught up in the drug-testing mania of the U.S. workplace.)

His former girlfriend, however, was willing to help—to a degree. Alice Embree had once been the secretary of the local SDS chapter, though she was in Chile as part of a student exchange program when her friend George Vizard was slain. Meeting with Ruiz one night in Les Amis Cafe across from the university, she was unable to identify Zani from photographs as anyone she had known. She agreed to ask around, though, and phoned the next day to say that she had spoken with Frances Rogers, one of Zani's co-workers in the Bexar archives on campus.

That afternoon, Ruiz visited Rogers. Zani had worked there as a Spanish translator, she recalled, an intelligent, neatly dressed young man who was quite likable, though he tended to keep to himself. She remembered her surprise when he returned from a brief vacation in the early summer of 1967 and announced that he had married in Mexico. He left his job not long after that, Rogers said, and she never heard from him again.

Back at the Twin Towers, Ruiz looked through the pile of papers he and Martinez had subpoenaed from UT just before the second Acapulco trip. There were no employment records from Zani's time in the Bexar archives. He understood they couldn't just issue some giant subpoena in the sky, but it seemed ridiculous to have to ask for each specific document only after each specific lead. Ruiz consulted with Turner, who promised to dog the university until they had in their possession every last scrap of paper with Zani's name on it.

The documents they eventually shook loose were fascinating. One unsigned memo in the files of the University of Texas police contained a curious notation. Written in April 1966 or 1967 by a campus cop checking into "the use of peyote, barbituates [sic], and other drugs by groups" around UT, it detailed a meeting in his office with Robert Zani. "He stated that he was approached by a person on the campus who is trying to get him to go to Lareado [sic], to bring back some dope," the investigator wrote. "I have a meeting with Mr. Zani in the Texas Union [a student center that housed, among other things, the Chuck Wagon] at 4:30 tomorrow. He is to point out the person who is trying to get him to go with him."

The officer continued his report the next day: "This person did not show up. I took Mr. Zani to the DPS where we talked with Det. Doug Nealer, the head of the Narcotics Division. It was suggested to Mr. Zani that he try to obtain the marijuana that was offered to him and then report immediately to myself or either to Mr. Nealer." There was no indication that the plan was ever carried out, and the report ended with a general discussion of the professor, students, and ex-students whom the investigator suspected as sources for "some of these dopes."

According to the records, Zani was given a job as clerical assistant in the Main Library on May 26, 1965. He continued to work there five days a week each semester, receiving a promotion to library assistant in September 1966 and, finally, to translator in the archives section on June 1, 1967. Later that month, he took eight vacation days—to marry Irma in Mexico and adopt her two children, Ruiz and Martinez knew. Upon his return, Zani worked the entire month of July, showing up on time every morning—including July 24, the day after Vizard's murder—and then took leave without pay from August 1 through August 16.

On July 26, 1967, in response to a request from Zani, his boss had written to Jacob Snyder, the immigration chief at the U.S. embassy in Mexico City, assuring the functionary that "his work is satisfactory and we hope to retain his services." Zani had apparently applied for a visa to bring his Mexican bride to Texas. Then, on September 1, Zani submitted his resignation. He was going into the military, he explained.

A subsequent check revealed that Zani had actually enlisted in the Marine Corps reserves' officer candidate course on July 5, two months earlier, pledging to serve at least six years and erroneously listing his marital status as single with no dependents. On September 15 he backed out of the commitment in a letter to his commander. "At the time I signed the forms, I was married—and am," he confessed. "Financially, I just cannot be gone from work, with a loss of income. My wife and children would be placed in extreme hardship; besides, I am deeply in debt." The Marines had quickly granted Zani an honorable discharge.

On August 4 an Alcohol, Tobacco and Firearms Bureau agent called with the information Ruiz and Martinez had requested on the Rossi .38, serial number D341906, the weapon brought back from Acapulco with the .357. The gun had been sold on July 10, 1979, to James Wilheim Morrison of Austin, who bought it from E-Z Pawn Shop on North Lamar. A quick check with the pawnshop owner confirmed the details.

Just before midnight two days later, Ruiz traced Morrison to Houston and got him on the line. Morrison admitted having once owned the gun but said he sold it for $125 in the fall of 1979, after a man answered a want ad Morrison had placed in a local shopping guide. "Seems to me the guy mentioned that he worked for a company that imported goods from Mexico," Morrison said, "and that he wanted the gun for his wife, who lived on a farm somewhere in the Midwest."

Ruiz perked up. "What did the man look like?" he asked.

Morrison was vague on the description. He was in his mid-thirties and not very tall, maybe 175 pounds, dressed in a loose-fitting shirt and black-rimmed glasses. The man had said it was dangerous to travel in a foreign country without a weapon—which struck Morrison as odd since the man had already said the .38 was for his wife. Morrison was certain he could identify the man if he saw a photograph, but Ruiz let the matter drop. He and Martinez had no murder to fit with the gun, and they had plenty of other work to do without trying to establish a definite link. Besides, there was no doubt in Ruiz's mind that the man Morrison described was Robert Zani.

At eight-thirty in the morning, August 14, Ruiz sat down at his desk. Martinez was already there, having left work early the day before and come in early this day to make up the hours. Ruiz, on the other hand, had been at APD headquarters until after one-thirty that morning, begging and cajoling the woman in charge of central records to make photocopies of the entire original Vizard offense report, the missing portions of which had finally been located on microfilm. The copies sat on his desk now, neatly arranged in a stack about three inches high.

Ruiz sipped his coffee and slowly began to read through the full report for the first time since he and Martinez had become involved in the case back in March. Many of the entries were familiar by now: how Kelton and Landis had grasped at every flimsy lead that came their way, how Donald Kidd had pursued his own misguided angles, how the entire investigation had finally been left to wither in the back of some file cabinet. Even if Ruiz and his partner had arrived at a better understanding of the myriad political relationships of Austin in the sixties, it was still difficult for him not to shake his head now and then at the silly clues the original investigators had judged important enough to follow thirteen years earlier.

"Robert!" Ruiz suddenly shouted, slamming his fists on the desk.

Martinez looked up. "What's the matter with you?" he asked. Ruiz was speechless, an uncommon occurrence. Martinez rushed across the room to see what his partner was reading and there, on page 39, he saw Robert Zani's name, identified as a suspect.

At 10:25 on the night of Wednesday, July 26, 1967—three days after Vizard's murder—a man had called APD to say that he might have some information concerning the case. On the desk that night was Sergeant Jimmy Freeman, a veteran officer who had cut back his work hours because of a nagging illness eventually diagnosed as cancer (he died a few years later). Freeman grabbed a notepad and jotted down the information the caller offered. Afterward, he gave the sheet to a secretary, who then typed up the report on a supplementary offense sheet and placed it on Merle Wells's desk for the lieutenant to review in the morning.

Thirteen years and nineteen days later, Ruiz and Martinez read Freeman's report, barely able to conceal their astonishment:

Interviewed Harlan Cooper, WM of 2216 Rio Grande, after he had called this Department stating he might have information on the Vizard murder.

He stated that Friday or Saturday night [July 21 or 22], he and a friend, Robert Riggs, were at the Chuck Wagon on the UT Campus. When they were there they met a friend of Riggs, Robert Zani. Zani kept saying that he needed money and would like to go hold up a place. He asked them both to go with him. Cooper states he passed it off as a joke, but the more he thought about it, the more he thinks Zani was serious.

He stated that Zani is employed at the Library on the Campus. He does not know where he lives. He describes Zani as follows: A WM in late 20s, dark hair, beginning to thin on top, 5'8" (approx), 160 pounds. Cooper states that if he finds out any more information he will call this Department.

In the margins, someone had written "Wit," connecting it with a line to Cooper's name. Below, he had written "Sus" and drawn an arrow to Zani's name.

Later, after staring at page 39 for what seemed like hours on end, Ruiz and Martinez noted that the report was signed by Wells, Landis, and Kelton at eight o'clock the following morning. It was entirely possible, they knew, that only one of the three had actually read it; all of the names, in fact, were signed in the same slanted scrawl. But with every freakish lead that had been followed back then, each oblique clue that had taken priority, why no one had ever interviewed Zani, Cooper, or Riggs was beyond their comprehension.

"I can't truthfully say that you really look at all of those reports closely," Lieutenant Roger Napier commented years later. "If it's a run-of-the-mill murder case and there's a shit-pile of paper coming across your desk, you may not read them all. But that particular case—the kind of case it was, with all the publicity—I can't imagine somebody not reading the goddam thing, not snapping on it. It wasn't the kind of case you just took lightly, after all."

SIXTEEN

For the next week, Turner, Ruiz, and Martinez scoured the complete offense report as if it were a treasure map containing secrets that would reveal themselves if the men revisited its pages often enough. In fact, the missing entries had already yielded some rather startling information. Page 39, for example, had provided two more names to check out: Harlan Cooper and Robert Riggs.

For now, however, Turner was especially intrigued by the interviews with the Mogoynes, Jerry Senior and Junior, who both said that the clerk in the Town and Country that early Sunday morning was someone other than Vizard. With an eye toward eventual prosecution of Zani, Turner decided that the Mogoynes should be reinterviewed—maybe, he suggested, even hypnotized and returned to the scene. He had a hunch the jury would find it difficult to ignore testimony from a couple of witnesses who might have been waited on by the killer. The defense would probably protest such circumstantial evidence, but after thirteen years, Turner's whole case was looking pretty damn circumstantial. He told Ruiz and Martinez to locate the Mogoynes.

On August 19 they tracked the elder Mogoyne to the small Central Texas town of Liberty Hill, where the former contractor had settled into retirement. Mogoyne was astonished to hear that the case had been reopened, and though he was unsure how helpful he could be to them after so many years, he readily agreed to a meeting. Ruiz and Martinez drove to his home the next day.

It was soon clear that Mogoyne had a remarkable memory. He and his son and a man named Dungan had stopped at the store to buy ice and snacks, he recalled. There were two men inside. The first, a slender dark-haired man wearing a maroon shirt and dark pants, was standing in the corner by the rest room. He was clean-shaven, Mogoyne said, about five feet eleven inches tall and 130 pounds. The second man, perhaps five eight and 160 pounds, with short hair and wearing a light-colored shirt, was standing behind the cash register.

While they were in the store, Mogoyne continued, a man came in and asked directions to U.S. 183, southeast of town. The one in the maroon shirt unfolded a map, draped it over the magazine rack, and pointed out the best route. Another customer entered the store, saying he needed to borrow an ice pick and some tongs to break apart the blocks of ice in the bin outside.

Ruiz and Martinez showed Mogoyne the five snapshots taken at the April lineup. He thought that two of the faces, including Zani's, might possibly belong to the clerk he remembered, but he stopped short of making a positive I.D. He was willing to be hypnotized if necessary and gave the officers a phone number where his son could be reached.

Jerry Junior now lived in Houston, where he was in charge of land development for the White Oak Development Corporation. He, too, was startled when Ruiz and Martinez phoned to explain that they had spoken to his father and wanted to set up a hypnosis session to see if the younger Mogoyne could help them with the description of the clerk who had made change at the register of the Austin convenience store thirteen years earlier. Mogoyne protested that he ran a tight schedule and probably couldn't come to Austin anytime soon. But after several moments, he warmed to the idea of an interview—as long as it could be conducted in Houston—and told the officers that if they would leave a message with his secretary when they had arranged the session, he would break away from his office for an hour or two.

The session began at two forty-five on Monday afternoon, September 8, 1980, in the offices of the Therapeutic Forensic Hypnosis Institute in the Montrose section of Houston. The institute's director, James Michael Boulch, was a thirty-three-year-old Texas A&M University professor whose lengthy résumé belied the newness of a field of forensic hypnotism. He let them in the door and made the introductions: first, Texas Ranger Carl Weathers, whom Boulch had trained; then Arthur Douet, a sketch artist frequently employed by Texas law enforcement agencies. Mogoyne took his seat, uncertain what to expect. Ruiz, the only officer who knew what Zani looked like, sat in the back of the room, away from the others.

In recent years the medical uses of hypnosis had gained a quiet acceptance among members of the American Medical Association and other powerful lobbies. Attempting to solve crimes through hypnosis, however, was still considered controversial. There was a common misconception among jurors that a person under hypnosis is compelled to tell the truth, although, in fact, even deeply hypnotized subjects are quite capable of lying if they choose.

After all, hypnosis is a state in which an individual's susceptibility to suggestion is heightened (the word comes from Hypnos, the mythological god of sleep). People tend to suspend critical judgment under hypnosis, eager to please the hypnotist by complying with both explicit suggestions and subtle cues that might be entirely unintentional. This process of confabulation, or filling in details as if they are actual recollections, has led many researchers to embrace the reconstructive theory of memory, in which both external information and a person's own thoughts can alter recall. As a result, critics declare, hypnosis is inappropriate as a forensic tool—and extremely dangerous in court.

Boulch and other proponents disagreed. They subscribed to the video-tape theory of memory, which holds that every piece of information a person is exposed to in his life is permanently stored somewhere in his brain and can be retrieved. The group seated in Boulch's office now hoped to reach into Mogoyne's memory and extract a detailed portrait of the clerk who had waited on him in the Town and Country more than thirteen years earlier.

As Boulch sat back to watch his student at work, Weathers took Mogoyne into what was later deemed to be "a deep medium level of hypnosis." Boulch looked for the physiological signs that told him the subject had gone under. He saw Mogoyne's muscles relax, heard his breathing shift from the upper chest to the lower abdomen, noticed an occasional twitching of his fingers.

Starting a metronome that would accompany them throughout the session, Weathers began to speak in a soothing, leisurely Texas accent, taking Mogoyne back to that Sunday morning, July 23, 1967. Before long, Weathers had guided Mogoyne's attention to the man behind the counter, asking him to focus on the image as best he could.

"About what age is the man?" Weathers asked.

"Tw . . . twenties," Mogoyne replied in a high-pitched, dreamy voice.

"In his twenties. That's fine, that's good. That's very good. Now I wish that you would describe him from his hair all the way down to his neck, taking each part at a time. Now . . . now he is in complete focus."

"Dark hair. Neat."

"That's fine. Neatly trimmed. That's fine."

"Kind of waxy," Mogoyne added, sweat beginning to bead on his forehead.

"Good," Weathers said. "You're doing very, very good. I need you to relax."

"Parted," Mogoyne continued, his shoulders loosening slightly.

"High forehead or low forehead?"

"Higher than lower. Kind of combs to the right."

"Can you tell me what side his hair is parted on?"

"I believe right part. To his right, I think. Kind of a round or squarish-looking face . . . neat eyebrows, not heavy."

"Are the eyebrows arched or straight?"

"A little arched, I think. Yeah, just a little arched."

"Very good. Can you describe his eyes?"

"No . . . kind of a boxy guy." Mogoyne seemed to be drifting, his eyelids fluttering.

"Very, very good," Weathers whispered. "Continue to relax, deeper and deeper, concentrating on the clerk. Now can you describe his nose? In your own words, describe each characteristic that you can see, from his hair down to his neck."

"His lips are defined, maybe a little . . ." Mogoyne hesitated.

"Do you mean thin?" asked Weathers.

"No, heavier . . . and the chin, the chin is defined. Maybe like a bulge on the end of it."

"Would you say prominent chin? Is there a mark on the chin?"

"I guess it just shows up."

"That's fine," Weathers said. "That's very good. Take one deep, deep breath and exhale very slowly. I need you to relax."

Mogoyne complied, letting the air out in a long, low sigh.

"In just a moment you will hear the voice of the artist, Mr. Douet," Weathers continued. "He will discuss what this man looks like to you. In just a moment he will begin asking you questions about the man you see, and each sound that you hear takes you deeper and deeper . . . relaxed . . . and makes the focus sharper and sharper."

Douet leaned forward. "Can you say if this man was wearing glasses, spectacles?" he asked.

"No," Mogoyne answered.

"Can you describe his eyes to me?" Douet gently insisted.

"I don't see anything that's . . . that I can describe. It just . . . I think the . . . the square or fat face . . . round. No, it's more . . ."

From the back of the room where he had been told to sit, Ruiz could not tell if Mogoyne was having trouble focusing on the image in his head or just finding the right words to describe what he was seeing. Boulch watched as Weathers scratched down a note. Douet waited, his sketch pad at the ready.

". . . kind of a boxy-looking face," Mogoyne continued. "That, and the hair is dark. It's . . . There doesn't seem to be a definite part. Neat. The eyebrows—they're neat. And the eyes, they just . . . just sort of fit into it. There's nothing . . . They're not wide. They're not narrow. They're not close to the nose. They're not away from the nose."

"Can you describe his nose to me?" asked Douet.

"It's . . . It's what I call defined. It's kind of rounded at the nostril, and it's not heavy or thick, and it's got a . . . It's not very significant, either. It's just . . ."

"Would you say his nose was, um, long?"

"No."

"Short or medium?"

"Uh . . . medium."

"Medium. Would you say that his nose was straight or somewhat curved in some areas?" Douet asked, drawing lines on his pad without looking at the witness.

"Curve there between the nose and the upper lip," Mogoyne responded, staring at Douet's sketch pad with an expression that seemed to come from another world. "Nose kind of curves around and comes out, ending at the top of the lip. The mouth doesn't blend with the face. They're not large lips, but they're not small lips. They're not . . . I guess they're just average, but they're defined. The bottom of the lip comes down like that same curve, out to the chin. The chin doesn't protrude . . . It just . . . got a lot of definition there that's . . ."

Douet interrupted him. "Between the mouth and the chin, would you say that, um, the chin was a long chin or a short chin?" he asked.

"Short chin."

"Was this man wearing a beard or a moustache, or was he clean-shaven?"

"I would say he is clean."

"Would you call him, um, somewhat good-looking, or would you say he was plain or . . ."

"Clean. Clean-cut. Yeah, neat."

"I remember you saying that his nose was well defined."

"Yeah, and the nostrils are a little curved."

"Down to where the nostril meets the . . . meets the face?"

"Meets the cheek, yeah."

"Meets the cheek," Douet repeated under his breath, drawing the line on his pad. "I see."

Mogoyne gazed at Douet's sketch. "It's not significant, but it's a little more defined than just the . . ." He let out a sigh.

"Is there a distance between the top lip and the nose? Would you say that it's close to the nose, the top lip, or would you say that there's a fair distance there?" Douet asked.

"No, no. There's not a long distance between the nose and the lips."

"What about his forehead? Was it receding or was it . . . coming forward?"

"I don't think so. It's not receding. Nothing unusual about it."

"Was his hair combed back? Or was it combed over the forehead somewhat?"

"Somehow, it's not back, and it looks like it could be to the side. But then it looks like it could be just slick and shiny."

"Slick and shiny. Would you say that the hair was exceedingly dark? Or would you say that it was somewhat brown or medium, medium dark, or—"

"Medium dark."

Boulch uncrossed his legs, inadvertently bringing both feet to the floor with a thud. Weathers, sensing that Mogoyne was weavering, broke in.

"You are doing very, very good, Jerry," the ranger said soothingly. "Just continue to relax. Each breath that you take, each ticking of the metronome, each sound that you hear, takes you deeper and deeper—relaxed, continuing your focus on the face of the clerk and describing him to Mr. Douet."

"Would you say that this gentleman has a wide neck or thin neck?" Douet resumed, a face beginning to take shape on the sketch pad before him.

"About a medium neck. Yeah, it's about medium."

"Is his mouth wide from corner to corner? Or would you say his mouth is somewhat short?"

"No, it'd be more wide than short, but not wide. It'd be straight. It wouldn't be a . . . Yeah, just a straight mouth."

"Between his eyes, is there . . . Would you say there's a . . . Were his eyes a normal distance apart from each other?"

"No. They're normal. And they, you know, they may be just a little wider than normal. But they're close to normal."

"Would you say his eyes matched his hair—being dark— or would you say he had light eyes—gray eyes, blue eyes?"

Mogoyne frowned in concentration. He rocked back in his chair, saying nothing.

"That's very good, Jerry, very good," Weathers spoke again. "Looking at his eyes now, can you tell what color his eyes are?"

Mogoyne continued to rock in silence.

"That's fine. That's fine," Weathers whispered soothingly. "Can you distinguish if they are dark or light? His eyes— are they dark or light?"

"Mogoyne's brow furrowed, the lines deepening like ruts

on a construction site after a weekend of rain. The metronome ticked on.

"You are doing very good," Weathers insisted. "In just a moment I am going to count from three to zero. When I reach zero, I want you to turn and look at your father and focus clearly on his face. You see your father's face very clearly. Three, two, one, zero."

Mogoyne stared into the middle distance, expressionless.

"When you are focusing on your father's face clearly, raise the index finger of your right hand," Weathers commanded him. Mogoyne complied.

Weathers went on. "When I say 'now,' I want you to turn back and look at the clerk once again, this time focusing even more clearly than ever before, while you continue to relax with each sound that you hear. Now. He is much more clear than before. Can you describe his eyes as to their size or anything that might be different about his eyes from anyone else's?"

"No."

"Looking now at his forehead from his hairline down to his eyes, describe what you see."

"Nothing abnormal. The distance is normal. The hairline doesn't . . . The hair is all the way across the head."

"From side to side?" Weathers asked. "Does the forehead appear to be narrow or wide?"

"Wider than narrower than normal. Not . . . It wouldn't be pointed or rounded. It would be square, but not, you know . . . Boxy, but not fully."

"Are there any lines in the forehead?"

"No."

"Can you describe his cheek and his cheekbones?" Weathers asked.

"They protrude. They have some definition under the cheek, under each cheek. Not puffy, just . . . I want to say the hair is kind of kinky or curly or wavy, but I can't do it. For some reason it doesn't . . . Maybe the way it's combed. He's not a big guy. About medium . . . Neat. Clean."

Ruiz, growing more and more certain that Mogoyne was describing Zani, shook his head in quiet amazement.

Weathers guided Mogoyne back to the inventory of the clerk's features. "Looking at his jaws—are they thin or wide?"

"Squared. Yeah. It's the boxy face. It just ties in. But it's not a mean . . . It's not a rough face."

"Can you see his ears?"

"Yeah. They're kind of flat. They're kind of . . . They don't protrude, and they're not high."

"Very good. Can you look now at his neck and tell me whether he has a long neck or a short neck?"

"It's about medium. It's, it's . . . like a sport shirt or a white shirt . . . Uh, collar fits in there."

"About how tall is this man compared to you?"

"He's about my height. Not heavy. Medium."

Ruiz, sitting against a bookshelf, shifted in his chair. Weathers was approaching the heart of the matter now, and Douet let his pencil hover slightly in anticipation of the next question.

"Now, as you look at the man, he is looking at you," Weathers continued, his words even and measured. "I want you to describe his eyes as he is looking at you."

Mogoyne wrinkled his brow. "Well, they don't . . . They aren't sunk in," he hesitated. "I can't see a color. I just . . . I don't see any more than that."

Weathers was now pacing around the room. When he spoke again, his voice came from another direction. "What about his complexion?" the ranger asked, trying to help Mogoyne arrive at a definitive description.

"Normal, Not dark, not light. Average."

Weathers stepped closer to Mogoyne's chair. "In just a moment, Jerry, I'm going to count from three to zero. When I reach zero, I want you to stay deeply relaxed just as you are, but I want you to open your eyes and look directly in front of you at the drawing that Mr. Douet is doing from your description. And as you look at the drawing—keeping crystal clear in your mind the picture of the clerk as you're looking at him—I want you to tell Mr. Douet any changes that you would like for him to make on the drawing and describe the features more fully as you picture in your mind's eye the clerk." Weathers counted backward from three to zero and asked Mogoyne to study the drawing.

"Yeah, yeah. The ears, they're perfect," Mogoyne said, studying the sketch. "The part, I . . . still doesn't come off. The hair looks good. The line looks good. The part—no, I don't remember that."

"Is the part more—" Weathers began to ask.

"I don't remember a part, actually," Mogoyne interrupted him. He studied the face emerging on Douet's sketch pad. "The lips . . . That little thing below the nose is good. The nose. Forehead."

"That's very, very good," Weathers said. "Looking at the eyes now, comparing the eyes on the drawing . . ." Weathers was trying one last time to establish an eye color.

"I, I . . . I really . . . I can't say about the color," Mogoyne apologized. "The whole deal looks good just like that."

"Looking at the eyebrows now . . . ," Weathers prompted him.

"They weren't heavy," Mogoyne replied, as Douet added some shading here, a line there. "They could be just a little heavier . . . Uh, okay. And he's got the curve over to the other side. Yeah . . . not much. Neat."

"Do you recall seeing any jewelry while you are looking at him now? Can you see any jewelry? Can you see his hands?"

"No."

"That's fine," Weathers whispered. "When I say 'now,' close your eyes, take one deep, deep breath, continuing to relax. Now. Continuing to look at the picture in your mind's eye of the clerk, you feel all the tiny muscles in your scalp becoming deeper and deeper relaxed, the muscles around your eyes relaxing even more, all the muscles in your neck becoming totally, completely relaxed."

Mogoyne tilted his head back and closed his eyes. Ruiz could see Mogoyne's shoulders react in almost imperceptible little shivers to each of the Texas Ranger's nonthreatening commands. Mogoyne's eyes closed tighter as Weathers continued: "Focusing on your father's face for just a few moments, I am going to count from three to zero. When I reach zero, you will look again at the clerk, and time will be standing dead still. It will be as if everything is completely out of focus to your eyes and your perception—except for the face of the clerk. And it will be very, very sharply focused. Clearly focused."

Weathers again counted down from three to zero. "Now I want you to describe to me the distance between the man's lips, his top lip and his nose," he said.

"Not long. It's not long enough to, say, have a long, heavy mustache. It's more shorter than long."

"Shorter distance than long distance?"

"Yeah. But it's not real short, either."

Weathers asked Mogoyne to open his eyes and study Douet's sketch once more, paying particular attention to the eyes this time.

"That's good, but . . ." Mogoyne hesitated.

"Is there anything you would like the artist to try with the eyes to see if it would look better to you, more like the clerk to you?" Weathers asked. "Does the drawing now look to you like the picture of the clerk in your mind's eye?"

'The part . . .," Mogoyne began, then faltered. He was still troubled by the part and the hairline of the face in the sketch. "I don't know what's happening to the hair," he complained, the frustration in his voice mounting.

"Should it be less defined?" asked Weathers. "Is the hair thin or thick?"

"You probably should remove that receding area towards the part," Mogoyne said. "And the hairline needs to be straighter."

Douet made the adjustment, but Mogoyne was still not

satisfied. "I don't know what happens to it up there," he said, gesturing to the top of the forehead.

Weathers tried to focus on the problem of the hairline with a number of pointed questions, but Mogoyne was unable to be more specific. Weathers moved him back in time to the point when Mogoyne and his father had first entered the store.

"I go straight to the cooler," Mogoyne said, "and I get out my . . . I think it's chocolate milk."

There were several moments of silence. Finally, Weathers decided that the session had gone on long enough. Counting slowly from ten to zero, he brought Mogoyne out of his hypnotic trance.

No one said a word as they marveled at the drawing on Douet's sketch pad. Ruiz thought about Mogoyne's difficulty in describing the clerk's hairline. If Zani had just chased Vizard around the storage cooler before executing him, he reasoned, his hair might be mussed sufficiently to have obscured his hairline when he emerged to find a customer at the register. All in all, it seemed, the hypnosis ploy had been quite helpful.

"I didn't go into the vault, I think, because I bought milk," Mogoyne said, commiserating with the others before heading back to his office. "Normally, when we went into this place, we went to the vault because the guy had his Cokes stacked in the aisles. We went to the vault because he would let us get the cold ones out of the cooler. But I think I bought milk that day. And milk would have been sitting right there at the front of the cooler."

If Jerry Mogoyne had followed his usual routine that distant Sunday morning, he would have entered the cooler—and discovered Vizard's body.

Ruiz reached into his briefcase and brought out the five color photographs that constituted his portable lineup, placing the photos one by one in front of Mogoyne. When he got to photo number 3, Mogoyne slapped his hand down on the table.

"That's it," he said excitedly. "That's the one."

Ruiz told him to take his time.

"That's him," Mogoyne repeated. "A little older, but that's him. I'm positive."

It was impossible for the five men gathered in Boulch's office that late afternoon not to see the remarkable resemblance of the face in the mug shot taken on the night of Zani's arrest in March to the face in Arthur Douet's sketch. The only difference between them was an interval of thirteen stark and unrelenting years.

Ad Ruiz drove back to Austin that night, he had little doubt that they had finally gathered the evidence they needed to press for an indictment against Robert Joseph Zani. Whether they had enough to convict him, however, was an entirely different question.

SEVENTEEN

Harlan Cooper. The more Joe Turner looked at the evidence, the more the name played in his mind. One of the seminal songwriters of the country-and-western music Turner so loved was Harlan Howard, a lumbering man who never quite achieved the acclaim he deserved for helping to put Nashville on the musical map. Turner knew it was strange, but he imagined Cooper to be a lumbering man as well, the two Harlans sharing physical characteristics as well as an unusual first name.

Harlan Cooper was in fact a slight, slender man with sandy-brown hair, blue eyes, and a passing interest in philosophy. In the early sixties he enrolled in UT's Plan II, a liberal arts program for honor students. According to those who knew him then, he was strange, a loner, the sort who shied away when the political debate inside the Chuck Wagon was at its most raucous. The original police report noted that potheads in the dorm knew Cooper as a small-time drug dealer who was "too squirrely" to get into the illicit trade in a serious way. Cooper, they imagined, went alone to midnight movies on campus, sitting in the back row and reading the credits aloud to invent companions for himself.

Just before the 1964 University of Texas–Oklahoma University football contest, an annual rivalry during which students took the opportunity to run wild in Dallas (midway between the two schools), Cooper gathered the courage to ask fellow student Nancy Clare to accompany him to the game. Clare already had a date but offered to fix him up with her friend Mariann Garner instead, and the two couples spent the weekend in the Dallas–Fort Worth area, staying overnight with Mariann's parents. Cooper seemed more interested in Clare, though everyone knew he had an on-again, off-again relationship with the daughter of a UT professor. At any rate, there wasn't much hope for a long-term commitment, and Mariann went out with him only one other time.

Now assistant DA Joe Turner's instincts told him that the man who had phoned in the report about the conversation he had with Zani and Robert Riggs in the Chuck Wagon one or two nights before the murder—page 39 of APD's offense report—was a pivotal character in the investigation. He decided to track Cooper down.

Meanwhile, Ruiz and Martinez were running checks on Charles Robert Riggs. They found him in Bastrop, a small town about twenty-five miles southeast of Austin. Riggs recalled Vizard and the feeling on campus that his murder was motivated by more than simple robbery. As a member of Young Americans for Freedom, Riggs had often argued with Vizard in the Chuck Wagon, where, he said, those who were involved in political movements met to "solve the world's problems" over cups of watered-down coffee. The name "Zani" failed to ring a bell with Riggs, but he was willing to submit to hypnosis if it might refresh his memory.

For three hours on August 26, Texas Ranger Joe Davis attempted without success to take Riggs under at DPS headquarters in Austin. Riggs apologized, complaining that he was distracted by the death of his three-year-old son in January and the fact that he was unemployed. He would like to try again and would even take a polygraph test to prove that he wasn't just another uncooperative witness.

Two days later, Ruiz and Martinez met him at the offices of Doug Farris, Austin's premier polygrapher. Farris spent more than two hours with Riggs and concluded that he was telling the truth when he claimed not to remember the meeting in the Chuck Wagon. Beyond that, however, the results were inconclusive.

A third session, conducted by local hypnotist Jerry Don Roberts, led to the conclusion that Riggs recalled the meeting but was hesitant to identify Zani and Cooper. Roberts suggested another visit, reminding the officers of his fee, but Ruiz and Martinez chose not to pursue it. As they left, they heard Riggs making an appointment for later in the week to work on "some personal problems" at his own expense. Although the investigators hadn't really cleared Riggs—could he have been the other person in the store with Zani on that distant Sunday morning?—they agreed that his willingness to cooperate spoke well for him.

Turner now insisted that the time had come to contact Cooper, whom he had already traced to Falls Church, Virginia. Ruiz and Martinez quickly placed the call. When Cooper came on the line, the officers explained that they were investigating a 1967 homicide and that his name had surfaced in connection with it. At first, Cooper, who took great pains to remind the officers that he was an "independent consultant for higher education," admitted to only a vague recollection of Riggs—perhaps as a professor of philosophy, he wasn't sure. They could hear what sounded like puffing on a pipe during the long pauses before he reluctantly answered each question.

After persistent peppering, however, Cooper's memory improved. Oh, yeah—*that* Robert Riggs. Sure, he said, they had shared a dorm just off campus back in '64. Riggs was usually broke, despite a job as grounds keeper and janitor at the UT football stadium. He was a very religious person, too, always talking about rushing off to India or some other exotic locale to study nonviolence—not that a couple of cops would understand such interests, of course. Furthermore,

Cooper said, his voice haughty and bothered, he had left Austin in 1968 and had never seen Riggs again, except for an encounter on a city bus during a brief return visit four years later. Even then, they had just exchanged greetings and gone their separate ways, nothing more. As for phoning APD three days after the Vizard murder, Cooper had no recollection of it.

Ruiz and Martinez hung up and rolled their eyes at each other. How many times does someone call the police to offer a tip in a murder investigation? Whether it was thirteen years ago or thirty years ago, it isn't something a person is likely to forget, they told themselves.

Turner agreed. He urged Ruiz to call Cooper at home again. In the meantime, Martinez checked with UT and discovered that Cooper and Zani had been enrolled in an English-Russian literature course together, a class that usually drew only a handful of students with a shared interest. Now they wanted to find out what else Cooper might know about Zani. Ruiz asked him to agree to both a hypnosis and a polygraph session to be administered by an investigator from the Falls Church Police Department, but Cooper was uncooperative. He no longer wished to be involved, he said flatly. Not only was he skeptical about hypnosis, but the results of polygraph tests were rarely admissible in a court of law. Why should he waste his time?

When Ruiz and Martinez reported to Turner, the assistant DA was livid. "Let's turn the snide motherfucker around," he said, reaching for the phone to make airline reservations. All three were beginning to harbor the same thought: Cooper may well have been the young man in the Town and Country with Zani on July 23, 1967. They needed to confront him face-to-face, Turner argued, by going to Virginia. At least then Cooper might understand that this was a murder case, something that was going to haunt him if he didn't come clean.

On November 19, 1980, Turner and Ruiz deplaned in Washington, D.C., and caught a cab across the Potomac to

Falls Church, where they checked into a hotel. Because it was too late to drop in on Cooper, they ambled down to the nightclub in the lobby. Turner struck up a conversation with a young woman and spent the next few hours teaching her the cotton-eyed Joe and other country-and-western dances. Ruiz sat glumly at the table, sipping white wine and wondering what they would find when they dropped in on Cooper the following day.

Cooper and his family lived in a Tudor-style home on an upper-middle-class street just outside the Beltway, where federal employees and the consultants who feed off the huge carcass of public policy in the nation's capital return each night. Turner and Ruiz arrived at the house in the early evening. They were greeted at the door by Cooper's wife, a petite woman who invited them in and offered them tea or soft drinks, explaining that her husband was due home from the office at any moment. Turner was reminded of June Cleaver, Ruiz of Betty Crocker, as they watched Mrs. Cooper bustle nervously around the living room. She was pleasant enough, though each sensed that she was only reluctantly playing the role of hostess. It was clear their presence was an unwelcome disruption in her family's middle-class life.

When Cooper arrived, they understood why. Dressed in a dark suit, his hair graying at the temples, the former UT student was surprised to find Turner and Ruiz waiting for him. Without removing his jacket, he took a seat and again displayed what the Texans regarded as a remarkably poor memory. He didn't remember a thing, he repeated. The names "Zani" and "Vizard" meant nothing to him. He had never phoned the police about anything, much less a murder. And he grew increasingly uncomfortable when the questions began to touch on his relationship with Mariann. Turner and Ruiz noticed that Mrs. Cooper kept shooting stern looks in her husband's direction, and they knew intuitively that she was unaware of his college days, when, according to the police report, he had been a small-time dope dealer operating on the fringes of radical politics.

"I read her like a book," Ruiz later recalled. "She may have been petite, but she held his nuts in her hands—very domineering, in a subtle way. Every time he said something, she would look at him as if to say, 'Watch your *p's* an *q's*, buddy.'"

The investigators knew they were going to have to get Cooper away from his wife if they hoped to open him up. When she left the room for a moment to freshen their drinks, Turner leaned in toward Cooper. "Listen," he said, "we're working on a murder case here. You're a citizen, and you would like to help us, wouldn't you?"

"Yes," Cooper allowed, nodding slightly.

"Well, then, what's the problem?" Turner asked. "We've flown all the way from Austin because you're important to the case. Do you understand that without your help, this murderer might walk free?"

Cooper seemed to waver but again became impassive as his wife returned to the room. Finally, Turner and Ruiz stood to leave, thanking Mrs. Cooper for her cool hospitality. The second round of refreshments sat untouched on the coffee table as they climbed into their rented car and drove to the Falls Church Police Department. Once there, Turner placed a call to the Cooper home and was relieved when Harlan answered the phone instead of his wife. They had a detective standing by to strap him to a polygraph machine, Turner explained, and they would appreciate it if Cooper would come down to the station right away.

"Let me think about it," Cooper whispered.

They were all a little surprised when he showed up a few minutes later. In the harsh light of police headquarters, however, Cooper underwent a change of heart. He again expressed his reservations about the admissibility of polygraph tests, but Turner suggested he leave the legal interpretations to the judge. Cooper was unswayed. Turner reminded him that a subpoena could be issued compelling him to testify. But after an hour, the meeting ended badly, with Cooper driving off into the night and the Texans heading to their hotel room, having been unable to turn the one witness who they were certain could have clinched their case.

On the flight back to Austin, Turner and Ruiz discussed the visit to Virginia. The assistant DA believed that Cooper had been walking an extremely fine line between failing to cooperate and trying to placate them enough that they would leave him alone. Ruiz was angrier, convinced that Cooper had something to hide. But one thing was certain: If they ever proved Cooper was involved in George Vizard's death, he could be prosecuted at any time in the future. There was no statute of limitation for murder.

By now Turner was as thoroughly caught up in the case as Ruiz and Martinez. Like them, he worked impossibly long hours, trying to puzzle out the mysteries that remained. But he came at the task from a slightly different angle. Not only did he want to know every fact, but he also wanted to thread them together in a way that would make sense to a jury. Judge Jim Dear had set an Austin trial date for the next week, and Turner didn't feel ready.

"I wanted to shore up the circumstantial evidence we had," Turner later recalled. "Someone else might have said, 'Hey, we have prints, we have an eyewitness, we even have a possible ballistics match.' But the case was thirteen years old. The ballistics didn't prove it beyond a reasonable doubt, and the eyewitness was tied up in the legally untested realm of hypnosis. Other prosecutors might have been willing to go on it, but I wanted everything."

A number of vital questions begged answers, including where Robert Zani was living at the time of the murder. As Turner saw it, the Town and Country was located at what had then been the northwest edge of Austin, far removed from the hub of university life and, thus, a unlikely stop for a college student on an early Sunday morning. It was not a store you ran up to for a loaf of bread, he argued, unless you lived right around the corner. It was crucial to pin down the suspect's address on July 23, 1967. For that, they needed time—and only Zani could give it to them.

Meanwhile, Zani was threatening to represent himself at trial. During the nearly eight months of his incarceration, he had refused to cooperate with a succession of court-appointed attorneys, dismissing them one after the other when they failed to meet his standards. Each time, Dear had moved the trial date back to give the new lawyer time to prepare. On November 13, Zani's latest attorney, David Allen Smith, had filed a motion for continuance, maintaining that he too needed time to bring himself up to speed, and as expected, Dear had granted it. Though incensed at the classic delaying tactic, Turner had to admit that the extra time helped him as well.

Now, however, Turner suspected that the judge's patience was nearly exhausted. The state legislature had recently passed the Speedy Trial Act, which allowed the prosecution a maximum of 120 days to get ready for trial; any case exceeding that limit could conceivably be thrown out of court. Though the act was eventually ruled unconstitutional, Texas judges in late 1980 were dismissing entire dockets that failed to comply with the strict time rules.

Turner desperately wanted to move for a continuance, pushing the starting date of the trial back by at least a few weeks. But he knew that the defendant's long months in custody—as well as Zani's contentious nature—worked against him. Consulting with Ralph Graham, a bright, young assistant district attorney who had been assigned to serve as his co-counsel, Turner reviewed their options. If they moved for a continuance, he guessed, Zani would almost certainly object, whereupon Dear might grant the defendant an immediate trial date—for which Turner and Graham were unprepared. Even if their motion was granted, he added, any possible murder conviction could eventually be overturned. The Speedy Trial Act was untested terrain for lawyers and judges, none of whom wanted to see their cases batted down on appeal by some inadvertent failure to comply with the latest legal wrinkle on the books.

"Look," Turner told Graham, "if we move for a continuance, Zani will oppose it. So this is what we do: We go into the pretrial hearing and say, 'This has gone on long enough. The defendant is delaying his own trial by filing motion after motion and dismissing his court-appointed attorneys every week or two. We're ready to go to trial—right now.' "

It was a high-stakes gamble, but it worked. As soon as Turner moved for an immediate trial date, Zani jumped up in protest. He wasn't ready, he complained. He was seriously considering the possibility of representing himself, and he needed more time to investigate his options, more time in the law library, more time—period. Judge Dear listened with a sympathetic ear as Zani himself moved for the continuance Turner wanted. "Granted," Dear said at last.

Turner's gamble had brought them time, but it was up to Ruiz and Martinez to put it to good use. They already knew that Zani had lived in a couple of campus dorms and a nearby rooming house during his college years. But the typical student's mobility and Zani's particular penchant for secrecy combined to make it almost impossible to pinpoint his residence in any given month.

The officers went to the public library, where they found a copy of the 1967 Austin telephone directory listing Zani's address as Rural Route 5, Box 371G. Using an old city map, they learned that Rural Route 5 was a tree-lined street in the far southeastern reaches of town. It had since been renamed Bluff Springs Road, caught in the throes of the development taking place all over Austin. Next they scoured records in the office of the municipal utility company and discovered that Zani had paid utilities at that address—the second in a row of eight tumbledown cottages on a quiet dirt lane—from February 14 through September 27, 1967. In fact, he still owed $10.93 and $8.18 from two outstanding bills. Turner's hunch had paid off. Not only did Zani not live near the Town and Country at the time of the murder, but he also lived about as far across town as one could get in those days and still be inside the city limits.

Ruiz and Martinez tried to contact those who had occupied the other seven houses during 1967. It was a painstaking task. Some still lived in Austin, others had long since moved away, and none had any special recollection of their former neighbor, except that he drove a sky-blue VW. The officers even interviewed a handful of letter carriers who had worked the route in the late sixties. They offered no real help, so the investigators shifted their attention to Zani's former co-workers at the UT library. One recalled often talking with Zani during lunch breaks and said that Zani had once mentioned he was having trouble getting a visa for his Mexican wife or girlfriend—she couldn't remember which. Another said she had taken to avoiding conversation with Zani because he was "so emotional." Still another recalled that Zani had disappeared for a time; when he returned, he was distressed by a family financial problem—he needed money to hire an immigration lawyer, he had said.

By the beginning of December, Ruiz and Martinez had followed so many leads that they began to slip into their "Amos 'n' Andy" routine on a regular basis: "Oh, noooh, Andy. Not another rabbit tail." In addition, the continuing press coverage of the investigation had brought a growing number of requests from reporters for interviews, and the officers found themselves answering more and more queries from police agencies across the nation who wanted background information on Zani in connection with their local crimes. Some days, it seemed, the toughest part of their job was simply finding the time to be a cop.

The Rhode Island State Police suspected that Zani might know something about the murder of Edna MacDonald, fifty-two, found strangled with her own nylons and hanged in the basement of an unoccupied home in the city of

Barrington. The police in Burlington, Iowa, wanted to question him regarding the 1969 murder of a forty-eight-year-old realtor named Dorothy Miller, who had been raped, stabbed twenty-three times with a pocketknife, and hanged after being lured to a vacant home by a man who gave his name either as Robert Clark or Clark Robert and drove a black Ford Econoline.

El Paso authorities were thinking of reopening an investigation of Zani for allegedly forging a $1,000 check at a local bank in the early seventies. From Fort Worth came word that Zani had been arrested in 1973 for cashing bad checks. A supervisor with the Church's Fried Chicken fast-food franchise in Corpus Christi called to say that Zani—he knew him as Bob—had worked there back in the early seventies but abruptly left town after $2,000 vanished during a faked armed robbery on Zani's shift. Authorities in Moore, Oklahoma, and Magnolia, Arkansas, were still pursuing leads in the murder of realtor Bobby Gene Thomas and the disappearance of Bobo Schinn, respectively. And even the National Defense Student Loan Program got into the act, wondering when it might expect payment of a $300 loan made to Zani in the sixties.

All very interesting, Turner agreed after hearing the reports. But he was trying to build a specific prosecution in Travis County, and such far-flung developments only muddled up his efforts to present a jury with clear choices in an admittedly complex case. He encouraged Ruiz and Martinez to focus on evidence directly related to the killing of George Vizard.

A small break came on December 6, 1980, when Ruiz received a call from Paul Landsfair. Landsfair lived in California, he explained, but had been told by a friend that the Austin police were holding Robert Zani as a suspect in the Vizard murder. He wanted to talk because he and Zani had been pals from 1964 until March 1968, when Landsfair left to join the marines. *Finally,* Ruiz thought, *someone who actually knew Zani at the time of the killing.* He grabbed a pad and pencil and told Landsfair to go ahead.

They had met on campus, Landsfair said, and spent many an evening in the Chuck Wagon. Zani was quick-tempered and aloof, usually hovering at the periphery of the political discussions taking place. He carried a Ruger .357 in a briefcase and often showed it off to the group around the table.

"How do you know what kind of weapon it was?" Ruiz asked.

"Because I had one just like it," Landsfair assured him, "a gift from my father."

What was more, during the Whitman incident, Landsfair and several friends had been pinned down on a sidewalk just off campus by the gunfire. He remembered how they wondered if Zani might be the maniac on the tower. He was that strange, Landsfair stated. If Ruiz wished to know more, he should contact Edward Carl Groscurth, Tom Jacob, and Walter DeBill, three of Zani's closest college buddies during those years.

Ruiz thanked him, cradled the receiver, and immediately ordered traces on all three men. Two days later, he received a report that Groscurth had died the month before in a traffic accident outside Boulder, Colorado. Jacob and DeBill, however, were very much alive.

He got in touch with DeBill first. A computer programmer in the Veterans Administration's Austin office, DeBill was more than willing to cooperate when Ruiz called him on December 12. Sure, he had known Zani back in school. They weren't close—Zani wasn't the sort you ever really got close to, he explained—but they had hung around some. DeBill recalled helping Zani distribute leaflets during his campaign for student-body president. DeBill planted himself in the audience to shout friendly questions when his friend debated the other candidates on the steps at the base of the UT Tower.

Once, DeBill and his wife, Stacia, had visited Zani at his house, a rickety wood cabin on what was now called Bluff Springs Road. He remembered seeing an accordion propped in a corner of the room and sheet music for "Lady of Spain" on the floor. The kitchen sink was piled high with dirty dishes, and several oily .357 ammunition shells sat on a grimy tablecloth. Later that day, they had gone outside to take target practice, firing at a five-gallon jug balanced on some old railroad ties. DeBill smiled at the memory of what a poor shot Zani was.

Stacia DeBill's recall paralleled her husband's, but she had a few details to add. Zani had gone off to Mexico during the summer of '67 to get married; his mother had come to Austin looking for him a short time later, without success; and during that same period, word had made the rounds that Zani was responsible for shooting up a car belonging to a fraternity member. "He hated frat rats," Mrs. DeBill confided.

On December 16, Ruiz phoned Tom Jacob, a professor at UT-Dallas. Yes, Jacob said, he too knew Zani, who had been introduced to him by a mutual friend, Paul Landsfair. They all used to get together at the Chuck Wagon, Jacob said, where Zani impressed everyone as a weird, ultraconservative individual. Zani and Landsfair were gun freaks; they each owned .357 magnums, which they weren't reluctant to display to those gathered around the table, where the conversation usually revolved around politics and the "damn fraternities."

As the pace of the city slackened in anticipation of the 1980 Christmas season, Ruiz, Martinez, and Turner took stock of where they stood. The assistant DA repeatedly insisted that building a circumstantial murder case was like erecting a wall—one brick at a time. He was satisfied that the first brick had now been securely put in place.

"Brick number one," he said aloud, unconsciously parroting Zani's manner of presenting his myriad motions in court, "where did the sonuvabitch live at the time of the murder? We've answered that. He lived all the way across town—and you don't drive from Southeast Austin to Northwest Austin on an early Sunday morning to get some Twinkies, right?

"Brick number two: the eyewitness. We know that Vizard was supposed to have been the clerk in the store the morning of July 23, and we've got Jerry Mogoyne, Jr., saying that the guy who waited on him was not Vizard but someone who bore a remarkable resemblance to Zani.

"Brick number three: motive. Zani needed money to pay an immigration attorney to help get his wife into the country legally—and what more time-honored way is there to pick up a little cash than by knocking off a convenience store?

"Brick number four: the fingerprints. Zani's prints were all over the items on the counter that morning—strong evidence that places him at the scene. But it doesn't prove beyond a reasonable doubt that he didn't just wander into the store several days earlier on his way to the lake or something. After all, how many dozens of other folks could have touched those same items sitting on the shelves in the days leading up to the murder?"

Ruiz and Martinez understood what Turner was getting at. Somehow they were going to have to place Zani in the store *on the day of the murder*.

They decided to try to establish where Zani had banked in July 1967 and then subpoena his records; perhaps they would get lucky and pick up a paper trail linking him to the Town and Country. Returning to the old telephone directory at the library, Ruiz and Martinez compiled a list of the eight Austin banks in operation at the time. After calling those that were still in business and tracing the new names of the banks that had since been rechartered, they narrowed the list to one. Turner immediately issued a subpoena.

In the pile of papers that arrived a few days later, the officers discovered two personal checks cashed at the Town and Country store on Northland Drive. Dated June 2 and June 5, 1967, each sported a rubber-stamp impression on the back with spaces to note the customer's driver's license number, telephone, and other personal information. On a line labeled "Taken by" were the initials. "R.J.Z."

It was incredible, they admitted, but Ruiz, Martinez, and Turner couldn't squelch the growing suspicion they now harbored. Employees, not customers, were supposed to fill out the backs of personal checks. Was it possible that Robert Joseph Zani had actually worked at the Town and Country in the beginning of June 1967, just six and a half weeks before Vizard's murder? If so, it would explain why he drove clear across town on a Sunday morning—because he knew the routine at the store and he knew the combination to the safe. It was just a gut feeling, and it would take a lot of work to prove. But they hadn't come this far by sitting on their butts.

Ruiz placed the first telephone call in the tenth month of the investigation—January 1981—to William Longshore, the former owner of the Town and Country convenience store chain. Longshore explained that in December 1966, he had sold all eighteen Austin locations to Stop and Go Markets of Texas, whose corporate headquarters were in Houston, though the name change at individual stores was not completed for another year. He had no records dating from that time, Longshore apologized, but he supplied the names of several past and present employees who might be able to help.

Ruiz and Martinez sat back, prepared to work their way slowly through the long list. On the very next call, however, they got close. Chuck Dinges, whom they knew from the original offense report as a Town and Country district manager at the time of the killing, wasn't sure, but he thought he remembered the name "Robert Zani." In late May 1967, Dinges had been promoted, he said. A few days later, about the beginning of June, he hired his friend Tom Mantle to manage the store on Northland. Mantle in turn hired his own friend George Vizard to work the three-to-eleven shift. As for Zani, it seemed to Dinges that he might have carried around an employee check issued to Zani, which he returned to the main office in Houston when the guy failed to come by for it after several weeks. It would not have been unusual for Mantle to hire someone like Zani part-time, particularly in the summer months, when store traffic increased with people headed to the lake.

By the way, Dinges added, they should get in touch with Manuel Flores. Flores, who preferred to go by the name "Manny Flowers," had also been a Town and Country district manager at the time; if anyone could help them, ol' Manny could.

The next call was to Tom Mantle, who had quit his job as manager of the Town and Country immediately after the murder, moved with his wife to San Francisco, and, after their divorce, wound up in Las Vegas, California, where he struggled to make a living as a musician and jewelry maker. Mantle's memory in early 1981 was consistent with what he had told the original investigators nearly fourteen years before, but he really couldn't add anything new. He suggested they contact Manny Flowers or Ray Pannell, who had been a senior supervisor for Town and Country and Dinges's immediate boss back in July 1967.

After several more calls, Ruiz and Martinez got in touch with Pannell, who was now retired and living in Irving, Texas. Pannell remembered the murder well because of what he described as the "Marxist literature" found in the store afterward. He also recalled his doubts that it had been a simple robbery. The register tape was gone, Pannell explained, and the safe mounted in a concrete block beneath the register showed no signs of forcible entry even though Saturday's receipts—"at least $1,500"—had been taken. Ruiz and Martinez thought back to the original investigation, at which time Dinges had stated that little or no money was missing.

On January 14, Ruiz and Martinez met with Pannell in his Irving home. During the three-hour visit, they learned more than they ever wanted to know about the inner workings of a convenience store. They hauled out their portable lineup again, having replaced the mug shot taken on the night of Zani's arrest with a photo supplied by Vera Tolbert picturing Zani in a bow tie around the time of his high school graduation, and showed Pannell the photographs. Pannell quickly pointed to Zani's, although he couldn't be positive they had ever met. Before they left, Pannell too suggested they contact Manny Flowers.

That was easier said than done. Flowers had left Austin in the late sixties for Nashville, Tennessee, where he continued to work for Stop and Go. Next he had been transferred to Ohio, but authorities there were unable to trace him. While Ruiz worked down the list of names supplied by Longshore, Martinez tried to track Flowers through every state and national organization he could think of. Finally, on January 20, he located Flowers in Lumberton, Texas, just north of Beaumont, where he had taken a job as vice president of operations for the Bell Oil Company.

Flowers was shocked to hear from the officers. Yes, he remembered the murder and had even attended Vizard's funeral service, but the name "Robert Zani" meant nothing to him. Asked whether Town and Country employees had been in the habit of cashing personal checks for customers, he said that the normal procedure called for the store manager to approve it first. When Ruiz and Martinez mentioned they had uncovered two personal checks signed by Zani, made out to Zani, and approved by Zani, Flowers suggested that it would be unusual for either an employee or a customer to approve his own check, though it probably had happened more frequently than he would have wished back then. Finally, Flowers confirmed that Town and Country managers were permitted to hire part-time help on an ad hoc basis in 1967, usually UT students who worked evenings and weekends for minimum wage. Record keeping for those folks was especially lax because the corporation wasn't overenthusiastic about filing W-2 forms with the IRS for every Tom, Dick, and Harry who happened to work a week or two behind the register.

A sense of frenzy had set into the lives of Ruiz, Martinez, and Turner by the beginning of February, 1981. Judge Dear's latest trial date, February 9, was only a week off, and despite their gut feelings, it was abundantly clear they were never going to prove conclusively that Zani had ever worked in the Town and Country on Northland Drive. Turner especially had taken to pulling out clumps of hair as he envisioned facing a jury without brick number 4—why were Zani's fingerprints at the scene?—firmly mortared into place. There was only one thing to do. They had to show that there was no reasonable explanation for Zani to have left his prints unless he went there to kill George Vizard with three shots from a .357 at close range.

With Turner phoning once every hour or so to check on the progress, and Martinez tracking phone numbers as he hovered over Ruiz's shoulder, Ruiz called and recalled witnesses. From Pannell in Irving, he learned that bread deliveries at the Town and Country were designed to make sure the stock turned over daily. Bread never stayed on the shelf longer than one day, Pannell said. As a safeguard, the loaves were coded so that both the routeman and the store clerk could tell at a glance if a day-old delivery had inadvertently been left behind. As for the items found on the counter after the murder, store clerks were expected to clear the register area of merchandise every night before closing.

John Wesley Marshall, a retired salesman for Mrs. Baird's bakery in Austin, recalled the murder at the Town and Country because it happened the day after he left on vacation. Marshall worked six days a week, with Wednesdays off, delivering bread each morning between six and seven o'clock, including Sundays. The clerk who was usually on duty at the convenience store was a young man with dark hair, glasses, and a mustache that "came off and on about as often as a whore's panties." It was unclear whether Marshall was describing Mantle or Vizard, but he remembered the clerk because they sometimes argued politics while Marshall stocked the shelves. As far as who had taken over his route when he went on vacation, it was probably a choice between two men: Lloyd Heckman and Tom Erdman, the swing-shift guys.

Martinez found a phone number for Heckman in Corpus Christi, and Ruiz placed the call. It had been a lot of years, Heckman said, but he was pretty certain he hadn't filled in for Marshall on July 23, 1967. That left Erdman, who was quickly located in Plano, Texas. Erdman remembered working the route every third Sunday of the month, and because July 23 was the fourth Sunday, he was probably not their man, either. But company policy called for the routeman to fill out a receipt and get the store clerk's signature after each delivery. If the officers would send him a copy of the receipt for that morning, he would tell them for sure; all he had to do was look at the handwriting on it.

When Ruiz hung up and reported the conversation to his partner, Martinez was flabbergasted. Receipt? Of course, he exclaimed, pounding his forehead with his palm. As a former grocery store manager, he should have known that whoever was on duty in the store that morning had been asked to sign for the bread delivery. Frantically, the officers searched through the evidence not included with the original offense report to see if they had overlooked anything. There they found the receipt clipped to an affidavit taken on July 28, 1967, from one John Henry Maddox, a Town and Country clerk who worked at another location but was called to the Northland Drive store on the day after the murder to fill in for Mantle, who had taken time off to help Mariann make funeral arrangements. The receipt was dated July 22, but Maddox's attached statement explained that he had actually signed it on July 24.

Turner was disappointed. The misdated receipt failed to prove a thing and, in fact, raised more questions than it answered. Was the bread delivered on Saturday but signed for on Monday, contrary to routine? If so, why? Had the routeman filling in for Marshall forgotten to have the clerk sign the receipt on Saturday? Had he hoped to correct the oversight on Monday, when Maddox happened to be in the store? Did Maddox merely sign for the regular Monday delivery as he was supposed to, in which case the receipt was dated wrong? Or was it possible no bread was delivered on Sunday at all—either because Vizard arrived late to open the store or was already dead on the floor of the walk-in cooler?

In any case, Turner concluded, they were going to have to run with Pannell's story before the jury. Bread was delivered daily, precluding the possibility that Zani's prints were left on the loaf of Mrs. Baird's bread the previous night. That would have to be that.

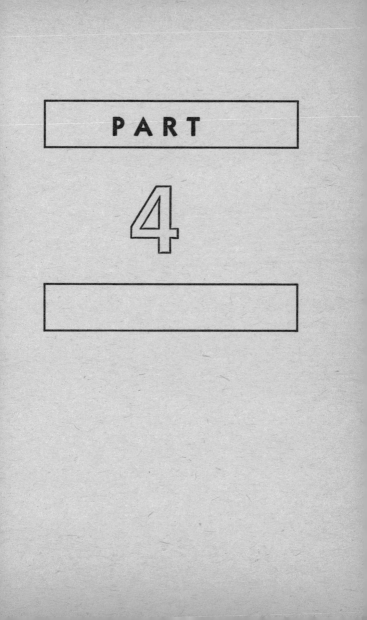

PART

4

EIGHTEEN

Texans are known for having a particularly vicious view of the criminal—as long as he remains at large. Once arrested, though, the defendant acquires a face. His picture appears on the news, his name in the press. He is shown being led in shackles from the jail to the courtroom, his eyes downcast, his demeanor filled with an underdog's understanding that the system now holding him captive lacks even the slightest concern for mending the cracks in his existence. That's when the sympathy syndrome kicks in, public pity replacing hatred.

To a DA, a reputation for being tough on crime rather than vindictive toward criminals can make all the difference at the polls. The DA's prosecutors are therefore under an unspoken pressure to go easy on suspects, finding it prudent to avoid actions that might cast their elected boss as a bully. Not only are they bound by law and professional ethics to be reasonably certain of a defendant's guilt before bringing him to trial, but they must also provide the defense with any evidence that even suggests innocence—because prosecutors have as much obligation to the accused as to the state, their oaths commanding them "not to prosecute, but to see that justice is done." Such constraints, further encouraged by an attitude at the appeals-court level that no defendant be unduly detained or inconvenienced at the time of his arrest, make the job for prosecutors like Joe Turner difficult.

By contrast, defense lawyers have only one obligation: to defend their client. They regularly defend the guilty, and nothing in the law or professional ethics requires them to bring a scrap of evidence to the attention of the prosecution. Even if a murderer confesses his guilt privately, his lawyer is still allowed to plead him not guilty and fight to have him freed.

Roy Greenwood and Patrick Ganne, Zani's latest court-appointed attorneys, seemed especially equal to these standards. Greenwood, big and tall and given to the garish ties and pin-striped suits that matched Hollywood's stereotype of the defense lawyer, was a longtime staffer at the Texas Court of Criminal Appeals—a man, many said, who never should have strayed from the appeals process, where his real expertise lay. As for Ganne, he had honed his reputation to an even split between those who said he tended to pick up a file and try a case with little preparation and those who admired his ability to play to a jury's sympathies.

As case number 61,076 came to trial in Judge Jim Dear's 126th judicial courtroom on Monday, March 9, 1981, two things became clear. The first was that, as lead counsel, Greenwood regarded the proceedings as a test of the merits of hypnotically induced testimony—a case that would put his name, if he prevailed, in the record books for all time. The second was that Ganne should have been lead counsel. In either case, Zani seemed ill served.

The first two days of the trial were consumed by voir dire, the tedious task of jury selection. Aware that the case was close, Turner seized the initiative. Most trials, he believed, were won not during dramatic final arguments, as shown in the movies, but at the outset, when jurors got their first look at the attorneys in the case and made up their minds whom they would trust. Turner wanted an older jury, weighted with women, because experience had taught him that he enjoyed a natural rapport with such people. But he also wanted at least one person on the panel who might emerge as a leader, someone familiar enough with the law to guide the others, once they retired to deliberate, through the complex evidence and legal arguments presented during the trial. Turner hoped to establish momentum early and instill a sense of common mission, then "play the jury like a symphony" until they were left with no alternative but a guilty verdict.

For many of the abnormally large panel of sixty-three prospective jurors, the sketch of the case they received during voir dire brought back memories of their own college days. Others viewed the times from a different generation, recalling the exploits of their children. One man was excused because he had known George Vizard, another because he used to hang out at the Chuck Wagon and argue with SDSers and other student activists. A woman was dismissed because she was eight months pregnant, another because she believed that evidence obtained through hypnosis was inherently untrustworthy, still another because she was morally opposed to life sentences. No one had to wrestle with his conscience regarding capital punishment, however; Zani had already exercised his legal right to be sentenced, if convicted, under the penal code in force at the time of the murder, which precluded the death penalty.

In the end, twelve Austinites were selected to serve on the jury of what had already become one of the most talked-about murder trials in Austin history. Turner took one look at them and smiled. He had his panel: ten older women and two men, one of whom was a lawyer. Turner then reached two decisions he had been mulling over for months. First, he would leave the politics aside and prosecute the case as a straight robbery-homicide; it may not be as sexy, but these jurors were unlikely to feel much sympathy for a victim who had been a member of both the SDS and the Communist party. Second, he would meet the issue of hypnosis head-on because that was where he expected Greenwood to mount the strongest attack.

Judge Jim Dear was not about to yield control of his courtroom to the brash young assistant DA without a fight, however. In his late thirties, Dear already affected the country-lawyer mannerisms associated with Senate Watergate Committee chairman Sam Ervin and other old-timers. "I'm way behind you," he would admonish lawyers appearing before him. "I'm a country boy, a little bit slow." A former justice of the peace and county court-at-law judge, Dear in fact derived much of his considerable power as a political mover from his friendship with federal district judge Jack Roberts and longtime local attorney Paul Holt, with whom he played dominoes several times each week. Many assumed he was first in line to replace the aging Roberts, and Dear did little to discourage them. Dear had a flair for the dramatice and was not against reminding lawyers in his courtroom just who was running the show.

Some thought Dear had displayed inordinate restraint toward Zani during the endless pretrial hearings of the past year. It was a once-in-a-lifetime case, and if it took a lifetime to bring to trial, so be it, he said. He had endured frequent outbursts from the defendant, patiently explained the law to him, and entertained countless oblique motions. Now Dear was prepared to spend eight or nine hours a day over the next week and a half with a parade of witnesses rumored to number over fifty. "Obviously," he joked to a colleague, "both sides intend to try this case by inundation."

On Wednesday morning, March 11, Dear called for a final pretrial hearing to decide the merits of hypnotically induced testimony in general and, specifically, whether Zani should have been allowed to have an attorney present during Jerry Mogoyne, Jr.'s hypnosis session. Turner introduced his first witness: James Michael Boulch. With the jury out of the room, Turner took Boulch through a detailed description of the dangers and benefits of hypnosis, a trancelike recitation that inadvertently pushed the bailiff to the brink of sleep.

Then, for the next hour and a half, Greenwood pressed the hypnotist on the details of the session with Mogoyne back in September. Did Texas Ranger Carl Weathers, Boulch's student and the man who conducted the session, have any prior knowledge about the case? Had anyone involved shown Mogoyne a photograph of the suspect or in any way prejudiced the hypnosis session? Were the questions that sketch artist Arthur Douet directly asked Mogoyne standard procedure during a session? Boulch was adamant. Hypnosis was a reliable investigative tool, and this particular session had been conducted according to the strictest standards. Even under questioning by Judge Dear, Boulch refused to waver.

Next up was Weathers, who defended his conduct of Mogoyne's hypnosis session. "Briefly, would you tell the court the procedure you followed in putting Mr. Mogoyne under hypnosis?" Turner asked. "Tell the judge the whole procedure you generally follow in inducing hypnosis."

Greenwood objected. "Not generally, Your Honor, but what he did in this case," he protested.

"What he did in this case will be fine," Turner agreed.

Dear adjusted his glasses. "When y'all get it worked out, let me know," he said. "Otherwise, go back to courtroom procedure, which is asking the witness a question—something we learned in law school, remember?" He was obviously losing patience with the drawn-out lecture on hypnosis.

Just before lunch, Dear sprang another surprise by moving for a quick identification hearing out of the jury's presence. He rearranged the courtroom, seating Zani in the audience and someone else at the defense table. Then he told the bailiff to bring in Mogoyne and, after placing him under oath, asked him to identify the defendant. Turner was dumbfounded. Mogoyne had come face-to-face with Zani only once—fourteen years earlier. Since then, Mogoyne had conjured up Zani's face during hypnosis and briefly studied a lineup photo after the session. But on none of those occasions had Zani been wearing glasses, and Turner was well aware of the defendant's uncanny ability to alter his appearance by the simple act of donning a pair of black horn-rims, which he had just pulled out of his pocket.

A hush settled in as the witness slowly surveyed the crowded courtroom. Turner began to perspire, watching Mogoyne's eyes move from side to side. He saw them reach Zani, then move on. When Mogoyne got to the end of the courtroom, he repeated the process in reverse. Then, after a long pause, he looked up at Dear. "That's him right there," he said at last, pointing directly at Zani.

The afternoon session got under way with Mogoyne on the stand. He testified that he had been shown no photographs of the defendant before being placed under hypnosis. After the session, however, Mogoyne remembered Ruiz's handing him a stack of five snapshots. "I laid them out in front of me one by one," he said. "I recognized the third picture as the person that I had been looking at while I was hypnotized. You can place a million photographs in front of me, and I will be able to go through and eliminate all but the one." Turner looked toward the jurors' box, wishing they were present. Dear ruled that the hypnotically induced testimony was admissible.

Turner followed with his opening statement before the jury, delivering without notes a detailed version of the case he intended to present. Then he called Chuck Dinges. Judge Dear asked Dinges if he had ever been a witness in court before.

"No," Dinges said.

"There is no magic to how it is done," Dear assured him. "The lawyers are going to ask you questions. You answer as best you can. If you don't understand their questions, don't be afraid to tell them. You won't be the first person, okay?"

With that, Dinges took a seat. He recalled hiring Robert Zani to work part-time in the Town and Country store on Northland Drive about mid-May 1967—a transitional time during which Dinges, who had been promoted to supervisor needed someone to help Tom Mantle, the new manager, get a handle on the store. Dinges's memory seemed to have improved substantially.

Turner waved at a diagram of the Town and Country he had asked an artist to draw from Sergeant Robert Kelton's original, showing how the store was laid out in 1967. "Would you point out on there where your safe was located?" he asked. Dinges complied.

"What kind of safe was this?" Turner wanted to know.

"Just a safe in the floor. It had a combination at the top and a metal shield over that and then a rubber mat that we camouflaged it with."

"Did Robert Zani have the combination of that safe?"

"He would have, yes. Anybody that either closed or opened the store would have a combination to it."

"Originally, it was reported that three hundred dollars was missing from that safe. Do you know how that report got out?"

"It was probably me, because we had a policy that we would not give the media the amount of money. We didn't want anyone to know the amount of money in the store."

"Did Zani ever work on Sundays? Did he ever open the store on Sunday?"

"Yes."

"Did he know how to run that cash register?"

"Yes." Dinges added that he had called the police department after reading news reports of the renewed investigation a few months earlier and left word that he might have information about Zani. But Ruiz and Martinez never got the message, and no one returned Dinges's call.

Greenwood sensed that his client's defense had sustained a serious hit. Under cross-examination, he tried to shake Dinges's memory. "How many Sundays did Zani work?" Greenwood asked.

"Three would be the maximum," Dinges replied.

"And he left before the fourth of June?"

"That was his last weekend, I would say. It was a transition period for me."

"And how many temporary or part-time people did you hire during that time?

"Just one."

"Would that be Mr. Zani?"

"Yes, sir."

Turner then called Tom Mantle, who had flown in from California. Greenwood and Ganne objected, saying that Mantle and several other potential prosecution witnesses were unknown to them and, thus, ineligible to appear. For several minutes, the lawyers shouted at one another.

"Does anybody here have training as a referee in boxing?" Dear asked at last. "I'm going to settle this lawsuit real easy. I'm going to lock you guys up in the jury room and let you all have at it. He who walks out wins."

Mantle was finally called to the stand. He repeated what he had told police at the time of the original investigation and what he had been able to add when Ruiz and Martinez contacted him just weeks before the trial. He refused to budge under Greenwood's cross-examination.

Mantle was followed on the stand by Richard Furlong, the UT professor who discovered Vizard's body, and Clifford Wolff, who had gone into the Town and Country with his three fishing buddies on the morning of the murder. Neither added anything new to their previous statements, and the grateful jurors were excused for the day.

That night Ruiz and Martinez were called to Turner's office for a midnight strategy session and were surprised to find Robert Kelton there. In their opinion, Kelton and his former partner, Bill Landiss, had blown the original case, and they wondered what Turner wanted with the sergeant now.

Turner laid out his plan. Contrary to popular belief, he explained, a criminal trial is not a search for the truth. After a solid year of the most outstanding investigation he had ever seen, he said, the only question that remained was how much evidence Judge Dear would let them present to the jury. It was critical to let the jurors know that Zani had been a suspect at the time, according to Harlan Cooper's phone call three days after the murder. But Cooper had refused to cooperate, and the only other person who could tell them anything—Irma Zani—was prohibited under state law from testifying against her husband. That's where Kelton, who was scheduled to testify the next morning, came in.

Turner guessed that Greenwood would ask Kelton about any suspects he might have interviewed back in 1967. Greenwood had studied sections of the original offense report enough to know that Kelton and Landis had questioned a long list of people. What he didn't know—because Turner had kept secret the existence of page 39, detailing Cooper's call to the police department—was that Zani had also been a suspect.

"Tomorrow," Turner told Kelton, "Greenwood will ask you about some of those names to show that you had a lot of suspects but his client was never one of them. When he does, I'll object on the basis of hearsay, even though Judge Dear will probably overrule me. So I want you to give Greenwood two or three names. And when he asks, 'Well, who else was a suspect?' you drop Zani's name on him. That'll allow me to ask why he was a suspect. If Greenwood objects, I'll argue that he opened the door, not me.'

Turner smiled. "Even if Dear rules against us, it'll be too late. Not only will he look partial to the defense, but the jury will already have heard the question, and they will see that the defense is trying to hide the answer. Remember, you can take the skunk out of the jury box, but you can't take the stink out." It was a complicated plan, and Kelton was a simple man. They went over it half a dozen times until Turner was satisfied that the sergeant understood.

When the fourth day of the trial began Thursday morning, Greenwood led Kelton through a lengthy discussion of the original investigation and, after about an hour, began asking about suspects. Turner sat back and tried not to look smug as Kelton listed a couple of names, then stopped.

"To your knowledge, were there any other reports of any suspects?" Greenwood asked.

"No, sir," Kelton replied.

Turner was red-faced. He jumped up from his chair and approached the bench. "I have an obligation to tell the court that in fact there were some more reports, he whispered to Dear. "This witness has evidently forgotten about it, but there was a report of another suspect, a person who called and described a suspect," Turner glared at Kelton.

"I appreciate that, Mr. Turner," Dear said, genuinely grateful. "Y'all have a seat and go on."

Greenwood resumed his cross-examination, unaware that he was about to be broadsided. For several minutes Kelton hemmed and hawed, failing to mention Zani while Turner sat at the prosecution's table, narrowing his eyes at the sergeant in anger.

"Do you have any recollection of any other suspects?" Greenwood asked one more time. It was clear the defense attorney was about to move to another line of questioning, and Turner leaned forward in his chair. *If Kelton blows it this time, I'll kill him,* he thought.

Kelton seemed to react to the silent threat. "One of them is the defendant," he finally answered, "Robert Zani."

Greenwood looked stunned. "As a suspect?" he asked.

"Yes, sir."

"Pass the witness," Greenwood mumbled.

On redirect, a still-seething Turner took Kelton through the list of suspects again, asking one by one if each had been cleared, to which Kelton nodded affirmatively, afraid to look Turner in the eye. "You said Robert Zani was a suspect. Why is that?" Turner demanded when he got to the defendant's name on the list.

It was Ganne who objected this time. "Your Honor, that's clearly hearsay," he shouted.

Dear sustained the objection, and Turner rephrased the question. "Just state why he was a suspect at the time."

"We received a telephone call, and later two men was interviewed," Kelton replied. Riggs and Cooper had never been interviewed, of course. Kelton had let the killer slip from his grasp fourteen years earlier, and he didn't want that fact to get into the trial record now.

"Why was he a suspect?" Turner increased the pressure.

"He had told one of the men that he wanted somebody—"

Ganne was back on his feet. "Objection, Your Honor," he yelled.

"Sustained."

Now Turner exploded. "They've opened the door on this issue of suspects, Your Honor," he shouted, gesturing toward the defense table.

Dear peered over the bench. "I sustained the objection to what he was about to say," he roared. Then, lowering his voice. Dear smiled thinly. "Go ahead with your questioning."

"Your Honor," Turner pleaded, "this is not offered for the truth of the matter, but just for the purposes of showing—"

Dear asked the jurors to step into the jury room. Then, turning to the lawyers, he vented his anger. "This trial is not going to get out of hand again today," he warned. "I'm not going to argue with lawyers about my rulings. You may not like them, you may not like me—I don't care."

By the time the jurors were brought back, the heat and intensity in the courtroom were so high that condensation had formed on the windows and ceiling. The jurors didn't know what had been discussed in their absence, but from the muffled shouts they had heard through the door and the look on everyone's face, it had not been a pleasant conversation. Turned hoped they understood that there was more to the case than they were being permitted to hear. He looked at Kelton, who was still on the witness stand.

"You said a moment ago that Robert Zani was a suspect at the time," Turner began, determined to make Kelton pay for his poor execution of their plan. "Did you have his finger-prints on file?"

"Not that I know of."

"Did you ever interview him?"

"No."

"Did you ever make any attempt to find out whether or not he had any connection with the store?"

"I didn't, no."

"Pass the witness," Turner said, not even trying to conceal his disgust. Dear dismissed the jurors for the evening.

As he gathered his files and prepared to leave, Turner caught sight of Kelton huddled with Greenwood, Ganne, and Zani around the defense table. "I'm not going to tell you twice," Turner hissed, pulling the sergeant aside. "I want you to leave this courtroom. If I have to call your shift captain to get you to go back to work, I will." Kelton ambled out the door.

Years later, Turner was still angry. "If Kelton had simply interviewed Zani or Cooper or Riggs back in 1967, if he had just taken the fingerprints and matched them, the case would have been solved. Kelton was responsible for the man getting away."

"**G**ood morning, and welcome back," Dear said as he smiled at the jurors when they had been seated for the morning session on Friday, March 13, the bad-luck implications of the date lost on few. "I want to tell you this morning that there will be times, as you have already seen, in which there will be some rather heated and angry exchanges among all of us. That's simply the way lawyers and judges conduct their business sometimes when things begin to get a little out of hand. The reason is that everybody feels very, very strongly about what they're doing, and sometimes that strength comes through more than it ought to. So please disregard any outbursts we engage in. We will try to keep them to a minimum." As it turned out, Friday's proceedings would be even more explosive.

The morning brought surprise testimony from Rufino Salas García the Guerrero state police officer who had arrested Zani in January 1980, and Miguel Angel O'Campo Oliveros, the state prosecutor who had lent Ruiz and Martinez the jam box with which they recorded Irma's interview. Both had readily agreed to fly to Austin to testify about the chain of custody on the murder weapon because they were anxious to shop for gringo goods. Ruiz and Martinez had taken them out the evening before their court appearance, and the Mexicans had purchased six trunkloads of videocassette machines and other electronic equipment, which they assured the skeptical cops would be *no problema* getting through customs upon their return.

Speaking through an interpreter, Salas García testified that he received a report from Irma's mother in January 1980 that Zani had threatened the family. He went to the Sands Motel in Acapulco, where Zani was staying, to check into the matter, he said. When he arrived, Zani pointed a .25 out the window of his room. Salas García broke down the door and seized the weapon and two others—a .357 and a .38—after which he placed Zani under arrest.

Next, O'Campo Oliveros testified that he was given the guns by Salas García and had placed them in the "arms vault" in his office, where "belongings of people who are arrested" were kept. Ruiz and Martinez looked at each other and tried not to laugh, recalling how they had been forced to call on Florentino Ventura, Mexico's top cop, to get the weapons turned over.

"Are you required to keep a record of the transfer of weapons from the time they are seized until the time they are introduced into court?" Turner asked.

"It's not a general requirement," O'Campo Oliveros replied, in what may have been the understatement of the trial.

"But is it done?" Turner insisted.

"Yes, it is done," O'Campo Oliveros answered.

"Was it ever taken out of the vault and fired?" Turner asked.

"Never, no." O'Campo Oliveros replied with a straight face.

"Who did you turn this weapon over to?"

"The weapon was delivered to Captain Rendon of the Corpus Christi police," O'Campo Oliveros said, reciting the lines he had rehearsed, "on June twenty-fourth of this past year."

"Pass the witness." Turner knew that search warrants and chain-of-custody rules did not exist in Mexico. But such legal technicalities were of little importance to the case anyway, and he hoped that bringing witnesses all the way from Acapulco would impress upon the jury the serious nature of his prosecution. By the end of the morning session, he had a feeling that the gamble, not to mention the cost to Travis County taxpayers, had been worth it.

After lunch, Fred Rymer was called to the stand. The DPS expert who had run the original tests on the bullets recovered from Vizard's body was now testifying in his final trial before retirement. Rymer was a legend, widely regarded, after forty years, as the premier ballistics expert in the nation. In 1967, he said, from 3 to 5 percent of all firearms contained the rifling characteristic of eight lands and grooves to the right, including the .357 Ruger Blackhawk and certain .38 specials. In 1980, he added, after Ruiz and Martinez returned from Mexico with those two weapons, he had attempted to match them with the original ballistics. Unfortunately, the lead buildup in the barrels of both guns prevented a positive identification.

Turner's next witness was Paul Ruiz, who recalled how Jerry Mogoyne, Jr., had identified Zani from the photographic lineup after his hypnosis session. Under cross-examination, Ganne asked how many people he and his partner had attempted to hypnotize.

"Three," Ruiz replied.

"Would you name them?"

"Jerry Mogoyne, Jr.; Mr. Mogoyne, Sr.; and Robert Riggs."

"Now, Mr. Riggs has been a mystery, has he not?" Ganne asked, the hostility in his voice obvious. A new name had been introduced.

"What do you mean by 'mystery'?" Ruiz responded, matching Ganne's tone.

"When I asked you specifically who had been hypnotized, did you ever mention Mr. Riggs?"

"I don't recall you ever asking."

"Let me make it clearer for you," Ganne said. "It was in Mr. Turner's office. Didn't I ask you who was hypnotized?"

"I don't remember that."

"There are a lot of things you don't remember."

"No, sir. I can remember a lot of things."

On redirect, Turner asked Ruiz why he and his partner had tried to hypnotize Riggs. Before Ruiz could answer, however, Greenwood shouted an objection, and Dear turned to the jurors, asking them to excuse themselves. "We're going to fight again, I think," he apologized.

With the jury out of the courtroom, Dear called the lawyers to the bench. "Paul is no dummy," he said. "He's played this game before. All I want to hear is what he's about to say—before he says it in front of the jury and I can't cure the problem."

Ruiz looked at the judge. "Robert Riggs was in a conversation with Mr. Zani at the Chuck Wagon on the Friday before the armed robberty," he explained. "Zani tried to solicit his help in holding up a convenience store. The police department received the information three days later, after the murder."

"That's what I was afraid you were about to say," Dear sighed.

"Hearsay," Greenwood sniffed.

Turner stepped forward. "I haven't lost my cool in this whole trial," he said, his voice rising, "but I'm about to."

"I don't suggest you do it now, either," Dear warned.

Turner ignored him. "They've tried to imply that we are

hiding Robert Riggs," he said. "And now they've opened the door with hearsay, and I think I ought to be able to shut it with the same hearsay."

"Yeah, well, let's pick our hearsay carefully," Dear cautioned him, "because some hearsay is so hearsay that we don't have a prayer of getting past a mistrial. Ask your question again, and let me see how he's going to put it together."

Turner looked at Ruiz. "Why did you attempt to hypnotize Robert Riggs?" he asked.

"To try to take him back thirteen years to that day when he had the conversation with Mr. Zani at the Chuck Wagon on the Friday before the armed robbery," Ruiz replied. "We wanted to see how much he could recollect."

"Why was that conversation important?" Turner asked.

"Because it was three days before the murder."

The discussion had grown more heated now as Dear tried to explain what he would allow before the jury and as Turner and Greenwood haggled over what they wanted in the record and what they would concede. "I'm not a commodities broker," Dear said.

"But there is no evidence anywhere that this conversation actually occurred," Greenwood yelled, "so I don't see how an officer can assume it did."

"That's why I instructed him how to answer the question," Dear shouted back.

Ruiz cut in. "I'm confused as to what I'm supposed to answer," he said.

"That makes two of us," Dear said with a chuckle.

Turner saw nothing funny about the matter. "Your Honor," he continued to protest at the top of his lungs, "the witness should be permitted to explain why this information is important. The reason we hypnotized Riggs is because we had information that a conversation with Robert Zani occurred the Friday before the murder. And in that conversation, Zani indicated that he was trying to get people to go hold up a convenience store—"

"Your Honor," Greenwood and Ganne cried in unison.

"Hold it. I'm talking," Turner yelled.

"Why are you objecting to what he is saying?" Dear asked Ganne.

"Because he's yelling it loud enough to go through the jury-room door," Ganne screamed.

"The only thing people can hear through that door is both of you yelling," Dear said, clearly out of patience.

"I'm perfectly willing to go to the Court of Criminal Appeals and argue this personally," Turner insisted.

"Do you want to do some time?" Greenwood sneered.

Dear stood up and motioned for silence. "Y'all have been at each other's throats in this thing, and all we are doing is trying a lawsuit here. We're not trying each other, okay? Stop yelling at each other. The only person on trial here that I know of is Mr. Zani. Bring the jury in."

When the jurors had taken their seats, Dear again apologized. "This is an aerobic trial," he told them, trying to establish a lighter mood. "You get your exercise going back and forth to the jury room." Then, facing Ruiz, the judge ordered him to answer the question.

"Yes, sir," Ruiz said. "Could I please have the question asked again?"

Turner stepped forward and stared at the bewildered jurors. Without taking his eyes off them, he addressed Ruiz. "Would you tell the jury why you were attempting to hypnotize Robert Riggs?" he asked.

Ruiz directed his answer to the jurors as well. "We had prior information that Robert Riggs had a conversation with Robert Zani," he said, measuring his words carefully. "By placing Mr. Riggs under hypnosis, we were trying to determine how many of the details of that particular conversation he could remember to further the investigation. This conversation took place—"

"Allegedly took place," Greenwood interjected.

"—allegedly took place two days before the murder on July twenty-third, 1967," Ruiz concluded.

"Pass the witness," Turner said, returning to his seat. The defense lawyers had made the mistake of allowing a question to which they didn't know the answer, opening the door on the reason Riggs was hypnotized. And if Turner hadn't exactly slammed the door, he knew he had succeeded in getting enough before the jury to at least close it gently. Dear dismissed the jury for the weekend.

In the hallway, Turner walked up to Greenwood. "Now tell me your client's innocent," he said, still angry. Until that moment, he thought, Greenwood had carried an air of moral supremacy into the courtroom. but as he walked away, Turner was confident the jurors would spend a long weekend wondering what Riggs and Zani had discussed a day or two before the murder.

As the trial moved into its final week on Monday and Tuesday, March 16 and 17, a sense of lost momentum lingered in the courtroom. Turner called a parade of witnesses to testify about Zani's university transcripts, bank accounts (including two hot checks for $3 and $4), and other evidence the prosecutor wanted in the record. Robert Martinez testified that he had traced the .357 Ruger Blackhawk to Zani, who had purchased it from Oshman's Sporting Goods in Austin on July 23, 1966—precisely one year before Vizard's murder. Later, Don Stallings, a former roommate of Zani's, took the stand to say that the .357 appeared to be the one his friend had owned back in the sixties. He had seen it a number of times in Zani's dorm, and he knew that Zani carried it around in a briefcase. Walter and Stacia DeBill each recalled the day in late spring or early summer 1967 when they visited Zani in his cabin off Bluff Springs Road to take target practice with a weapon very similar to the one in the courtroom.

William Richter, an employee of the Barker History Center at UT who worked with Zani in the Bexar archives section in 1967, remembered a conversation with Zani concerning a woman in Mexico. "He talked about going to Mexico, to a place called Boys Town in Nuevo Laredo," Richter said. "And he later spoke about marrying a girl from Mexico and the difficulty of getting his wife across the border." Then, Chester Kielman, Zani's former boss at the archives, testified that Zani had asked for advice on getting his Mexican wife into Texas legally. Kielman had suggested he contact an attorney specializing in immigration law.

Turner and his assistant, Ralph Graham, who handled many of the technical questions, were clearly trying to show the jury a motive for the robbery: Zani needed money to pay an immigration lawyer and was so broke he couldn't even make good on seven bucks' worth of bad checks. Not only that, but he also owned a gun from which the bullets could have been fired, the only one of its kind sold in Austin between 1961 and 1969. Some of the testimony was damaging but not damaging enough. And not even appearances by colorful characters such as Coleman DeChenar, the pathologist who performed the autopsy on Vizard, or John Williamson, APD's venerable fingerprint expert, could enliven the proceedings.

Late Tuesday afternoon, Greenwood asked Richard Bennett Garver, a San Antonio psychologist, to take the stand. Garver had an impressive résumé spanning some twelve years in the fields of clinical and investigative hypnosis, which Greenwood made sure to ask him about in detail. Then, for the next several hours—with a break for lunch— Garver delivered a free-flowing lecture on the unreliable nature of hypnosis and the dangers of its use as a forensic tool. Just as a hypnotized subject can be taken back in time, Garver said, obviously referring to Jerry Mogoyne, Jr., so too can he be "age progressed," a therapeutic technique whereby individuals describe quite realistically their surroundings and activities at some future date. "This doesn't mean they are clairvoyant," Garver argued. "What it means is that they are confabulating." As for the specifics of the case at hand, he hadn't heard the tape of Mogoyne's hypnosis session. But he felt certain that the qualifications of both James Michael Boulch and Carl Weathers were quite limited. In fact, he doubted if either knew enough even to enroll in a training school.

In many ways Garver was a more commanding presence than Turner's young hypnosis expert, James Michael Boulch. Garver's experience, his academic credentials, and his self-assured attitude were difficult to deny. The jurors were disturbed, however, by his willingness to criticize the conduct of a hypnosis session he had neither witnessed nor heard on tape. Even more troubling was a comment he made early on when Greenwood, attempting to impress the courtroom with Garver's expertise, asked if he had ever spoken to Joe Turner. "Yes, sir," Garver replied. "He was very kind. He said he wished he had gotten to me first." True or not, the inference left behind was that Garver might be willing to argue either side of the hypnosis issue in court, depending on which side's expert-witness fee was greater.

Lawyers tend to believe that their final arguments before juries make the difference. Rarely is this true. Most cases are decided during pretrial hearings or at voir dire, when jurors choose which attorney they trust. But in close cases— and this was as close an any—final arguments can weave the web that shakes a juror's confidence in one side or another. It takes only one of twelve people to hang a jury, after all.

With that in mind, Joe Turner had begun composing his final argument the day he inherited the case from John Dietz, and he didn't finish until two o'clock in the morning on Wednesday, March 18. He thought he had a pretty good read on his strengths and weaknesses as a prosecutor. When it came to pretrial preparation and jury selection, he was unbeatable. But he lacked the patience for the careful, ponderous questioning that made up the bulk of most trials. In an ideal judicial world, he often said, he should be allowed to move directly from voir dire to final argument. Now he and Ralph Graham reviewed the elements that had brought the trial to this point, putting the finishing touches on what each would say in the morning. They decided that Graham would make the closing remarks, after which Greenwood and Ganne would be permitted rebuttals. Then Turner would deliver the final argument.

It was surprising that hypnosis had played such a small role in Zani's defense. Turner and Graham had expected the issue to dominate the trial, and they considered it a blunder on Greenwood's part to have waited until the end—after Turner had a chance to counter with a preponderance of other evidence—to bring hypnosis to the fore. Still, only a small portion of the brilliant investigation by Ruiz and Martinez had made it into the trial record. Though personally convinced of Zani's guilt, Turner knew there were far too many loose ends left dangling, too many bits of partial testimony that might have left a question in some juror's mind. "What does all this mean?" he and Ruiz and Martinez had joked during the preparation of the case. In a few hours it was going to be their job to answer that question for the jury.

On that Wednesday morning, Ralph Graham rose to address the jury. Quickly, he led the jurors through the evidence. "Did Mr. Zani do it?" he asked, then went on to answer his own question. "Well, his fingerprints were on the goods by the counter, so we know he was in the store. We know that he needed money. He was a student, and students are always poor. This one was working part-time in a store. Everybody needs money, and whoever got that money knew he had to get it out of the floor safe without having to blow the safe, so it was somebody who probably worked there—like Mr. Zani.

"He had a gun, too, a rare gun. He just happened to have the kind of gun that did the killing. Remember that and the fact that he needed money, knew how the store worked, how to operate the register, and how to pose as the clerk. He knew when the money would be there, and he knew how to gain the confidence of the person who worked there so he could do the killing in the most expeditious manner.

"Mr. Mogoyne, Jr., after undergoing hypnosis, identified Mr. Zani as the person behind the register posing as the clerk while the body lay in the cooler, dead. We're not saying that hypnosis is infallible. But Mr. Mogoyne rememberd the face behind the counter, and you can determine for yourselves if it's just a coincidence that it happens to look like Mr. Zani out of all the faces it could have been. All of these coincidences, you see, add up.

"Now, we have to prove this case beyond a reasonable doubt. In such cases, it's not enough that the circumstances coincide, account for, and render probable the guilt of the defendant. We have to exclude every other reasonable hypothesis to prove this beyond a reasonable doubt. And in a circumstantial case like this, we have to prove it with little pieces of the puzzle, fitting it all together to show you the whole picture.

"We have his fingerprints on the food that was on the counter. View that as a piece of the puzzle. He has the gun, another piece of the puzzle. He knew about the safe and how to get it open. That doesn't prove that he is guilty all by itself, but you put it together and what have you got? You've got the whole picture—and it puts the gun in Mr. Zani's hand, and it takes the money out of the safe and puts it in his pocket. What a coincidence that he happened to have this rare gun. What a coincidence his fingerprints happened to be right there at the scene. What a coincidence he knew how to open that safe. What a coincidence that Mr. Mogoyne just happened to see a face that looked like Mr. Zani's. It *was* Mr. Zani's."

Patrick Ganne was next. Leafing through the defense exhibits, he selected the statement from Tom Mantle in the original offense report indicating that at 7:10 on the morning of July 23, 1967, about the time Mantle was dropping his wife, Mary, off at the Seton Hospital emergency-room door, Vizard had called for the combination to the safe. "Now, here was an employee who had been working there for some six weeks, and he can't remember the combination. I submit to you that a logical deduction is because the combination had been changed. So all of this balderdash about Zani being guilty because he knew what the combination was is trash."

It was an unexpected point, a good one, and Ganne pressed on. "One more thing I want you to consider—state exhibit number one," he said. "They have harped, they have yelled, they have hollered, trying to glamorize themselves on how fair they are. Well, look at state's exhibit number one and we'll show you what fairness is. It's a five-picture photo spread that Paul Ruiz, who is sitting like a vulture on the front row to see Zani go to the penitentiary, showed witnesses. It's so shocking I can't believe it. No wonder you can pick out that picture; anybody could. There is one picture of a full face in there—the four other pictures are side views."

Turner had to admit that Ganne's performance was admirable, playing to the natural tendency of most jurors to try to outguess the pros by discovering one or two pieces of evidence that set an innocent man free. Greenwood, however, was next—and any advantage his partner might have won was quickly lost. "This is the most disorganized trial I have ever participated in," Greenwood began. "We apologize for the tempers, the delays, but none of that is Robert Zani's fault. You can't hold it against him.

"Let's look at the evidence," Greenwood continued. "First of all, the gun. Fred Rymer is the number one ballistics expert in the country. Nobody questions his judgment, but the man cannot tell you if that thing right there is the murder weapon."

Greenwood lumbered to the defense table and glanced at his notes. "The state has put on gangs of testimony showing that Mr. Zani was living in Austin around the time of the shooting. No issue. Do we have flight here?

"Now, the next thing. Mr. Turner has touched on possible motives. First of all was, 'Well, maybe he wanted to get money to get his wife across the border.' Just a matter of administrative paper-shuffling is all that is. Takes a little time, but it's not a money matter. Besides, it was a month after he was married that this robbery occurred. How can you get motive out of that? I don't think it would have been very difficult to smuggle her across if that's what he wanted to do. But no, he goes and asks his boss, 'What procedures do I go through?' Is that the type of man that would take a gun and go out and blow somebody up for a few bucks?"

After pointing out that Chuck Dinges had reported no money missing at the time of the original investigation, then upped the amount to $300 and, finally, as much as $2,000, Greenwood slammed Kelton. "He didn't even know the floor safe existed," Greenwood said. "Nobody proved that there was even a robbery here—and if you don't know, you can't vote guilty.

"I have been an Austin resident for twenty-seven of my thirty-five years, and I have never seen a case like this prosecuted in Travis County," he concluded. "I am ashamed of it. I might get physically ill if somebody could be convicted on this evidence. This whole thing scares me. How can somebody in this time be put before a jury to fight for his life on evidence like this?"

After a brief recess, Dear looked at Turner. "The ball is in your court," he said.

Turner stood slowly. "Mr. Dinges testified that the bread was delivered every day," the young prosecutor began, meeting each juror's eyes. "In order to find the defendant not guilty, you would have to believe he went to that store on Saturday, put his fingerprints on three separate items, and left without purchasing those items—and the next day those same three items were brought to the counter by some other person. That's possible, but it's not reasonable. In fact, it's ridiculous." It was a refrain Turner would repeat throughout his final argument, a litany designed to be as memorable as the hook of a country-and-western song.

"Even though Zani worked at that store before," Turner continued, "it's possible that he went in there while George Vizard lay shot to death and, finding no attendant, didn't walk around to look for the attendant. It's possible, ladies and gentlemen, but it's not reasonable. In fact, it's ridiculous.

"It's possible that with all the publicity at the time, he didn't call the store manager to report the fact that he had been there. It's possible that he didn't call the police to report that he had been in that store. But, ladies and gentlemen, it sure ain't reasonable.

"It's possible that Robert Zani went into that store, found no one there, and, because he'd worked there before, decided to wait on Mr. Mogoyne, Sr. and Jr., and then left without taking his own groceries. That's possible, but it's not reasonable. In fact, it's ridiculous.

"Just consider the fact that he lived so far away. The only reasonable explanation is that Robert Zani went in there and committed this crime. He'd worked at the store before. He was familiar with the safe. He went in there and shopped, waiting for the customers to leave. And when everyone left, he marched George Vizard back to that cold-storage vault. Vizard was a dead man, and he knew it. He tried to make a move to fight him, and Zani shot him. He tried to make a desperate run around these boxes into a narrow passageway. And when he did, Zani hit him with a second bullet that went right through his chest.

"Zani put the gun back in his pants and walked out to get the money. While he was underneath that counter, appearing to be a person working behind the counter, Jerry Mogoyne, Sr., and Jerry Mogoyne, Jr., and Norman Higgins dropped in, so he had to pretend like he was running that store. He waited on them. After they left, he took his money and split. And then what did Robert Zani do? At the time of the killing, he was sixty-one cents overdrawn at his bank and faced with the possibility that his wife, who was pregnant with his child, would not be brought to the United States. The only reasonable explanation of where he got the money was that he killed George Vizard and went into that safe."

Turner also tried to dispense with the defense's objections about Mogoyne's hypnosis session. "How could James Michael Boulch or Carl Weathers suggest a picture of Robert Zani when they didn't know what he looked like themselves?" he asked. "It's possible that Jerry Mogoyne, Jr., just dreamed up some face that happened to look like Robert Zani. That's possible, but it's not reasonable. In fact, it's ridiculous.

"The defense has taken you down rabbit trails. One straw man they tried to develop was a political assassination. We have never contended this was a political assassination. It's possible that Robert Zani had his own political reasons, that it was a shooting over politics. But if this was strictly a political assassination, there would be no reason to take the money in the safe.

"Then the defense wondered why Zani knew the combination to that safe when George Vizard didn't know. If that combination had been changed, don't you know they would have subpoenaed some people to tell you about it? It's very much possible that George Vizard forgot the piece of paper at home that he had written the combination on. That has nothing to do with whether or not Robert Zani could remember the safe number. Don't run down that rabbit trail."

Turner was perspiring now. He had often said that trial lawyers are salesmen—they sell stories—and that nobody will buy a story from someone who bores them. He raised his voice and, standing in the middle of the room, swept his arms toward the defendant. "They had an opportunity, folks, to tell you what a good person Robert Zani was," he pointed out. "He could have gotten up here and told you why he was in that neighborhood, but he didn't. He could have told you he was on the way to the lake, but he didn't. He could have told you he was with some friends early that morning, but he didn't. Robert Zani could have told you a lot about this case—but he didn't."

"Your Honor," Greenwood cut in, "we would request a mistrial."

"Denied," Dear snapped.

Turner was on a roll. "You can use your common sense and make reasonable deductions," he told the jurors. "There was one person that Sergeant Kelton didn't clear, and to be frank with you," Turner stretched the truth, "it was embarrassing for me to force Sergeant Kelton to tell you. Robert Zani was a suspect, and yet Sergeant Kelton never interviewed him, never got his fingerprints, never checked to see whether or not he had followed up the lead whatsoever.

"Robert Zani got away with this murder for thirteen years," Turner continued, his voice booming. "Thirteen years later, his luck ran out. It's time to send a message to Robert Zani and anyone else that you might get away with it for a little while and you might get away with it for a long time, but sooner or later you're going to slip up, you're going to get caught, and then you're going to have to accept the responsibility for your crime—because for the offense of murder, ladies and gentlemen, the state never rests."

If the play on F. Lee Bailey's best-selling book *The Defense Never Rests* was a bit overdrawn, few seemed to notice. Turner slowed the pace and, resting his elbows on the railing, scanned the jurors. "What does all this mean?" he concluded. In the audience, Ruiz and Martinez smiled at the inside joke. "I have carried this case on my shoulders for the last several months, and it hasn't been easy. But the responsibility is now on your shoulders. The only reasonable verdict in this case is guilty, because the facts point to Robert Zani. He's the man, no question about it."

Turner moved back to the center of the room. "The easiest thing to do would be to throw your hands up in the air and say, 'Oh man, it's fourteen years ago.' That's the easy way out. But Paul Ruiz and Robert Martinez didn't take the easy way out when they started investigating this case, and don't you shy away from it. Grab that responsibility. I'm going to go home and sleep tonight because I know that you are twelve reasonable people. We can finally put this crime to rest. Thank you."

Robert Zani sat at the defense table and stared staight ahead as he waited for the jury to return a verdict. He had been remarkably quiet; other than a few whispered exchanges with Greenwood or Ganne, he rarely even participated. But for those who had caught him staring at them during the trial with what one observer later described as "those cold, dead eyes," Zani's presence was chilling.

Turner sat on a bench in the hall. His girlfriend, *American-Statesman* reporter Janet Wilson, saw that he was exhausted and drained, and she moved closer as his head slumped to his chest. Ruiz and Martinez milled about, chain-smoking and chatting with Betty Jo Mason, Vizard's parents, realtor Larry Flood, and others who had made the trial a priority in their lives. Just before two o'clock the bailiff stuck his head out to announce that the jury had reached a verdict. It had taken them three hours and forty-six minutes.

As they climbed into the jurors' box, Turner studied their faces. He had learned through the years that it was a bad sign when jurors refused to look at him before announcing their verdict. Now he saw several glance his way and felt a slow surge of confidence. Even better, a couple of the women looked at Zani and then lowered their heads. Judge Dear read the verdict to himself, and Turner leaned forward as if to read his lips. Then Zani was asked to rise and face the jury as Dear read aloud: "Number 61,076. The state of Texas versus Robert Zani. We, the jury, find the defendant, Robert Zani, guilty of the offense of murder."

Ruiz and Martinez looked at each other, and Martinez saw that his partner was shaking, his arms outstretched and stiff as he clutched the chair in front of him. All the tension, all the questions, all the late nights and missed weekends of the past year, seemed to be releasing themselves through his fingertips.

Suddenly Ruiz jumped up and walked to the defense table, where Zani, Greenwood, and Ganne were trying to gather their files in the general commotion. Pushing his way through the crowd, Ruiz fought back tears of relief and anger. He wanted to tell Zani so many things, but when he caught Zani's eye, he could think of only one. "I told you we'd find out," Ruiz said.

One more trial day remained. In Texas, guilt and punishment are decided in separate stages. After a guilty verdict, the jury is presented with new evidence—usually prior convictions, if any, and a series of character witnesses—to help them decide what sentence to pronounce. And though Turner, Ruiz, and Martinez were delighted with the verdict, they had seen before a tendency in close criminal cases for juries to balance convictions with light sentences.

That night the three again met in Turner's office to plot strategy. Because the murder was so old, the jury, with little information about Zani's history in the intervening years, might opt for the legal equivalent of a shrug as punishment. Besides, all the testimony about Vizard's radical politics had done little to win sympathy for the victim. They had to make the jurors understand what kind of man Zani was, and the way to do that was through reputation evidence. Long past midnight, they manned the phones in Turner's office, lining up witnesses and urging them to be in Judge Dear's courtroom at nine o'clock the following morning.

On Thursday, March 19, Turner's first witness was Austin real estate agent Marilyn Powell. The prosecutor launched into a litany whose cumulative effect would be devastating. "Are you familiar with Robert Zani's reputation in the community for being a peaceful and lawabiding citizen?" he asked.

"Yes," Powell answered.

"Is that reputation good or bad?"

"It's bad, very bad."

Next came realtors Mary Evelyn Lowder, Jean Shearer, Larry Flood, and Elena Smith; Betty Jo Mason; Adolfo Cuellar, a Texas Ranger whose jurisdiction included Bexar and Wilson counties; Secret Service agent Cecil Calvin; and, finally, Ruiz and Martinez—none of whom could find a positive word for the defendant. Ralph Graham delivered the state's closing remarks, and Greenwood and Ganne waived the defense's right to the same. It was a good strategy. By waiving their right, they also prevented Turner from presenting a *final* final argument in which he might hammer them even harder.

The jury retired to puzzle out the punishment. Three hours and thirty-five minutes later, they returned with the maximum sentence—ninety-nine years.

After the verdict, Ruiz, Martinez, Turner, and several of the jurors walked up the street to the Veranda for a celebratory drink. They discussed some of the pivotal points in the trial, laughing about this incident or that scrap of testimony. All agreed that Zani's defense had been pitiful. "We wanted to give *Greenwood* ninety-nine years," one juror claimed.

Despite the evidence they had been presented over the past ten days, the jurors were astonished to hear the depth of the yearlong investigation. Ruiz and Martinez regaled them with stories of leads they had pursued, many of which were never introduced at trial. They heard about the killing of J. A. Dess and the butchering of Zani's own mother, and most came away even more convinced that they had arrived at the correct verdict.

But as they left the bar late that afternoon, one of the jurors wondered aloud if, despite all the evidence, it was possible they had convicted an innocent man. "Sure, it's possible," the others quickly chimed in, "but it's not reasonable. In fact, it's ridiculous."

NINETEEN

On June 30, 1981, Irma Zani, her two defense attorneys—Allan Manka of San Antonio and a local co-counsel, John Winhoven—and a packed courtroom of onlookers gathered in Floresville. San Antonio judge Pat Priest, who had exchanged dockets with Robert Eschenburg for the week, informed them that they were there to select twelve jurors whose job would be to gauge Irma's psychological ability to stand trial for the capital murder of Julius Dess.

Many of the prospective jurors in the courtroom that day knew Winhoven, who not only had performed their legal work from time to time but also socialized with them at private parties, civic functions, and an occasional family reunion. Manka, too, was acquainted with some and even related to others, having grown up in Panna Maria, just twenty miles down the road.

But District Attorney Alger Kendall and his assistant, Stella Saxon, didn't raise a single objection during voir dire; as it happened, they also counted a number of the prospective jurors as friends. People were expected to know their neighbors in a dusty town that had to wrack its civic brain just to come up with favorite sons—former Texas Governor John Connally and Aberlardo Lopez Valdez, the chief of protocol in the Jimmy Carter administration. It took little more than an hour for twelve jurors to pledge their impartiality, the surnames of half of them (Pawelek, Jarzombek, Wiatrek, Pruski, Skrobarcek, Zunker) reflecting the heavy Czech influence in the area.

Unlike a murder trial, a competency hearing places the burden of proof on the defendant. Accordingly, Manka and Winhoven chose three witnesses who they calculated would help them win their case. They were wrong.

First, Dr. José Manuel Hernandez, a San Antonio psychiatrist, testified that he had given Irma a three-hour "main status" examination ten days earlier. "It was striking to me from the very beginning how she introduced herself," Hernandez said, his accent belying an English gleaned on the streets of his native Seville, Spain. "She said she was seeing me, she was seeing the judge, she was seeing the whole system, you know, as a plot that she was going to be the victim of. You would expect a person that would be saying that, it would be accompanied by anger. But she was giggling. She was smiling. She was, at one point, laughing.

"But the one that stands in my mind is, we were discussing her childhood. She stated, you know, that numbers have special meanings and there is a healing quality about numbers. She said, 'I have the power. I can dictate and perceive human quality in numbers.' She described it as seeing God in people when that person turns 'cloudy or dark.' And at the end, I shared with Mrs. Zani my findings, to which she responded, 'Don't you dare put your hands on the fire.'

"She was able to pinpoint that the reason she was in jail was that she made a confession once under specific circumstances, and she backed off from the confession she made. She said, 'There was a lot of pressure on me. Now that I have been able to think about it, I see I made the wrong confession. I was not a participant in the murder.' My final conclusion is that she is incompetent to stand trial."

Next up was John Winhoven. Manka questioned him about Irma's habit of almost constantly writing notes. Ruiz, Martinez, and others involved in the investigation had seen her scribbles over the past year—some in English, some in

Spanish, and some in a language all her own. To Manka, the notes were an indication of her mental instability. "Have you had an opportunity to observe her handwriting?" he asked his co-counsel.

"I have," Winhoven replied.

"Is there anything unusual about it?"

"Occasionally, Mrs. Zani writes in what would be termed a mirror image—upside down, backward, mirror-type image."

"Have you had an opportunity to discuss with her the legal aspects of this case?

"I have."

"Have you been able to fully communicate with her?"

"No."

"Have you been able to communicate with her to the extent you feel comfortable in defending her with her participation in this case up to this point?"

"No, I do not."

Finally, Texas Ranger Gene Powell was called to the stand. One year earlier, Powell had taken photographs of the walls in Irma's jail cell, which she had filled with scrawled pictures and gibberish. One read, "Christ I'm a police woman. I'm not good but I'm k-i-c-e." Another contained symbols, markings, and the name "Powell." Still another depicted a large bird wearing a hat and featuring a violent scribble in the groin area. Beneath the picture was a caption: "Poor Jercy Powell."

"Can you tell me what that means?" Manka asked the ranger.

"To me, it means she don't like me," Powell answered. "That's what it means to me."

Kendall got his chance next. He called two psychiatrists, each of whom had examined Irma during the past week. Dr. John Sparks, the director of psychiatric and psychological services for Bexar County, found nothing unusual about the defendant, save for a habit of giggling when she was nervous. As for her belief in the healing quality of numbers, he wrote it off to the cultural beliefs prevalent in her native village near Acapulco. "The same happens in certain parts of lower Louisiana, the Cajun area," Sparks offered.

Last up was Dr. Richard Cameron. A former assistant chief of psychiatry for the U.S. Army and Sparks's ex-boss in Bexar County, he had examined Irma the day before.

"Did you find any mental illness?" Kendall asked.

"No," Cameron testified. "She does not have any mental illness or defect, and I think one would be hard put even to put a psychiatric label on her. She is more a product of her origins or lack of education. Academically, she is somewhat limited, and her cultural situation leaves something to be desired. I think she is a survivor. I think she has done the best she can for herself. There is no doubt in my mind she is quite competent to stand trial."

Under cross-examination, Cameron stuck to his guns when Manka asked sarcastically how the doctor had arrived at the determination that Irma was able to consult with her attorney. "She said she essentially had three choices that you had given her," Cameron replied evenly. "First of all, she could plead guilty, and she might get twenty-five years. Secondly, plead no contest and let the judge decide the issue. And third, she said she would go to full trial and let the jury decide. Now, she understood all this, and this is more than most inmates understand, I can assure you."

At the end of the afternoon, the jurors returned with their unanimous verdict: Irma Zani was competent to stand trial.

The actual trial began about four months later, on October 12, 1981, with Priest and Eschenburg alternating days on the bench, as if neither looked forward to presiding over case number 5,370 by himself. There was good reason for their reluctance. Moments before Priest entered the courtroom on day one, the bailiff sent word that Irma was refusing to dress for her appearance. She was finally persuaded to put her clothes on, but Priest suspected that the incident foreshadowed events to come.

The first order of business was Kendall's announcement that the state would proceed on the lesser charge of murder, instead of the capital-murder indictment originally handed down by the grand jury. The DA knew that his case was weak, which meant two things to Irma: She could not be sentenced to death if found guilty, and she could waive her right to a jury, letting the judge decide her case. The irony was not lost on Kendall when she chose to place her fate "in Priest's hands."

With no jury to impress, Kendall eschewed his opening statement and called Pat Dix to the stand. The San Antonio realtor repeated her encounter with the clients she knew as Dr. and Mrs. Pech in the late summer of 1979. She described the incident on the stairway of the home in Helotes when she had turned suddenly to see Irma holding the green scarf above her head. "It was not the normal way that a woman would put a scarf on," Dix said, recalling how she had become frightened and gone down to her car to fake a call on the broken mobile phone while Robert and Irma peered at her through the living-room curtains.

Next up was José Bayardo, the Robstown man whose wife had met Irma when they shared a hospital room back in 1970. Bayardo recounted how the Zani brood unexpectedly dropped in on them on Monday, December 3, 1979, and how Robert and Irma drove off in the wee hours of the next morning, leaving the kids with Bayardo and his wife. Under cross-examination, Manka asked if either of the Zanis had mentioned killing a man from San Antonio when they returned on Wednesday.

"No, sir," Bayardo answered in his broken English. "They never did talk nothing like that."

Manka passed the witness, satisfied that he had scored a point by implying that if Robert and Irma really did kill someone, they would have blurted out a confession to their hosts when they got back to Robstown. He was playing to a jury that didn't exist.

Back at the defense table, Manka and Irma fell into an animated discussion, hissing at each other in stage whispers. Priest let it go on for a few moments, then called both lawyers to the bench. "Let the record reflect that the defendant did not want to put her clothes on for court this morning," he finally announced, struggling to keep a straight face, "and I state she cannot take them off now."

Kendall shook his head in wonder and called Donald Wilkey, the man who had identified Zani in the Austin lineup on April 2, 1980. Wilkey related his brief conversation with Dess when he saw him showing the Horwedel property to a couple. Barbara Wilkey then testified that she had also seen Dess showing the spread to a man and woman who "looked Hispanic." After a quick break for lunch, Kendall called Michael Chaney, the beachcomber from Corpus Christi who first discovered Dess's body. Park ranger Norm Bonneau was next, followed by FBI agents Norman Stutte and John Newton, each of whom repeated his previous testimony in detail. Manka's questions were perfunctory. And when the first-day session adjourned, most observers suspected that the trial was going to be a sleeper.

The second day brought appearances by Ruiz, Martinez, Solomon Ortiz, Lencho Rendon, and, again, Gene Powell. With Eschenburg on the bench, and under a running objection from Manka, Ruiz was asked if the defendant was present in the courtroom. "Yes," he replied, looking at Irma. "She's sitting between her two attorneys—with a green scarf on her neck."

Ruiz was also the target of Manka's most hostile questions. He was grillzd about minor discrepancies in Irma's original Acapulco confession and later developments in the investigation. For example, Ruiz had reported that Irma and her husband threw most of Dess's possessions into the water after burying him on Padre Island, including a pocket calculator that was in fact discovered in a hole some five feet from the body. Manka repeatedly insisted that Ruiz was uncooperative, complaining that the officer misstated distances from the burial site to the park ranger station, the Sand Dollar, the spot where Dess's T-Bird had gotten stuck, and other landmarks. Again and again, Ruiz explained that he was testifying from memory because his files were down in the car.

"Do you have any other evidence down there that might have a bearing on Irma's guilt or innocence?" Manka asked, rolling his eyes in exasperation, apparently for the benefit of the imaginary jury.

"Like what?" Ruiz retorted. "Give me an example of what you want."

"You tell me," Manka said.

Judge Eschenburg interceded, suggesting a brief recess while Ruiz retrieved his files.

"Go ahead and get most of what you have," Manka said, as Ruiz stepped from the witness stand.

"You can leave your spare tire," Eschenburg called after him as he left the courtroom.

The morning session continued with Nueces County medical examiner Joseph Rupp on the stand. Apologizing for using a Styrofoam mannequin skull—"Sometimes it's tough to find heads," Manka observed—Rupp explained his findings regarding the three bullets fired into the victim. They seemed to have been fired in rapid succession, he said, although the third could have been a few moments later. Gunshot wounds one and two ripped through the brain, and either one was capable of causing a quick death, Rupp added. Number three was more difficult to judge. It had penetrated the skull but missed the brain.

Kendall zeroed in. "What was the cause of death, sir?" he asked.

"Cause of death was a direct result of gunshot wounds to the head," Rupp replied.

"Are you saying, cumulatively they killed him or individually they killed him?" Kendall pressed.

Rupp rubbed his chin. "Well, gunshot wounds one and two would have been rapidly fatal in and of themselves," he repeated. "Gunshot wound number three was a potentially fatal wound and it probably would have taken some time for the person to die. But the person died of the cumulative effect of all three. Any of the three would have been fatal in and of themselves."

Eschenburg perked up. He knew Irma had originally told the officers in Acapulco that her husband fired all three times but had changed her story during the June 4, 1980, session with Gene Powell in Austin, admitting that Zani forced her to take the third shot. The judge looked at Rupp. "Let's assume that a period of time up to a minute or so intervened between the firing of shots one and two and the firing of shot three," he began, pausing to allow the significance of the scenario to sink in. "Would shot three have hit a dead man?"

"In a couple of minutes?" Rupp sputtered. "Not necessarily, no." He could not say with certainty that Dess had been alive when the third shot hit.

The courtroom fell silent. Eschenburg had just defined the heart of the case, but neither the prosecution nor the defense was able to revamp its legal strategy quickly enough to seize the advantage. That afternoon they returned to their previous lines of questions, which were now almost beside the point. Betty Jo Mason testified at length about her father's business and his movements on the morning of his death. Austin realtor Marilyn Powell recounted her experience with Dr. and Mrs. O'Farrell back in the fall of 1979. Gene Powell led them through his investigation, amusing observers at one point when Manka, still obsessed with his client's "inability to speak English and lack of intelligence," demanded to know how Powell or anyone else expected Irma to understand the severity of her legal predicament. "Sir," Powell answered, "I think she's probably smarter than me." Even Irma cracked a smile at that.

The third and final day of the trial began with Judge Priest back on the bench. Ruiz and Martinez played the tapes of their Acapulco interview with Irma and reviewed the terms of the immunity letter, reminding the court of the phrase in paragraph three that promised not to seek prosecution "if she did not directly cause the death of Julius Alfred Dess." Since then, the officers added, Irma had admitted to firing the last of three shots into the realtor's head.

Manka seemed distracted during much of the day, and Winhoven, who had never defended a murder charge, failed to object when Kendall repeatedly elicited information about Robert Zani's other crimes—even his 1973 arrest in Fort Worth on the check-forging charge. When Donald Wilkey was recalled, Manka tried to shake the witness's recollection of the woman he had seen with Dess on the Horwedel property. "How much would you say the woman weighed?" he asked.

"I'm not real good on women's weight," Wilkey said, hesitating. "She was a short woman, and the way she was dressed and all, she appeared heavier than the man did. The man was somewhere between five fix and five ten. She was a couple of inches shorter than him."

Manka told Irma to stand. Then, turning back to Wilkey, he asked him to estimate the defendant's height.

"Maybe five feet, five feet two inches," Wilkey guessed.

"No!" Irma shouted, jumping up. "I'm not that tall. I'll take my shoes off." She bent down and started to remove her flats.

"Irma, be quiet," Manka commanded.

There was a moment of tension as Irma sat down. Then, peering at the defendant, Wilkey repeated his estimate: "Seems she's about five feet, five feet two inches."

But Manka hadn't given up. Before letting Wilkey off the stand, he sprang a surprise. "Do you remember towards the end of May 1980, stopping at the Denny's Restaurant in San Antonio at Loop 13 and IH-35?" he asked.

"Very possible," Wilkey replied. "I drink coffee there now and then."

"Do you remember running into Sheriff Williams from Atascosa County and Gene Powell and that woman?" Manka insisted, pointing toward Irma.

"I remember them coming in with a woman," Wilkey admitted. "I didn't pay that much attention to them."

"So you don't remember if that was the same woman they had with them or not?"

"I couldn't say under oath it was, no, sir."

"You are saying you just happened to be in there when they came in?"

"Yes, sir."

"They didn't set up any meeting? There was nothing like that involved?"

"No, sir."

Kendall was taken aback. Apparently, Irma had been seen in a public restaurant with Williams and Powell by a potential witness in the trial more than seventeen months earlier. Maybe Manka was on to something.

"After that, did the sheriff call you or ask you about it, or how did you happen to talk about the woman afterwards?" the defense attorney asked.

"Well, when they came in, I was sitting there drinking coffee, so I didn't make any acknowledgment or anything like that," Wilkey recalled. "When we got over by the phone or the rest room, we was talking there for a second, you know, about it being a small world. I said, 'You know, Gene, this is a coincidence'—which it was."

Manka gestured toward Irma. "You don't remember if this is the same woman you saw in that Denny's or not?" he asked, the tone leaving no doubt that he found the entire episode incredible.

"I couldn't take an oath on that, no, sir," Wilkey answered. "I don't know if you are familiar with that Denny's, but you come in the door like so"—he drew a picture in the air with his finger—"and there is a little bar and a booth and what have you. The ranger and sheriff and the lady were all sitting in one of the booths down there, and I was in the coffee row."

"So you didn't get a really good look at her, but it was approximately the same type of person?" Manka asked.

"Uh-huh."

"Pass the witness."

Kendall decided to downplay the encounter while making sure the judge understood what he took to be the essence of the scene. "Do you remember telling Sheriff Williams and Gene Powell that the woman looked similar to the one you had seen with Dess?" he asked Wilkey.

"I remember a conversation something like that, yes, sir."

"What did you tell them?"

"That there was a similarity there." Wilkey stepped from the witness box, at a loss, like the others in the courtroom, about what to make of the Denny's incident.

The remainder of the day was tied up with legal maneuvering as first Kendall and then Manka pressed their arguments on Judge Priest. Kendall's position was that the promise not to prosecute contained in Irma's letter of immunity was nullified by her subsequent admission that she fired the third shot at Zani's insistence. If the autopsy was inconclusive about which bullet had killed him, Kendall suggested, it could just as easily be concluded that Irma "directly caused or was one of the persons causing the death of Julius Dess."

Manka countered that what they were trying was not really a criminal case but an issue of contract law. "Mrs. Zani came to this country in exchange for this offer made by the prosecution," he said. "The prosecution breaches his agreement by prosecuting Mrs. Zani." Irma had changed her story only after returning to Texas, giving a "coerced statement" to Gene Powell. For that reason, Manka concluded, the most trustworthy statement was the Acapulco interview, given at a time when "there was no compunction upon her to lie."

Priest surprised them with the swiftness of his verdict. Immediately after closing arguments, he found Irma Zani guilty of murder and sentenced her to thirty years' confinement in the Texas Department of Corrections. Three days later, she arrived at Gatesville, a brand-new women's unit less than a hundred miles north of Austin.

PART

5

TWENTY

J ury selection in case number CRF-81-3065, *State of Oklahoma* v. *Robert Joseph Zani*, began early on the morning of December 7, 1982—Pearl Harbor Day, as Zani was quick to note. He had been charged with first-degree murder more than two years earlier and had fought extradition from the politically charged environs of Austin (a city, like Washington, D.C., founded almost solely on politics) with a tenacity unfamiliar to those around the more laid-back Tulsa County courthouse. In June 1981, however, he had finally been forced to appear in district court before special judge David Peterson, whose role was roughly that of a grand jury in Texas: to decide if enough probable cause existed to order the defendant to stand trial.

During the early hearings, Zani acted as his own defense attorney, though local lawyer Pete Silva had been appointed to stand by as a legal consultant. The defendant had surprised observers with his rhetoric. He asked Bob Bivens, the former police investigator who had lived next door to his mother, if Bivens's relationship with Gladys was ever more than neighborly. Later, when Irma took the stand, Zani called her a "born falsifier," adding that she was "a self-confessed harlot, a self-confessed liar, and a self-confessed murderer." So by the time the actual trial rolled around, Tulsa County district judge Margaret Lamm, a diminutive woman in her seventies who was affectionately known around the courthouse as "everybody's grandmother," was ready to put a stop to Zani's explosive courtroom antics before things got out of hand. In chambers, she conducted a preemptive strike of her own, admonishing him that he was expected to behave like an attorney.

"You don't make snide remarks about people," Lamm warned him. "You can question the jurors like an attorney would or you can question the witnesses like an attorney would, but you don't make remarks outside of that. Do you understand what I am saying?"

"I think that advice should go both ways," Zani answered tersely, looking at assistant district attorney Mark Lyons.

"Just so everybody understands," Lamm said, standing up to signal that the time had come to move to the sixth-floor courtroom and begin the trial.

At twenty-eight, Lyons was prosecuting the case for his boss, David Moss, who had just been elected to replace S. M. "Buddy" Fallis, Jr., the recently retired DA. Moss was generally regarded by the public a an interim officeholder, certainly no match for the popular Fallis, and Moss was keenly aware of the need to establish his own reputation by winning a major case. Even though the first-degree-murder charge against Zani had been reduced to second-degree to comply with Oklahoma statutes in effect at the time of Gladys Zani's killing in 1974, Lyons had been given instructions to get a conviction if at all possible.

The courthouse sat just west of a six-block-square area known as the heart of downtown Tulsa, a city with a population of about 500,000 and lying along I-44 in the relatively populous northeast corner of Oklahoma. Tulsa had boomed back in the twenties when oil suddenly spurted out of the dirt, earning it the nickname "Terra Cotta City" as ambitious petro-millionaires erected gaudy art-deco skyscrapers to trumpet their new wealth to the world. But the buildings were largely empty now in the face of slumping oil prices, and civic leaders were switching to a different promotional tag—Tulsa as an Indian town, an area that boasts the highest percentage of native American residents of any metropolitan region in the country.

To some, though, Tulsa was primarily the home of Oral Roberts University, derisively known as the University of Mars among locals, who pointed to the campus's futuristic architecture and the heavyhanded Christian bias of students who often seemed to worship the school's evangelical founder as much as the Lord. Over the next three weeks, twelve of those locals—seven men and five women, all ordinary Tulsans—would sit in judgment of a man who had once been one of them but who now seemed as alien as Oral Roberts.

Zani and his new court-appointed assistant, local attorney Allen Smallwood, sat impassively at the defense table the next morning when prosecutor Lyons rose to make his opening statement. The jurors eyed Lyons with a quiet skepticism he had seen before, the look of people prone to agree with what their fellow Oklahoman Will Rogers once said: "A jury should decide a case the minute they are shown it, before the lawyers have had a chance to confuse 'em."

Nevertheless, Lyons gamely led them through the sequence of events Irma had described to Ruiz and Martinez two and a half years earlier in Acapulco. He recounted—a bit too graphically, some thought—how Zani had forced his wife to participate in his mother's murder. "The minute that towel goes up, *bam!* There goes the hammer on the back of Gladys Zani's head, and she falls down on the floor," Lyons told the jurors. "He bludgeons her until white material starts coming out of her head. Then the real gore comes out."

The jurors fidgeted in their seats, increasingly uncomfortable as Lyons related how Zani had bought a saw, cut the corpse into half a dozen pieces, and stuffed them into suitcases after washing the blood down the basement drain.

"So they get in the car, and they start driving," he went

on, fixing each juror with an intense, unsparing glare before moving to the next. "And they stop every now and then and throw out a piece of the body here, drive a little further, throw out a piece of the body there, until they get over to Arkansas. They have got the torso and the head left. And Irma says, 'What are you going to do with the head?' And he says, 'I'm going to hang it in a tree.' "

The assistant DA continued to map out the state's case, letting his voice rise as he worked to impress upon them the horror of the defendant's actions. Some of the jurors, he noticed, had begun to steal glances at Zani. Lyons told them about Gladys's neighbor, Bob Bivens. The former cop would testify that he had last seen Gladys in July 1974, Lyons said. Same with Vera Tolbert, Gladys's sister. Two Secret Service agents would then state that the victim's signature on her social security checks had been forged for a least another five years.

"The house in Tulsa gets sold," Lyons concluded. "The land in Arkansas gets sold, bank accounts get closed out, social security checks get cashed, retirement checks get cashed—and Gladys Zani is never heard from again. That's basically what you are going to hear. And I am going to ask you, ladies and gentlemen, when we get finished, to find Robert Joseph Zani guilty of murder. Thank you."

The presentation had been intense. Lyons was going for a conviction in a seven-year-old crime for which there was no body, little hard evidence, and a main prosecution witness—Irma—who was herself a convicted murderer. And as he took his seat, Lyons couldn't help feeling that his opening statement had been pretty damned effective.

If Zani was aware of the old adage that anyone who represents himself in court has a fool for a client, he didn't let on when his turn came. He descended from his cell on the eighth floor of the courthouse and gave a performance that ranked as one of the most bizarre the professionals gathered in the courtroom that day had ever seen.

He began by making two requests of Judge Lamm. First,

he wished to move the blackboard on which he had written a number of points to illustrate his case closer to the jurors' box.

"Denied," Lamm said.

Zani then asked to be allowed to make his opening statement without a coat.

"I have no objection if you want to take your jacket off," Lamm informed him. "Just so you stick to what you intend to prove."

"I understand, yes," Zani agreed, facing the juror's box. "Judge Lamm, Mr. Lyons, ladies and gentlemen of the jury, in the words of one of America's best-known newscasters, Parul Harvey, 'And now the rest of the story.' First Corinthians, Chapter 13, Saint Paul writes—"

Lyons was up on his feet. "Objection, Your Honor."

"You are merely to make an opening statement," Lamm reminded the defendant.

"I understand, Your Honor," Zani assured her. "Well, for now, we see through a glass darkly, but then—"

Lyons was back up. "Same objection, Your Honor."

"I would sustain the same objection," Lamm sighed. Impatiently, she reminded Zani to confine his remarks to the case at hand.

Zani walked to the easel that held the blackboard. "First of all, let me explain this number one," he said, scrawling notes in the margins of his giant outline as he addressed the jurors from over his shoulder. "The first thing is very simply a promise. The defense will tell you where this story originated. Number two, the defense will tell you that you will not hear from the person who originated this story. The third thing I will tell you is, the prosecution has not subpoenaed the person who originated this story, and I will also tell you that I am not able to subpoena the person who originated that story."

The jury had no idea what Zani was talking about. He jerked from side to side, making it hard not to notice that his thoughts were as awkward as his physical movements.

"Two, three, and four tie together, and they are very much a part of what the defense will show," Zani continued, pointing at the blackboard. "Number two is obviously one. You see, self-representation in this case will be very much different than what many people had assumed. It has been printed in the media that this man is representing himself because he knows more than an attorney, wants jury sympathy, or what have you. That is, of course, not true.

"The purpose of self-representation ties into a portion of my defense. I am going to be right in front of you where you can make the best decision of all. You can look me in the eye, and I can look you in the eye. That is my purpose in standing before you, not because I know the law or don't. I want to be that close that you can look and take as close a look as you will ever get at anyone in the courtroom."

Shaking his head ever so slightly, Smallwood looked down at the pad in front of him and pretended to make notes. *They've probably had too close a look already,* he thought.

"The third point ties in with the second," Zani went on. "I will tell you from the witness stand that, if believed, the whole story is a deranged act. This is going to lead to some interesting conclusions. The fourth thing ties in with two and three—that is, my conduct during the trial. I am going to be in front of you as close as I can get. In fact, I have tried to get even closer, but that's been denied by the court."

"Objection, Your Honor," Lyons reacted, leaping up again. He would remain standing throughout most of the remainder of the trial—to save wear and tear on his knees, he later joked—as he objected again and again to Zani's fumbling attempts to be his own counsel. Lamm once more admonished the defendant to stick to what he expected to prove.

Zani continued. "The fifth thing is, the state's case rests upon perjury, massive perjury. The sixth thing is immunity. Defendant will tell you from the witness stand himself he was offered immunity to testify. The defendant will also tell you he turned that down, and he is going to tell you exactly why he turned that down.

"The seventh point is money. The state is going to talk about money. The defendant is going to talk about money also. The defendant is going to tell you about certain instances when he was entrusted with large sums of money and carried out those trusts. He is going to tell you of at least two instances, one involving a personally made bank deposit of a little over one million one hundred thousand dollars. The second instance is a bank deposit of approximately four hundred thirty-five thousand dollars. He is going to tell you he was given that trust and that he carried that trust out."

Those who, by some miracle or chance, had followed Zani's opening statement from the beginning were thoroughly lost by now.

"The eighth thing," he continued, "the defendant is going to tell you in no uncertain terms that some of the state's witnesses are biased and prejudiced. And there are a couple of other points which, for now, I am going to lump together. This case is illogical. Number ten, Mr. Smallwood will be in the courtroom with me from time to time. He wanted me to explain this to you, and I think I should. All right. Now we come to the main point—well, there is three."

Even Zani was losing track now. He impugned testimony that Irma had yet to give and, after Lamm sustained Lyons's objection, returned to the outline that rested on the easel in front of the jury. Apparently forgetting that he had already recited the first ten points, he listed number one again—except that it was different this time.

"I have been through this process before," Zani assured the jurors, who at that point knew nothing of his previous trials. "This is a fishing expedition. Number two, I will tell you under oath that I am here in this courtroom primarily because of my beliefs. They are a little different, but I think they are right."

Lyons looked at Smallwood, who shrugged and went back to his doodles on the yellow legal pad in front of him.

"Very well," Zani said at last, "we will skip to point number five. I am going to tell you I have worked mentally on this case for over two and a half years, and I am going to tell you under oath that I have put my case together. I have ninety-nine pieces of a one-hundred-piece puzzle put together. I am going to tell you ahead of time what the one-hundredth piece is—the translator. When I see a translator in this courtroom, I will make my case."

There was a long pause during which the judge, the lawyers, and the jurors all tried, without success, to figure out what the hell the slight man in the black horn-rims was talking about. Finally, Zani brought them back to what he considered to be the heart of the matter.

"The defendant is going to tell you under oath again that since 1966 he has had a rather unusual employment," he said. "He is going to tell you that he has been employed in regular jobs, just as most all of you have been. But since 1966 he's been engaged in a moonlighting job. I will tell you that that employment for fourteen years was to save lives, not to take them. I will also tell you that fortunately or unfortunately, it is not what was done but how it was done that hurts the defendant. I will also tell you truthfully that other people have another definition of what I do—'a fixer.' I'm going to tell you about certain cases that I have personally worked. I'm going to tell you from the witness stand that in 1967 I failed. And I am going to tell you what happened when I failed—I'm going to tell you about the people that could not be brought back to life."

For months, word in the corridors of the Tulsa County courthouse had been that Zani claimed to be some deep-cover intelligence agent. Now those who had heard the rumors perked up.

"I am also going to tell you about involvement in a case which received national publicity in the early seventies," Zani went on, "one of the most strange and unusual cases in the United States, which was, at that time, written about by *Time* magazine. Yes, I will tell you I have gotten myself involved in some strange things. Ladies and gentlemen of the jury, in order to achieve what has been achieved, I have had to do some things that some people would rather not admit. I will tell you from the witness stand what brought me here. This case began with a bribe, another bribe, another and another bribe. I should know—I paid them. Yes, I did pay a judge, I paid a district attorney, I paid a judge's secretary, and I paid a court reporter. That initiated this case. And I will further tell you that it was the payoff to a judge that brought this whole thing about. I am sorry, that is true.

"I will tell you that during the past fourteen years I have picked a low number. I will tell you that, yes, I have made payoffs. Nearly every one of them was made to save a life. Some people may disagree, but I will talk about those cases.

"I will tell you how I got embroiled in other problems due to this. I have made more than twelve payoffs to judges. I have made more than twelve payoffs to district attorneys. I have made more than six payoffs to judges' secretaries. And I have made more than six payoffs to court reporters. That is the tip of the iceberg. I will tell you how doing this work—for which I was well paid, most of the time—I met some very strange and unusual people from other countries. I have learned a lot. I have met other people in the same type of business. I will tell you how other governments perform their functions, because I have seen it. I'm not talking about just one country, either."

Zani was inching his way across the room toward the defense table, choreographing his conclusion for maximum dramatic effect. "Ladies and gentlemen of the jury," he said, reaching his chair, "I will tell you from the witness stand that I am innocent. I have never taken a life. The state and other individuals have dipped their hands in innocent blood—and it is my blood, and it is my children's blood. That is all."

* * *

After a five-minute recess, Lyons played Zani's bluff. Just before bringing Irma to the stand, he called as his first witness Connie Stevens, a Spanish teacher and translator with more than a decade of experience. "When I see a translator in this courtroom, I will make my case," Zani had predicted. Well, here she was, the last piece in the defendant's puzzle.

Lyons couldn't wait to see how Zani dealt with this unexpected turn and, after asking Stevens a number of questions to establish her credentials, passed the witness. Zani immediately objected to the presence of a translator. He knew that she was there to help when his wife took the stand, and he contended that Irma spoke English well enough to do without an interpreter. Besides, he didn't want his wife's testimony translated for the jury with some subtle twist that might shade the case against him.

Zani then offered eighteen legal objections based on the issue of marital privilege. Each was overruled. He next moved for a mistrial, which also left Lamm unfazed. Finally, he demanded a translator for himself, but Lamm sidestepped that request by appointing Stevens "translator for the court," which meant she would be available to both sides.

When Irma was called to the stand at last, observers in the packed courtroom leaned forward. No one wanted to miss the unusual spectacle of a woman testifying against her husband—especially when, as his own counsel, the husband was going to have the opportunity to cross-examine her.

But first, it was the prosecution's turn. Lyons began slowly, letting his star witness settle in at her own pace. Gradually, though, he led Irma into Gladys's alleged sexual molestation of Zani when he was a teenager and, from there, to her husband's belief that everything his mother owned really belonged to him. "He said his daddy was sending money to his mama, and the money belonged to him and he never saw it," Irma testified.

"Had he ever said before that he wanted to kill his mother?" Lyons asked.

"Oh, yes, he did say it lots of times."

Pausing now and then so that Stevens could translate his questions, Lyons brought the testimony around to July 1974 and the day of the picnic at Gladys's property in Arkansas. Irma recalled that Zani and his mother had quarreled and that the drive back to Tulsa was tense and silent.

"All the way back to Tulsa?" Lyons asked.

"Yes, sir. She would not say anything, nor him. They were just quiet."

"Okay, what happened when you got back to Tulsa?"

"When we got back to Tulsa, it was late in the evening, about six-thirty. Zani said, 'This is it,' and I saw him grabbing a hammer."

"Did you know at this time what he was going to do with the hammer?"

"No, sir, I didn't."

"What happened after he grabbed the hammer?"

"Well, he grabbed a towel in the car and he told me to take it. I didn't understand, but I took it."

"What happened after he told you to take the towel?"

"We got out of the car, and she came in her house first. She was in front and I was next and Zani was next, the last. When we got inside her house, he turned the television on real loud. I just went with her to the kitchen."

"Did he say anything to you?"

"Yes. He said it was time for him to do something about her."

"Did you know what he was talking about?"

"Kind of, but not . . ."

"Did you think he was serious about doing it?"

Zani objected angrily. "That calls for a conclusion," he yelled.

"Sure does, Judge," Lyons shot back. "She was there. She had the ability to look at his emotions and know what was going on."

Lamm suggested that Lyons ask the question in a different form. She seemed determined to treat the legally unschooled Zani as fairly as possible, though his abrasive personality—to say nothing of the horrifyng events his wife was now describing—made it difficult.

Lyons switched tracks. "What happened after you had the towel in your hand?" he asked Irma.

"She was getting a drink of water, and he told me, you know, to put the towel on her. I did it."

"And then what happened?"

"Then he just hit her with the hammer on the back of the head. She fell on the floor and just . . . I don't know whether it was a question or just a word, but she said, 'Why,' and that was it. She said it, and then after that he just kept on hitting her."

"Where did he hit her?"

"On her face. She was wearing glasses, and the pieces sunk in her face, and he beat her ugly. She had all this white stuff coming out of her brain, and she was . . . Everything was destroyed on her face."

Lyons let her words sink in for a moment, then went on. "Now, what was Gladys's condition after he finished hitting her?" he asked.

"It was . . . She was dead. To me, she was dead."

"Was she breathing?"

"No."

"Was she moving?"

"Sir, she was not moving at all."

"Was she speaking?"

"No, nothing. She was destroyed."

The jury sat stunned as Irma recalled what Lyons had already told them: how she and her husband cut the body into pieces with a band saw and drove to Gladys's Arkansas property the next day, dispersing body parts one by one along the highway; how they later sold the house at 218 Xenophon and moved to La Feria, Texas, living on the forged social security checks and other proceeds from the sale of

Gladys's belongings; how they continued the pattern after moving to Buffalo, Missouri; and finally, how they fled to Mexico because her husband "was not satisfied on how people were doing things here in America."

None of the jurors could have been prepared to hear the gruesome details. More than one later recalled wishing at that point that they had come up with some reason not to report for duty.

When his turn came, Zani began the cross-examination of his wife true to form. Standing in the middle of the courtroom, he straightened his blue necktie and fixed Irma with a cold stare. "Mrs. Zani," he began in a voice full of sarcasm, "do you know Mr. Lyons?"

"Yes."

"Have you ever spoken with Mr. Lyons before?"

"Yes."

"How many times?"

"I did not count them. Not too many."

Zani turned toward the jurors' box and smirked. "Would you define 'too many'?" he asked his wife.

Irma was confused and requested a translation. After a brief discussion, Stevens interpreted her reply for the jury's benefit. "From when? From what time?"

Zani faced Judge Lamm. "Your Honor, I'm going to object to the way the translation is being done. If the question cannot be understood, it should be brought back with no conversing. The question was, 'How many times?' Obviously, since Mr. Lyons and she have had some sort of relationship—"

"My God!" Irma exclaimed.

Bill Musseman, a former assistant DA then in private practice (now a special Tulsa County judge) who had been appointed to represent Irma during the trial, leapt to his feet. "Your Honor, I will have to object," he shouted.

Lamm sustained the objection, frowning at Zani and motioning him to continue. Zani arched his brow in the overinnocent manner of a man who would have you believe he has been wrongly accused. "There is a relationship whenever anyone meets anyone else," he explained. "If anyone takes that the wrong way, to me that is in someone else's mind."

"The question can certainly be rephrased," interjected a disgusted Lyons.

"Yes," Lamm quickly agreed.

Zani spent most of the next ten minutes asking a series of peculiar questions, to which Musseman objected time after time. "What is your true and correct name? Are you Mr. Zani's first wife? Are you a citizen of Mexico by birth? How long have you lived in the United States? Have you ever applied for American citizenship? Have you ever sued an attorney?" Lamm sustained each objection, admonishing Zani to move on to a topic relevant to the case at hand.

"Well, Mrs. Zani," the defendant asked at last, "have you been promised or granted immunity in this case?"

"Here in Oklahoma, no," Irma replied.

"Mrs. Zani, has anyone indicated to you in any way that you would not go to prison in this case?" Zani insisted, drawing an objection from Musseman that the question had already been asked and answered.

Fed up, Lamm decreed a recess until the following morning. Few of those who had anticipated the revelations of a world of international intrigue to which Zani alluded in his opening statement now looked forward to another day. They were beginning to suspect that Robert Zani was, in the homespun ken of Oklahoma, "all hat and no cattle."

The third day of the trial began with the granting of a juror's request to be dismissed for personal reasons. She was replaced by the first alternate, a man, which realigned the balance of the jury at eight men and four women for the remainder of the trial. After that bit of business, Zani picked up his cross-examination where he had left off the day before.

"Mrs. Zani, has anyone indicated to you in any way that you would not go to prison in this case?" he asked.

"Yes. Mr. Mark Lyons. He said that as long as I said the truth . . ."

"Mrs. Zani, what is your permanent address?"

"I do not have a permanent address in America. I am staying in prison."

Zani thought he saw the jurors perk up at this news, and he moved in for what he hoped would be the final blow in his effort to discredit the witness. "Have you ever been convicted of a felony?" he asked his wife.

"Yes," Irma replied.

"What was that conviction for?"

Irma leaned forward slightly in the witness box, looking directly into her husband's eyes. "A death of a man I didn't do," she said, "a crime that *you* done."

Zani wheeled toward the bench and triumphantly moved again for a mistrial. To his dismay, Lamm was unmoved. "I would overrule that," she said matter-of-factly. "The jury would be admonished not to consider the answer."

Visibly deflated, Zani stumbled through a number of questions designed to show that Irma's command of the English language was limited. The jury was clearly unimpressed, having already heard her respond to convoluted questions they themselves often found hard to follow. Finally, Zani zeroed in on what he hoped to prove was his wife's illegal extradition from Mexico.

"When these police officers approached you in Acapulco, which one of them did most of the talking?" Zani wanted to know.

"Mr. Paul Ruiz," Irma responded.

"Mr. Ruiz. Did Mr. Ruiz tell you that he wanted you to go with them to the United States and that they would take you?"

"Yes, he did."

"Mrs. Zani, isn't it true also that you accused Mr. Zani only after your conversation with Paul Ruiz in May of 1980?"

"No, I didn't accuse you. I told him the truth, everything. I just told them at the time when they asked me everything concerning other crimes—"

"Mrs. Zani, didn't you go to the police in Acapulco, Mexico, on January 6, 1980, and accuse the defendant of killing his mother?"

"I didn't say that, no."

"When Mr. Hunt interviewed you on May 28, 1980, didn't you tell him that you had, in fact, gone to the police prior to May of 1980 with this story?"

"I don't remember that."

"You don't remember?"

"I don't remember saying that, no."

A number of other questions followed in quick succession, all objected to by Musseman, who approached the bench to say that while he understood Zani was "unschooled in the technicalities of legal proceedings," it was his duty to protect his client. Judge Lamm warned Zani to cross-examine the witness in "the proper way."

Zani retrenched. "Mrs. Zani, when you described the alleged scene of the murder yesterday, I believe you stated that you did not leave the scene. Is that correct?"

"Yes. Because I had been threatened."

"Mrs. Zani, are you stating that you couldn't go to the police or call the police that day or the next day or the day after? Who was threatening you at that time?"

"You," Irma replied firmly. "I have been threatened by you. I just couldn't do anything."

Zani spent several minutes more asking questions, all legally clumsy and objected to by either Musseman or Lyons. It was beginning to seem to the jury that the defendant was his own worst enemy. In desperation, Zani returned to this attempts to impugn his wife's character.

"Mrs. Zani, do you remember the date when you first met the defendant?" he asked.

"1967," Irma answered. "1967."

"Have you ever been employed in Mexico?"

"Yes."

"Would you state how and when and where?"

Musseman was standing now. "Your Honor, I will object to the form of the question. I know what he is getting into. It is improper impeachment, and I would object to the relevancy of it."

Judge Lamm, with little background on Irma, was completely lost. She asked the attorneys to approach the bench, where Musseman tried to explain.

"Your Honor, he is getting into a line of questioning that is improper before a jury," Musseman whispered. "Many years prior to this incident, she was a prostitute. That has no basis in this trial whatsoever. It is improper."

Lamm agreed. Turning to Zani, she said, "I would not let you ask that. I think it is improper in a jury trial."

Zani returned to his table and bent over his notes. He didn't know how to proceed. After several minutes, he straightened, having decided to pursue one last line of questioning. He had heard that Irma was told she would walk on the current charges if she implicated her husband and agreed to make things "look real ugly" for him.

"Mrs. Zani, when officers Paul Ruiz and Robert Martinez and others approached you in May of 1980 in Acapulco, Mexico, did any one of them make any promises to you for your statements or testimony?" he asked.

"Yes, they did."

"Who?"

"Mr. Paul Ruiz."

"What promises for your statements or testimony did Mr. Ruiz make to you?"

"He promised that if I said everything you have done, they were going to help me."

"How did they say they would help you?"

"I didn't have any money."

"Were you promised any money?"

"No."

"Were you then tricked into coming back to the United States?"

"Yes."

"By police officers?"

"Everybody there."

"Your Honor," Zani said, turning toward the judge, "I need about five minutes to rephrase several questions."

Lyons sensed that Zani might be on to something. More amused than worried, he wondered what would come next. After the recess, however, Zani demonstrated that he lacked the legal expertise to nail it down. "For the purpose of the record," he continued, "I'd like to ask Mrs. Zani if she has any makeup on."

Musseman objected to the bizarre question, but Lamm looked at the witness and observed, "Yes, she has makeup on."

Largely because no one present understood what he was getting at, Zani was allowed to continue. For close to thirty minutes, he read through the transcript of Irma's interview with Tulsa sergeants Hunt and Parke, getting his wife to admit that minor details of her account were inaccurate. Nothing, though, altered the essence of her story, and to everyone's delight, Judge Lamm finally called a recess so that they could all grab a bite to eat.

The afternoon included testimony from Bob Bivens, the former Tulsa homicide cop, who repeated that he and Gladys had been casual friends until July 1974, when she disappeared. Upon returning from vacation that month, Bivens and his wife had been surprised to find Gladys gone and Robert and his family living in the house.

Lyons then called Ronald Morris, an examiner of questioned documents with the Secret Service in Washington, D.C. Lyons regarded Morris's testimony as critical. Under Oklahoma law, no one can be convicted on the uncorroborated testimony of an accomplice; there must be independent evidence linking the defendent to the crime. That's what Lyons, who contended that Irma was not an accomplice but an unwilling participant, hoped to establish with Morris on the stand.

After leading the agent through a long and complex explanation of his inquiry into the forged signatures on Gladys's social security checks, Lyons asked for his conclusion. Morris replied that Robert Zani had "very probably" signed the checks. "Very probably," Lyons noted, was Secret Service code language for proof just sort of certainty.

Next Lyons called Tulsa PD detective Roy Nuttle, who testified about lifting Zani's palm prints from the forged checks. Then came James Bartee, a retired FBI agent who had gone to work as a fingerprint specialist with the Secret Service. Sitting perfectly straight and answering Lyons's questions while looking directly at the jurors (a technique most law enforcement personnel are taught before court appearances), Bartee delivered a long lesson on fingerprint identification. He concluded that prints on some of the checks supposedly signed by Gladys Zani after her disappearance actually belonged to Robert Zani, including a latent "writer's palm" just under the signature line.

By the time Margaret Lamm brought the session to a close, several jurors' eyes seemed to have glazed over. In fact, they had heard what may have been the most crucial testimony of the trial.

The fourth day, December 10, brought brief appearances by a couple of witnesses who were better at holding the jurors' attention. Bertha Epperson, who bought the house at 218 Xenophon, told the court that she and her husband dealt exclusively with Zani during the transaction, which had taken place on May 5, 1975, in the offices of Ralph Zimmerman, a local attorney. After the initial down payment, Epperson said, five more monthly checks were issued to Gladys Zani and cashed before she and her husband received notice that further payments should be made to an

Oklahoma City investment company, which they presumed, had taken over the mortgage from Zani.

Next up was Vera Tolbert, Gladys Zani's sister. Tolbert related that she had last spoken to Gladys by phone in the spring of 1974. She sent a couple of letters after that and even tried to call a few times, but the line was disconnected. By October of that year, when the new Tulsa phone directory was published, Tolbert became worried—it contained no listing for Gladys. "My sister lived for her telephone contact with friends," she told Lyons. "I knew Gladys would never drop her name out of that telephone directory unless there was something wrong, really seriously wrong."

When Zani took his aunt under cross-examination, he displayed the same disdain for her that he had shown for his wife the day before. "Mrs. Tolbert, in trying to locate Gladys Zani, did you ever make contact with anyone in any mental institutions?" he asked.

"Not personally," Tolbert replied, barely able to conceal her hatred of her nephew. "I made inquiries of how I could find out about it because I felt perhaps she had been sent to a mental institution."

"Mrs. Tolbert, would you tell the jury why you would think that?"

"I thought that perhaps you had figured out a way to get rid of her. That would be a sure way to get her out of circulation."

Zani abruptly turned and walked back to the defense table. "No further questions, Your Honor," he said, slumping into his seat.

Judge Lamm asked Lyons to call his next witness. The assistant DA suppressed a smile as he approached the bench. "The state is ready to rest," he said calmly. One glance around the courtroom was enough to indicate he spoke for nearly everyone there.

* * *

Just before the jury was brought in on Monday, December 13, Allen Smallwood made one last effort to give his client some sound legal representation, which Zani had clearly failed to provide for himself. Having spent the weekend studying the case, Smallwood argued that the prosecution had not corroborated the testimony supplied by Irma, who, he pointed out, was a codefendant and thereby not considered a reliable witness under Oklahoma's criminal statutes. He asserted that the existence of Zani's prints on his mother's social security and retirement checks proved little other than that the defendant had touched them, understandable given that they lived together. In light of the state's failure to prove its case beyond a reasonable doubt, Smallwood concluded, he was asking Lamm to direct a verdict of not guilty.

Lyons countered that Oklahoma law required only that the prosecution present evidence that tended to connect the defendant with the crime, not necessarily beyond all reasonable doubt. He told Lamm it would be a "travesty of justice" not to let the case go to the jury. Lamm agreed.

But Smallwood was not finished. He informed the judge that he had subpoenaed Dr. José Hernandez, the San Antonio psychiatrist who had testified the year before that Irma was incompetent to stand trial in Floresville for the murder of Julius Dess. In fact, Smallwood added, Hernandez was waiting in the hall outside, ready to take the stand.

Lyons had also done his homework over the weekend. He argued against letting Hernandez testify, reminding Lamm that two other San Antonio psychiatrists had refuted his findings during the Dess trial. To make matters worse for the defense, Musseman announced that he would be forced to invoke Irma's doctor-patient privilege if Hernandez was allowed to take the stand.

Lamm leaned back in her chair and considered their various positions. After a long pause, she ruled against any testimony from Hernandez. "Shall we bring the jury in now?" she asked.

Smallwood still had one more trick up his legal sleeve, though. Before admitting the jury, he asked for a motion to suppress evidence based on what his client claimed to have been his illegal arrest at the Austin Ramada Inn back on March 28, 1980. "I have a detective from Austin I would like to put on," Smallwood said.

Robert Martinez had been surprised to receive a subpoena in the mail two weeks earlier while working at his desk in the Twin Towers. What was odd, he noted, was that he was being asked to appear for the defense. Nevertheless, he drove to Tulsa on the appointed date, wondering what the man he and Ruiz—who had left the Austin Police Department ten days before—had pursued for so long might possibly want from him now. After three days of waiting to testify, he was going to find out.

"Can you tell Judge Lamm what information you had when you made the arrest of Robert Joseph Zani?" Smallwood asked.

"We had information that a man was registered at the Ramada Inn and that he was acting real suspicious," Martinez said. "We went to check the register, found that it was under a name of Richard Womack. Turned out the credit card had been stolen out of a house."

"Okay, how did you come to arrest Robert Joseph Zani?"

"We were in the manager's office. We saw him climbing up the steps heading for his room, and we went out the door and hollered at him. When we did, he ran to his room."

"What room did he run into?"

"Two-fourteen [*sic*]."

"What did you do as a result of that?"

"We knocked on the door for about ten minutes. Finally he came to the door, and we asked him what his name was. He said his name was Richard Womack. At this time, we arrested him."

"Did you conduct a search as a result of that arrest?"

Martinez realized at last what Smallwood and Zani were up to. They were going to try to get the case thrown out based on what they hoped to demonstrate was a faulty arrest. But Martinez had been down this route before, and he began to measure his responses. "No, sir," he replied carefully. "We secured the apartment, locked it, went to the police station, got a search warrant."

"You conducted no search of the person of Robert Zani when you arrested him?" Smallwood insisted.

"No, sir. Just frisked him for weapons there at the scene."

"Did you discover anything?"

"No weapons on him."

"I assume that you executed the search warrant immediately thereafter. Were you present when it was executed?"

"Yes, sir, I was."

"Who else was there?"

"My ex-partner, Paul Ruiz, and a detective named Jimmy Brown."

"What did you find there?"

"In the toilet bowl, I found four [*sic*] credit cards and one Texas driver's license belonging to Richard Womack."

"Did you find anything else?"

"Yes, sir. We found a twenty-five automatic hidden under a pillow in the closet. Suitcase, papers, a notebook containing an address in Acapulco, Mexico."

"As a result of getting that information, what did you do?"

"Called the American embassy in Mexico City. They in turn told me to call the American consulate in Acapulco."

"When the search warrant was executed, the affidavit contained a named informant to support the probable-cause allegations, did it not?"

"Yes, sir."

"Is it not a fact that the named informant turned out later not to exist?"

"Yes, sir. The name was wrong on the search warrant." During the Austin trial, he recalled, Zani's attorneys had tried to make a great deal of the fact that Brown had misrecorded realtor Larry Flood as "Jack Flood."

"And that named informant in the affidavit was necessary

to supply probable cause for the issuance of that search warrant, was it not?"

"Right."

"Detective Martinez, are you absolutely certain the search which was made as a result of the issuance of the warrant took place the same day that Mr. Zani was arrested?"

"Yes, sir. Positive."

"As a result of the search, you made contact with Irma Zani. She stated that Robert Zani was involved in a homicide in Oklahoma, right?"

"Uh-huh."

"Other than what Irma Zani told you as a result of your going to Acapulco and seizing her, did she tell you anything else which has resulted in any information which is being used in this case?"

"No.,"

"That is all I have," Smallwood said, returning to his seat.

Lyons had just one question on cross-examination: "Mr. Martinez, did she come back with you freely and voluntarily?"

"Yes," Martinez answered. *No doubt about it,* he thought, *this guy Smallwood was slick.* Martinez couldn't be sure, but he may have given the wrong room number at the Ramada. Was it 214 or 219? And now that he reflected further, maybe the search warrant hadn't been executed the day of the arrest. It was so close to midnight, after all, that it could have been carried out on the following day. And what about this bit of "seizing" Irma in Acapulco. Were these the technicalities upon which modern law enforcement was based?

On Tuesday, December 14, Smallwood called Zani to the stand. It was a calculated risk, he knew, but there seemed little to lose. After establishing that Zani had been employed in two jobs at the time of his mother's disappearance—as a pipe cutter at Tulsa's Dover Corporation and as "a cook and bottle washer" at a local Denny's Restaurant—Smallwood asked his client what other activities he was engaged in at that time. "In the summer of 1974, did you have an occasion to be out of the continental United States?" Smallwood wanted to know, thinking about the answers they had obviously rehearsed.

"Oh, yes," Zani replied. "Southern Mexico. Basically, I went there because many of my in-laws were being killed."

"As a result of what situation occurring in Mexico?" asked Smallwood.

"Well, it's a rather long story," Zani said. *Indeed,* thought several jury members. They had heard the defendant's allusions about shadowy top-secret missions but had been presented little evidence so far.

"Without going into details," Smallwood continued, "was it an earthquake or—"

Zani cut him off. "Oh, no," he said. "What happened was, the Mexican government had initiated a tax program. The people who lived north of Acapulco had never paid tax before. Some of them lived on their land for two and three hundred years. The government decided in order to raise revenue that they would tax these people for the first time, and the people resisted."

"And your in-laws were among some of the people who were resisting?"

"Oh, yes."

"Did you see your mother during the summer of 1974?"

"Yes, I did. Probably twice, maybe three times."

"Did you speak with your mother, if you recall, during the month of August 1974?"

"I believe so, yes."

"Was it in Tulsa?"

"Oh, yes."

"Did she inform you of anything regarding her intentions?"

"She was going to Fort Myers, Florida."

"Did she in fact go to Fort Myers? How do you know that?"

"Because I talked to her."

"Who made the phone call to Fort Myers?"

"There was more than one, and I did. I am certain I made two there. Might have been more, and they were made in the spring of 1975."

Zani went on to testify that his mother had visited him in La Feria, Texas, in early 1976, though he couldn't say whether she had come alone, where she had stayed, or anything else about the trip—except that she had been "a little different, a little more unusual than normal." Smallwood then guided his client into a discussion of a New Year's Eve party that had taken place in Acapulco on December 31, 1979. "Did anything unusual occur that evening?" the lawyer asked.

"I suppose unusual for those people. For me, no," Zani replied, his enigmatic tendencies in high gear.

"What happened?" Smallwood asked.

"During the party the conversations turned around to things that were happening inside the city. Still quite a bit of resistance north of Acapulco to the taxation program. And it was mentioned to me that there was a young American woman who was locked up in the city jail at Acapulco."

"Is there any particular reason that you would have been informed of this?"

"Yes and no. The people that were there, some of the people knew that I had gotten people out of jail on numerous occasions, and they knew also that no Mexican person in that area would have helped because she was—their word is *guaracha*—just a gringa."

"What is that?"

"Well, in southern Mexico it is a derogatory term for an American. Within a couple of days I went down to see her and discovered that she and another young girl had come down to Acapulco on one of those tours. I guess because she was away from mom and dad, she had purchased some marijuana, and she had gotten arrested for that. I went to Judge García, who had authority over this woman."

"What happened when you talked with Judge García?"

"A certain amount of money was required to so-call pay her fine. In the state of Guerrero, that is not very odd. We secured the funds and got her out."

"Did your wife ever get involved in this?"

"No. However, the judge and I—he was very happy because he made his . . . Well, he came out well on the deal. I talked with the judge there for about an hour and a half, and as I say, he was in a very good mood. As a matter of fact, he was in such a good mood that we had a drink or two, and we got to talking about why I was in Acapulco. We talked back and forth, and the subject came up of who I was married to. I told him that I married into the Serranos clan, and he was quite shocked. He said, 'I want to show you something,' and I went in with him where they keep the prison records. Judge García showed me some documents."

"Okay. As a result of seeing those documents, did you do anything?"

"Yes, I sure did. I paid for them and copies thereof, and I took them to my mother-in-law's house. This was January fifth, 1980."

"What happened in your mother-in-law's house?"

"I read the documents, which were in Spanish. I told my children that we were leaving tomorrow."

"Not including your wife?"

"No."

"Did you get out of Mexico with your children?"

"No, sir, I did not."

"As of this day, do you know where your children are?"

"No."

Smallwood paced around the room, letting the implications of what his client was saying sink into the juror's minds. Apparently, Zani was testifying that his wife was involved in some undefined but nefarious deeds down in Mexico, though just what was uncertain. At last, Smallwood rested his hands on the witness box.

"You have heard, Robert, your wife testify to as grisly a set of facts as this courtroom has probably ever heard," he said. "Is any part of that true?"

"No," Zani answered, without hesitation.

"Do you have any explanation why your wife would tell this jury that you murdered your mother?"

"I surely do."

"What is that?"

"If I may," Zani began, "subsequent to when I took my children on January sixth and attempted to leave Acapulco, we stopped to spend the night. Now, when I had talked to the four children, three of them had determined that they would go with me; one had decided that she would stay with her mother. We stopped that night at a condominium in Acapulco, and about twelve o'clock that night, while we were asleep in the bed, the *judiciales* broke in the door, arrested me, and assaulted my children. We were taken downstairs, and there was my wife and mother-in-law, and they were infuriated and saying all sorts of things. I was taken to the police station, as were my children.

"My mother-in-law was ranting and raving in Spanish. She was saying, 'He killed his mother!' And the Mexican police took me over to one side of the room where they had a table, and they told me in Spanish, 'Well, you killed your mother.'

"I said, 'You're crazy,' and they beat the hell out of me. Eventually, I was unconscious, and they revived me and put me in front of a table, and the officer in charge pulled out a piece of paper, and he said, 'Sign this.' I said, 'I'm not signing anything. There's nothing on it.' And he said, 'You sign it, and we'll fill in the rest of it.' Well, I've heard stories like this before, but it was my first experience."

"Did Irma witness any of this?"

"Oh, yes. Oh, yes. Oh, definitely yes. The next morning when I woke up, there was people in this same hole along with me that functioned sort of as a holding cell. It was about nine o'clock in the morning, and I was taken out. The police officers told me they wanted me to wait, the state prosecutor would be there shortly, about ten-thirty or eleven. It is a little difficult to explain what a state prosecutor is, but basically he is someone who has not only authority over all what you would call district attorneys and assistant district attorneys, but he has an unlimited authority. He is over the chief of police. He is the man, so to speak."

"What happened next, Robert?"

"The state prosecutor [Miguel Angel O'Campo Oliveros] arrived and introduced himself. I sat on a sofa. I wasn't in very good shape, but I sat on a sofa. He was there, I was there, my wife was there, my mother-in-law was there. My children were right outside, and there was an investigator there also. Mr. O'Campo said, 'We have heard what your wife said.' And I told him that it was not only false, it's malicious and it's not true. And he said, 'Well, Mr. Zani, why is your wife here this morning and your mother-in-law? Why did they bring you food?' I said, 'I can't answer you that. You will have to ask them.' "

Lyons finally objected to the hearsay testimony, and Lamm sustained the objection.

"So as a result of this conversation, what did you do?" Smallwood asked.

"My wife was brought in."

"Was she interrogated?"

"Yes, yes she surely was. After the interrogation and after my wife admitted that she lied—"

Again Lyons objected. "I ask the jury be admonished not to consider it," he said angrily. "I ask the witness be instructed again not to relate any hearsay conversations or any other evidentiary harpoons that he normally uses."

It was Smallwood's turn to stand in anger. "To which I will object, Your Honor," he protested. "Mr. Lyons is making a closing argument while trying to make an objection. I ask he be admonished not to say those kinds of things in front of the jury."

Lamm sighed. "I expect you both to act like lawyers," she

warned them. In a stage whisper loud enough for everyone in the crowded courtroom to hear, someone observed, "Now we're really in trouble." The tension in the courtroom was temporarily diffused by a burst of eager laugher.

Under cross-examination, Zani matched Lyons's unfriendly queries with questions of his own. He was repeatedly warned by Judge Lamm to cooperate but either refused, claiming not to understand the questions, or suffered memory lapses that reduced his answers to a vague mumble. After several minutes of trying to get the unresponsive witness to give straightforward answers about how his signature happened to find its way onto his mother's checks, Lyons vented his frustration.

"Mr. Zani, you seem to remember a lot of specific dates and times, but you seem to forget others that seem pretty crucial," he said. "Any particular reason why?"

"That is because this was not important," Zani replied. "What I did I had the authority to do and have the authority to do, Mr. Lyons."

"How do you have that authority?"

"I have that authority—in fact, so does my wife—through a series of powers of attorney."

"To cash her checks and deposit them and use the funds?"

"You bet."

"Do you have that power of attorney somewhere?"

"As far as I know, it should be filed wherever my mother filed it."

Lyons moved to another subject. "Do you remember ever telling anybody that your mother was sick, that she was tired of family intervention in all her problems, and that from a given day forward you were going to be the only one to know where she was, and if family members wanted to talk to your mother, you would let them know if she wanted to talk to them?"

"Not like that," Zani said. "That's a very gross misrepresentation. But there is some truth in what you say."

"I am just asking a question, Mr. Zani."

"I was just answering it."

"Did you ever dislike your mother, Mr. Zani? Did you get upset with her when she cut off your money to go to school in Austin, Texas?"

"I'm sure I did."

"Didn't you in fact write your grandparents and say how upset you were?"

"Yes, I had a better relationship with my grandmother and grandfather than I did with my mother, that's true. I had an excellent relationship with my grandparents."

"What about your mother?"

"That is a very hard question to answer."

"Do your best," Lyons commanded, the sarcasm rising in his voice.

"Will you give me the time?" Zani shot back.

"You have the floor," Lyons said, sweeping his arms in a gesture of exaggerated invitation.

"Thank you," Zani said with a sigh. "Basically, the relationship that I have with my mother is not love—I can't lie. It is not hate—I can't lie again. But for what I know she went through for so many years, I tell you this: I have undying respect."

Lyons was not the only one in the courtroom who smiled at the choice of words. Leaning toward the witness stand, the prosecutor looked directly at Zani and asked him if he had ever tried to gather any evidence to back up his various assertions that his mother had been alive long after July 1974.

"No, I have no reason to," Zani replied.

"Because she's dead, isn't she?" Lyons yelled. "She's been dead since July 1974, and you butchered her in her own basement. That's why, isn't it?"

"That's a stinking lie, and you're a liar!" Zani screamed.

"Give us one shred of evidence to show she's been alive

since then," Lyons insisted, shouting as he looked toward the jurors' box.

"Give me one shred of evidence to show otherwise," Zani retorted.

After a brief noon recess, Mark Lyons stepped toward the jury to take Zani up on his challenge. He seemed to have gained confidence over the past few days, and now he offered his closing statement, threading a verbal prose that alternated between grim details of the crime and legal eloquence. He reminded them of the expert testimony showing that Zani had forged his mother's signatures on the checks. He suggested that such efforts made no sense in light of Zani's claim to possess power of attorney over his mother's finances. And he pointed out that Zani's sole defense was built on his insistence that Gladys was alive and that he was being persecuted for certain shadowy intelligence missions, which the defendant alluded to but never even attempted to prove.

"You have been subjected to the biggest bunch of cock-and-bull that you will ever hear," Lyons told the jurors. "There is not one iota of evidence to support any position that he's taken. You're just hearing incessant ramblings here—Mr. Zani saved lives, he's a fixer—but you're not hearing any evidence. What about some of his witnesses that were eliminated? Do you remember that? What witnesses have been eliminated? There is only one witness that's been eliminated in this case, and that's Gladys Zani.

"This isn't ring-around-the-rosy or some namby-pamby game. This is for all the marbles. Why didn't Zani search for his mother? It's very simple—because she is dead. He butchered her, and he mutilated her, and he threw her out between here and Arkansas. This isn't just a good dime-store mystery. This is what really happened."

Lyons moved to the center of the courtroom. "Here stands before you now a murderer, and I want you to tell him so," he concluded. "I want you to convict him. I don't want you to give this man a good number of years. I want you to give him *hundreds* of years. I want you to give him thousands of years to keep him off the streets forever and ever and ever and ever. I want you to give him as many years as you can put down on that jury verdict form. Tell Robert Zani that he will never walk free again. And if it takes ten thousand or ten million years to do that, I ask you to give it to him. Thank you."

Lyons sat down, satisfied that he had summed up the absurdity of Zani's defense. But Smallwood, whose client had shut him out of most of the trial, was unwilling to see another loss added to his judicial scorecard without a fight.

"The state of Oklahoma has found itself in a spot," he told the jurors. "They don't have a body. I don't know how long you folks have lived here in Tulsa, but it defies belief that human severed parts could be thrown out of a car window by the side of the road on Route 33 and not some shred of them be found. They don't have any scientific evidence that somehow Robert Zani had a motive to kill his mother. I have yet to see a handwriting expert say that this was his handwriting because this is his palm print and he was sweating because he was committing a crime. If that's the case, I hope nobody looks at this yellow notepad, because my hands are sweating. And if you can come to the conclusion that I'm committing a crime, then I'm in a lot of trouble.

"Irma Zani is an admitted liar. She lied to the Austin authorities. She lied to other people. She fabricated evidence to make Zani look ugly, and yet she has the guts to take this witness stand with a translator down here—who was totally unneeded, since she speaks perfect English—and tell you that you should believe her now. Why should you believe her now? She's concocted stories all her life. Ladies and gentlemen, I ask you to deliberate this case and give Irma Zani's testimony the credit it deserves. You can come to one verdict. That is a verdict of not guilty. Thank you."

It took six hours and eighteen minutes for the jurors to

return with their verdict: guilty of second-degree murder. Punishment was assessed at ninety-nine years. Margaret Lamm affirmed the sentence on December 28, and Zani was returned to Texas. The next day, Tulsa County DA David Moss dropped the second-degree murder charge against Irma.

Mark Lyons had pulled off a remarkable conviction—but it wouldn't stick.

EPILOGUE

There is an old adage among cops in southeast Texas, where severe weather can blow in from the Gulf at a moment's notice: "Don't spit into the eye of a hurricane if you don't plan to evacuate." As the murder convictions of Robert and Irma Zani began to unravel in the appeals process, the legal storms that resulted proved the wisdom of those words.

The first case to come apart was the thirty-year sentence given to Irma in Floresville. Represented by her new court-appointed attorney, David Weiner of San Antonio, she quickly appealed the verdict. Because of the immunity agreement, Weiner argued, Irma should never have been prosecuted as a party to the murder. And because the state had failed to show beyond a reasonable doubt which of the three bullets "directly caused the death" of Julius Dess, the evidence was insufficient to convict.

Nevertheless, on August 31, 1983, the Fourth Court of Appeals in San Antonio upheld the conviction. "The pretrial evidence, standing alone, might fall short of the legal mark of guilt beyond a reasonable doubt," the decision read, but when added to the testimony of Corpus Christi medical examiner Joseph Rupp, it was enough to sustain Irma's conviction. In addition, the court stated the the immunity agreement had been rendered "unenforceable" when Irma lied about her participation in the murder during the initial interview with Ruiz and Martinez on her mother's Acapulco porch.

"Weiner filed a petition for discretionary review with the Texas Court of Criminal Appeals, and on December 11, 1985, in a majority opinion written by Judge W. C. Davis, the lower court's decision was reversed. District Attorney Alger Kendall, who had recently been reelected, may well have shown that Irma fired one of the bullets, Davis wrote, but he failed to prove that she "directly" caused Dess's death. As a result, she shouldn't have been prosecuted under the terms of the immunity letter. On Valentine's Day, 1986—more than five and a half years after returning to Texas—Irma Zani was released from prison.

There is no record of where she went at first, but a year later she applied for and received a Texas ID. On March 9, 1989—her forty-sixth birthday—Irma married Gene Franklin Sells, a San Antonio native whose lengthy arrest record belied the fact that he was twelve years her junior. Sells had been arrested at least fifteen times for an assortment of crimes ranging from burglary to assault to indecency with a child. He was paroled in July 1987 after serving slightly less than seven years of a twenty-year murder sentence. It was unclear when or where Irma secured a Mexican divorce from Zani, but she clearly had hooked up with another loser.

The couple bought a mobile home and moved it onto a lot in a trailer park along Corpus Christ's South Padre Island Drive—about six miles from where Irma and Robert Zani had buried Dess's body a decade earlier. When Irma and her new husband left the trailer park a few weeks later, the other residents were relieved; although they had liked Irma, several described Sells as "worthless." He beat his wife, according to a neighbor, and expected her to earn the family income, apparently by plying her former trade, while her four children remained in Acapulco.

Three months after their marriage, the couple moved to San Antonio. Police continued to keep loose tabs on the two, particularly after a number of real estate agents—three in

Corpus and another up the coast in Galveston—were found murdered in vacant homes. There was nothing to connect Sells or Irma to the crimes, but Texas law enforcement agencies were unwilling to take chances.

Then, on June 9, 1989, Irma phoned a friend in Corpus Christi to say that she had left Sells. She lives today with an elderly San Antonio couple, keeping house and running errands for them in exchange for room and board.

The Tulsa conviction was the second to be overturned. On March 31, 1986, the Oklahoma Court of Criminal Appeals ruled that the Interstate Agreement on Detainers Act, which gives a prisoner the right to be tried within 180 days, had been violated. According to the court, the 180-day period had begun on January 20, 1982, when Zani filed an offer to deliver temporary custody, and other documents, with the Tulsa County district clerk. After the lower court granted one 28-eight-day continuance, the deadline for trial should have been August 16, the court concluded. Yet Zani wasn't even arraigned until the end of July, and the trial didn't begin for another four months.

Even if the violation of the Detainers Act alone was sufficient grounds for reversal, the court made a point to state clearly that it considered the error just one of many in the case. According to the judges, Zani should not have been tried and sentenced under murder statutes passed after the date of the crime. Sweeping reforms of the Oklahoma penal code in the intervening years had required that defendants charged with murder before July 1976 be tried under the old statutes. But both the original charge (first-degree murder) and the amended charge (second-degree murder) contained language from the current law, and the appeals court found that the first clear indication of Lyons's intent to try Zani under the old law had come far too late—just before the jury retired to deliberate.

Another problem concerned the difference between Irma's legal definition as "accomplice" or "involuntary participant." The court contended that Lyons had taken the untenable position of charging her as a principal in the crime while denying that she was even an accomplice. Irma was in fact an accomplice "as a matter of law," the judges wrote, and the jury should have been so instructed.

Finally, there was a question of whether Irma may have been offered a deal in return for her testimony. Under cross-examination by her husband, Irma seemed to have indicated her understanding that she wouldn't go to prison if she told the truth. The timing of the DA's dismissal of the charges against her—one day after Zani's conviction—was suspicious, the judges wrote, especially because the motion came "pursuant to negotiations with her attorney." They pointed to an Oklahoma attorney general's brief stating that "the jury was aware of . . . the fact that Mrs. Zani had been promised immunity from prosecution for testifying." Even a florid account of the trial published in the June 1983 edition of *True Police Cases* contained an admission from Musseman that he at least had kept his client in the dark about what would become of her case.

"I wanted her testimony to be untainted as far as knowing she was going to get any specific thing for it," Musseman was quoted as saying.

Lyons denied that any deal existed, and the appeals court judges stopped just short of ruling on the issue. They left little doubt as to their suspicions, though. "If this were the only question on appeal," they wrote, "it would be necessary to remand the case to the district court to resolve the issue of whether an agreement for non-prosecution was reached before Mrs. Zani testified against her husband."

Although the genuine merits of his case had not been in dispute, Lyons was frustrated by the reversal. In time, he left the district attorney's office and is today a partner in the firm of Lyons and Clark, one of Tulsa's most successful private law practices. His colleagues, trying to raise his spirits, reminded Lyons that Zani still had time to serve for the murder of George Vizard. Besides, half a dozen police agencies from around the country were investigating other crimes in which Zani was a suspect.

In fact, those investigations had long since run aground. The 1978 case of real estate agent Bobby Gene Thomas, whose nude, bullet-ridden body was found stuffed into the trunk of his car in Moore, Oklahoma, remained open but inactive. Frank Brady and Leighton Stanley, the original investigators who traveled to Austin to interview Irma, were no longer on the case, but Moore police sergeant Scott Singer had zeroed in on a local suspect. "I doubt we have enough to ever bring it to trial," he says today. As for the complete handprint lifted from Thomas's trunk, it turned out to belong to a bumbling Moore police sergeant with a reputation for obliterating crime-scene evidence.

In Barrington, Rhode Island, the site of Edna Mac-Donald's brutal strangulation, the police hinted that the sexual aspect of the crime and the weapon used—nylons—were uncharacteristic of Zani. They turned to a man jailed in Virginia on another crime and got an indictment against him for MacDonald's murder.

In Burlington, Iowa, where Dorothy Miller was raped and hanged, police still hoped for a break. A description of the assailant was sufficiently general to match Zani—as well as tens of thousands of other men. And in the absence of any evidence that Zani was ever in the state, investigators ultimately crossed him off their list of suspects.

Authorities were at a similar loss in Magnolia, Arkansas, where realtor Bobo Schinn had vanished in July 1978—but they were reluctant to admit it. Mike Lowe, the Arkansas State Police investigator who originally contacted the Austin Police Department after receiving Jimmy Brown's Teletype, today professes no interest in the parallels between the Schinn case and Zani's known method of operation with more than two dozen Texas realtors. Zani lived three hundred miles away at the time, Lowe points out, as if that alone were proof of his innocence. Officially, Moore police lieutenant Lester Lancaster is reluctant to eliminate Zani as a suspect in the case. Privately, however, he says that Zani "ain't got nothing to do with it." Ruiz and Martinez still strongly believe that Zani is probably good for the murder.

Having spit into the eye of the Zani hurricane, law enforcement efforts now centered on Zani's conviction for the murder of George Vizard as the only legal means to keep him behind bars. To no one's great surprise, Roy Greenwood had immediately filed an appeal containing almost two dozen legal complaints, all presented in a cantankerous prose that revealed Zani's helping hand and ranged from the court's refusal to pay Zani's investigative expenses to seven separate attacks on Mogoyne's posthypnotic testimony. The Sixth Court of Appeals in Texarkana was unimpressed; on September 25, 1984, a three-judge panel unanimously affirmed the trial court's judgment.

With that, Greenwood began preparing a petition for discretionary review with the Court of Criminal Appeals in Austin, his old stomping ground. The decision was coincidentally assigned to Judge Sam Houston Clinton, the venerable liberal whose daughter's affiliation with the SDS had surfaced during the investigation by Ruiz and Martinez.

This time Greenwood wisely limited his appeal to four main points addressing the specific issue of Mogoyne's hypnotically induced testimony. The first was that Zani should have had counsel present during the hypnosis session. The second was that the jury should have been instructed not to assign "disproportionate weight" to Mogoyne's testimony. Next Greenwood argued that Judge Dear erred when he refused to hear from the defense's hypnosis expert during the pretrial hearings. And finally he contended that hypnotically induced testimony was inadmissible in Texas, period.

Judge Clinton quickly disposed of the first two points by arguing that because the hypnosis session took place more than two weeks before Zani was indicted, his Sixth Amendment right to counsel had not been breached, and that any instruction to the jury regarding Mogoyne's hypnosis testimony would have been, of itself, a comment on the weight of the evidence. He agreed with Greenwood's third point—that the trial court should have allowed the defense's expert witness to appear at the pretrial hearings—though Clinton pointed out that it was unlikely the expert would have testified any differently at that time than he did later at trial. The oversight was insufficient grounds to overturn the conviction, Clinton wrote, and he chose instead to fold the issue into Greenwood's fourth and final complaint: the admissibility of hypnotically induced testimony.

Here Clinton ran into trouble with at least two of his colleagues. Finding testimony enhanced through hypnosis to be admissible in some broad instances, he remanded the question to the Sixth Court of Appeals to decide the issue in Zani's specific case. In a dissenting opinion, Judge Marvin Teague blasted the majority for allowing "juries to convict accused persons on what many, including myself, consider to be nothing less than irrelevant 'gypsy-voodoo' evidence." Judge John Onion had a different gripe. He decried the lack of "judicial economy in the ever-expanding remand procedure indulged in by the majority" and accused them of failing to answer the admissibility question while they had the chance. "The offense occurred almost 21 years ago," Onion wrote. "Appellant was not apprehended until 1980. His trial occurred in 1981, and seven years later the case is still in the appellate orbit—and by the action of the majority today it will continue in orbit for months or perhaps years to come."

Nevertheless, on June 29, 1988, the petition was sent back to the Sixth Court of Appeals in Texarkana to address what the higher court was unwilling to confront. On February 28, 1989, a panel of three judges, including two of the three who had upheld the conviction in 1984, ruled that Mo goyne's testimony was admissible and again affirmed the judgment of the trial court.

On July 26, 1989, the Court of Criminal Appeals in Austin refused to hear Greenwood's final appeal, with Judge Teague the lone dissenter. Greenwood was granted fifteen days to file a motion for reconsideration, and when the deadline quietly passed, Zani's legal options in Texas were limited to one. He could file a writ of habeas corpus in state district court at any time in the future—probably citing, like most such writs, that he had received ineffective legal counsel. In the meantime, it had taken twenty-two years and three days for George Vizard to find a measure of posthumous relief in the Texas criminal justice system.

Zani spent his days in a small, tidy cell in the Wynne Unit, an aging facility set on some 1,400 acres near Huntsville, where operations ran to the traditional prison manufacture of license plates, mattresses, and corrugated boxes. His college degree set him apart from a prison population in which 85 percent never made it out of high school, and he quickly won jobs in the typing pool and data-entry sections of the unit. In his spare time he pored over lawbooks to prepare his many lawsuits.

He filed no fewer than nine against the state of Texas, alleging, among other things, that the state "relies on, as their entire basis for any/all conclusions: A) the hocus-pocus of hypnosis, B) numerology, C) hallucinations, D) perjury, E) suborning, F) bribery, G) apparent witness poisoning." All of Zani's suits were ultimately dismissed as meritless.

Zani's personality remained unchanged—by turns, sullen and arrogant. Shame did not seem to have a place in his emotional repertoire. He rarely discussed the charges against him and tended to speak in bumper stickers, advising the few inmates in whom he confided—usually those who sought his help with their own legal writs and mo tions—that "corn can't expect justice from a court composed of chickens." Still, prison officials considered him a model inmate, and he accumulated good time at a rate that alarmed those who feared the day he might be set free from the overcrowded facility.

In early 1988, however, Zani began failing to report for his latest job—taking care of the grounds surrounding the Wynne Unit with a group of inmates known as the garden squad. When asked for an explanation, he had a simple reply: "H-88-1600," the number of a lawsuit he had filed in federal district court alleging civil rights violations and harassment by prison officials. Zani's disciplinary captain, after limiting his commissary privileges and issuing other lighter punishments, chipped away at the inmate's good time. On May 17, 1988, Zani lost 730 days for refusing to report to work. His file of disciplinary actions grew to two and a half inches, according to Wynne warden Lester Beaird, and by August 1989, Zani had lost a total of 4,690 days of accumulated good time.

"Never in all the years I've worked here have I seen so much good time lost," remarked Daniel Guerra, a Board of Pardons and Paroles official.

Although there was an outside chance that Zani could earn new good time—or have a large portion of his previous time reinstated—it was unlikely he would become eligible for parole before the year 2000. If he had built up credit with the intelligence community in whose shadowy midst he claimed to have operated, there was no evidence of it now. If the government functionaries on whose behalf he said he had traveled to foreign lands were grateful, they didn't show it. And of the many people who owed him their very lives, as he had assured his Tulsa jurors, not a single one felt compelled to come forward.

At forty-six Robert Zani is assigned to a routine job pressing license plates in what inmates call the tag plant.

* * *

In September 1988, Florentino Ventura Gutiérrez, the Interpol commander who helped retrieve the .357 and the .38 for Ruiz and Martinez in Acapulco, died in a bloody shoot-out on a road near Mexico City. News stories reported that after an afternoon of drinking, Ventura, his wife, and another couple quarreled. Ventura killed the two women and then turned the gun on himself. The other man survived to tell the story. No autopsies were performed, and the bodies were buried the same day.

The Mexican press speculated that the incoming administration of President Carlos Salinas de Gortari ordered the death of Ventura—whose power had grown almost beyond control—in part because his long years at the top of the Mexican federal judicial police and Interpol made him privy to secrets about Salinas de Gortari or someone else in the new president's government.

The incident took another bizarre turn the following spring when authorities unearthed the bodies of fifteen victims of apparent ritual slayings in Matamoros, near the Texas border. Sara Aldrete, described as the high priestess of the drug cult responsible for the murders, named Ventura and other top police and government officials as members of the sect. She also named a number of popular entertainers, including the singer Irma Serrano. United States authorities were skeptical. Ventura, a former priest who had been forced into retirement by Salinas de Gortari's predecessor and was then brought back to help direct the search for the killers of U.S. drug enforcement agent Enrique Camarena in 1985, was known as one of the most violent law officers in Mexico, a man who killed with near impunity. He was not thought to engage in anything resembling cult behavior, however. As for the aging Irma Serrano, she denied any involvement with the cult. "I am diabolic, and I go to black masses," she explained to the Mexican press, "but I don't eat people."

* * *

Others whose lives were touched by Robert Zani went about their days in less dramatic fashion. Sheriff Solomon Ortiz was elected to the U.S. Congress from the newly created Twenty-seventh District in 1982, and Lencho Rendon went to Washington as his chief aide. They hope to be returned by the voters in November 1990.

When the authorities last checked on Harlan Cooper, he was still living just outside the Beltway in Falls Church, Virginia. He drove to work past government complexes and high-tech headquarters that reflected the enormous changes that had taken place in the national life since July 23, 1967. If the date represented any kind of personal watershed, Cooper wasn't talking.

In Tulsa, Vera Tolbert no longer harbors the hope that her sister Gladys will be on the line when the phone rings. Virginia Warner often recalls her friend as she sits in her Westminster, Colorado, home. Neither Tolbert nor Warner has any interest in contacting Robert Zani.

Bob Bivens, the former Tulsa PD detective who lived next door to Gladys, has since passed away. The Eppersons still live at 218 Xenophon, the house they bought from Zani.

Betty Jo Mason is a schoolteacher in San Antonio. Her mother lives quietly in the Castle Hills home from which Julius Dess left to keep the appointment with a couple who called themselves Ray and Mary Thomas a decade ago.

Jerry Mogoyne, Jr., who was waited on by Vizard's killer in the Town and Country, today lives in the small town of Elgin, about twenty miles east of Austin. As the single most important witness in a case that set a national legal precedent, Mogoyne still marvels at the Houston hypnosis session that drew Zani's face from deep within him to Arthur Douet's sketch pad.

Burt Gerding, the wily APD lieutenant whose job was to keep the lid on the student movement, retired from the force in the early seventies. Today he is a deputy constable in northwest Austin and the chief of security at Dobie Center, a high-rise dorm on the UT campus. Sometimes he rues the days when popular television shows like *The Mod Squad* helped him recruit student snitches who enjoyed playing the roles in real life.

Paul Pipkin now lives in San Antonio. He was a Jesse Jackson delegate to the 1988 Democratic National Convention in Atlanta and, as chairman of the local Progressive Democrats, is finally living up in some degree to the grass-roots activism he espoused in the sixties.

Mariann Vizard lives in Austin with her son and his father. For the past eight years she has served on the local cable television commission and helped run Oat Willie's, Austin's venerable head shop. She is now known as Mariann Wizard, a name bestowed upon her by fellow SDS member Alice Embree in the days following George's murder. Embree is now a researcher in the child-support enforcement division of the Texas attorney general's office.

The Methodist Student Center where Mariann and George Vizard were married in 1965 is now a parking lot. On the wall of the nearest building is a mural painted by Alice Embree's husband, Carlos Lowry. At the center of the mural stands George Vizard, surrounded by a group of students on campus, circa 1967.

"I still meet people who were influenced by his life and/or his death, and who have been trying to live for twenty-plus years as he lived," Mariann recently wrote. "When I think of him, I see him up in the face of narrow-minded official-dom, fearlessly challenging what is permitted—demanding the most of life."

A two-day seminar was held in Austin in April 1989 to present the latest information on forensic hypnosis to district and county attorneys, investigators, and other law enforcement professionals from around the state. The second day of the seminar was devoted entirely to the case *Texas* v. *Zani.*

The man who successfully prosecuted the case wasn't

invited. Joe Turner had left the Travis County DA's office in early 1982 and joined the U.S. attorney's office of Edward Prado (now a U.S. district judge), impressing his colleagues as brilliant and brash as he went after cases in the western district of Texas, from San Antonio to El Paso. In January 1983, Turner saw another opportunity to go into private practice. This time no one could dissuade him. Having put in half a decade as a public prosecutor, Turner jumped to the other side. Today he is one of the most successful defense attorneys in Central Texas. The lecture on *Texas* v. *Zani* at the hypnosis seminar was delivered by one of his successors in the U.S. attorney's office.

Paul Ruiz also failed to get an invitation. In December 1982 he had left the police department when Travis County DA Ronnie Earle created a new investigator's slot and asked Ruiz to fill it. With his former APD partner Frank Maxwell, Ruiz worked high-profile cases involving confessed murderer Henry Lee Lucas and the still unsolved slaying of a local topless dancer. But when he was asked to check into allegations that a powerful county commissioner named Bob Honts had charged taxpayers for thousands of dollars of personal phone calls made from the mobile unit in his Porsche, Ruiz sensed trouble. Honts was indicted just as the commissioners' court went into budget hearings for the following fiscal year—and when it emerged, the investigator's job in the DA's office had been eliminated. After a stint as a private eye, Ruiz is now the chief investigator for the charitable trusts section of the Texas attorney general's office.

Robert Martinez wasn't invited to the hypnosis seminar, either. In the years following the Zani investigation, he had cemented his reputation as one of the premier homicide investigators in the Southwest. For two years after Ruiz left the force, Martinez worked undercover in OCU. In 1984, when Lieutenant Bobby Simpson retired, he transferred to the special missions team, or SMT, a SWAT-like unit whose rigorous physical training aggravated an old knee injury. He was assigned to a walking beat on Austin's Sixth Street, an area of nightclubs, fern bars, and UT students.

On October 14, 1985, Martinez hit the streets of East Austin as the senior member of the Hispanic crimes unit, or HCU, an elite unit whose commander, Sergeant Hank Gonzalez (now a Travis County commissioner), had been issued a simple order by new police chief Jim Everett: Put an end to the violent crimes committed mostly by local Hispanics against undocumented workers from Mexico and Central America. The first night out, Martinez made the unit's initial bust when he interrupted a burglary in progress. And over the next two years the unit solved twenty murder cases, disbanded countless street gangs, and earned national acclaim for reducing crime by 75 percent in the area known as Charlie Sector. Martinez became the most decorated officer in APD history. Today he is in APD's community services program, where he works closely with citizens concerned about gang violence.

Although the careers of Ruiz and Martinez diverged in the years after the Zani investigation, they remained the best of friends, united by a hard-earned pride in their work. Martinez felt burned that among his hundreds of commendations there was none from Frank Dyson, the Austin police chief who retired in 1984 without so much as a thank-you for Martinez's part in clearing up the longest unsolved murder case on the department's books. Ruiz, attaching less significance to official recognition, resented more the petty jealousies that tended to win scorn instead of praise from officials and fellow street cops in return for a job well done on the three murder cases.

The onetime partners were still partners in another sense: Each had invested great faith in the court system's ability to deliver justice and make it stick. When they got together over a drink, they discussed the investigation that had consumed so much of their lives. They relived the high points, laughed about this incident or that, and regretted the time they had spent away from their families while working on the case. They discussed a criminal justice system that seemed intent on letting the criminals out of prison before the victims got out of the hospital. Most of all, they confided in each other their common image of how Robert Zani might live out his life—and they hoped the system wouldn't let them down this time.

Their image of Zani's last days went something like this: He reaches old age. With the arrival of each new morning, light filtering through catwalks and metal bars, he struggles awake, momentarily confused and unable to decide if he is returning from a dream or stepping back into one. Despite the years, it's no easier to grasp a new day dawning in Huntsville.

Zani lingers awhile, bringing himself to consciousness bit by bit, pausing to let the morning light turn pink beneath his eyelids in the last quiet moments of the day. From this point on, the scrape of steel upon steel and the collective complaint of human confinement reverberate through the Wynne Unit. There is no peace again until the wee hours, if then. After days of bone-numbing boredom, he shuffles back to lockup with a cellblock's worth of men who all seem about half the age he was when he first arrived.

Then, late one night after lights-out, when the unit is as close to silent as it ever gets, he props himself on a brittle elbow, runs his fingers across his balding pate, and surveys the man he has become—a serial killer who once found people's viscera and made them twitch but who is now a melancholy old con whom no one visits or awaits. The guards find him during final rounds, openmouthed and slumped on the edge of his cot, wearing a solid white T-shirt and baggy cotton drawstrings—and stroking the cold, hard floor with fingers already gone blue and beginning to bloat.

INDEX

385